Self

A biography of Claude Keith

by

Crispin Keith

Introduction

Introduction

My grandfather, Claude Hilton Keith, died in 1946, six years before I was born, and yet it is possible for me to feel that I really know him. That's because he recorded everything about his life, often with excruciating candour.

In 1926, Claude left his wife and one-year-old son to serve the RAF in Iraq and the Persian Gulf. While he was away, he had much time on his hands to write a memoir for his son, and to record all his adventures in these exotic locations. He also kept carbon copies of the all the letters he sent from Iraq, and copies of the letters he received. One collection of letters covers in horrendous detail the break-up of his marriage. Once divorced, Claude [certainly lonely] took to recording his life in the hope that one day he would see his son and give him all the stories and fatherly advice that a son should have. To this end, he compiled a book called 'My Rosery', which devotes a chapter to each of the women in his life, together with photos and even a lock of hair, with a foreword to his son in which he outlines advice on how to treat women.

Claude also had some extraordinary and important jobs, playing a largely unsung but significant part in shaping the 20th century. He travelled all over the world before 1914 as an engineer and wireless pioneer with Marconi, served in the Royal Navy Air Service during World War I, was a founder officer of the RAF, was a pioneer of 'air imperialism' and an explorer who was the first European to cross the Oman peninsula on land. He played a key role in arming the Spitfires and Hurricanes to compete with Hitler's M111s in World War II, and then during the war he commanded the largest British bomber airbase, playing a significant part in the propaganda war, both at the BBC and in print. He wrote two published books about his time with the RAF and was recognized by the RAF and by MPs as being a figure of significance. He was a thinker and innovator, discussing before 1939 how nuclear energy might be harnessed for peaceful power.

Claude was also undoubtedly vain. This resulted in him collecting a considerable photo archive, mainly from the years 1910 to 1930, some of it certainly of national historical importance, often with 'self' often posing in the foreground. There are boxes of loose photos, mostly of Iraq, the Gulf States and Oman in the 1920s, but also photograph albums containing pictures from all over the world, many taken from planes, some of stunning quality. To historians, it is his meticulous labelling of the photos which makes them valuable.

Claude was fascinated by family history. Given the extraordinary and insecure childhood that he had, hidden away from the Keith family by his mother's family, pursued by Keith investigators with a mother undergoing progressive mental illness, he probably felt the need to research and record his roots, and then to pass it on to the son whom he never got to know. Some of his research was fanciful, but a lot of it fascinating. His books for his son all say 'for your eyes only', but I think that his vanity and love of family history would greatly enjoy the fact that his writings are being resurrected nearly a hundred years later, and that later generations can enjoy his memories and ideas, even if they find some of them highly debatable.

While I was writing this book, there was one crucial gap in the material – his last three years. Then, on the very day I finished proof-reading, a new source turned up to plug that gap: my sister Juliet rang up to say that her husband Christopher had bought a copy of 'I Hold My Aim', which had a dedication signed by Claude to Suzanne Bavard, an American friend whom Claude had visited in Illinois in 1935 and again in 1942. Tucked in the book were four long typed letters from Claude, outlining his life and thoughts in 1945! Next day, my third cousin was able to email me Claude's death certificate. It is extraordinary the footprint that some people leave.

This biography contains extensive extracts from Claude's writings. It is tempting to sit back and allow Claude to regale you uninterrupted with the yarns of his life, but actually such a book would sag in places. However, I have kept large chunks, because they illustrate the extraordinary person that he was, and because he knew best about his life [usually].

Some sources

1. My Life – by Claude Keith, as a memoir for his son, 1927. Bound, unpublished.
2. My Rosery – being Intimate Tales of My Love Affairs, by Claude Hilton Keith. Written for his Son. 1928. Bound, unpublished.
3. Letters between Claude and Angel, 1926-1930. Bound, unpublished.
4. Letters from Iraq. Bound, unpublished.
5. Flying Years [A British Airman's Overseas Tour], by Claude Keith. Bound, published by J. Hamilton in 1937.
6. I Hold My Aim [The Story Of How The British Air Force Was Armed For War], by Claude Keith. Bound, published Allen and Unwin in 1946.
7. Per Ardua Ad Astra, a collection of poems by Claude Keith 1940 – 1943. Unbound, unpublished.
8. Marham Memories, an account of Claude's time as station commander during the Battle of Britain, 1940. Bound, unpublished.
9. Letters to Suzanne Bavard, 1945. Unbound, unpublished.
10. The Rogers Book, a set of family history notes compiled by Claude, 1920.
11. Three photograph albums, compiled by Claude, and a box of loose photographs.
12. Claude Keith Wikipedia entry, posted by RAF historians:
    http://en.wikipedia.org/wiki/Claude_Hilton_Keith
13. Masonic regalia and records.
14. Records written by Ellen Keith, Claude's aunt, in 1912.

Chapter 1   Parents and birth: latent tragedy

Claude Hilton Keith was dealt a mixed hand at the start of his life. He was born on October 1st, 1890, to parents from very respectable families. His father Hilton Keith was the son of the Accountant-General of the British India Office, and his mother Nettie Rogers was the daughter of a well known London solicitor. It might be assumed that young Claude could expect a life of calm convention, privilege and comfort, at least until the advent of the First World War. Nothing could be further from the truth.

Beneath the veneer of respectable upper middle class Victorian England, family life was seldom simple. It certainly wasn't simple on either side of Claude's family. In his memoir for his son, Claude started by describing his maternal grandfather, who had the nickname 'The Adonis of Cambridge':

In the days of many years gone by, there dwelt at Trinity College, Cambridge a young undergraduate famed for his perfect complexion and his wonderful brown eyes. That was my grandfather, John Bellas Rogers [pictured right], son of a well-to-do London solicitor and Captain of the Surrey Militia, John Rogers of 40, Jermyn Street. In the town of Cambridge lived a very quiet old-world country family of the name of Ringwood, who, having no daughter of their own, had adopted a daughter named Ellen Moore from her foster father, John Goode, a gentleman who resided in Kensington. The youthful Ellen was according to all accounts I have heard and as I judge from her photographs and pictures, endowed with more than her fair share of womanly looks. Living in such a town as Cambridge it was but natural that she should attract the attention of many of the undergraduates, and great was the care of her adopted parents to shield her from such attentions. In turn, my grandfather seems to have fallen under the spell of her looks, for when every effort to make her acquaintance by ordinary methods failed, I have been told how he used to sit behind the fair Ellen in the old town church and pass her little notes.

Be this as it may, the fact remains that he earned a place in her affections and eventually, she being tired of the close supervision of her adopted parents, made a runaway match of it with young Rogers. They were married at St. Mary Abbot's in Kensington and from the register it seems as if the former foster father John Goode was present, for the name of John Goode is signed alongside that of John Rogers.

The following year, whilst the young couple were staying with friends near Paris, my mother was born on 22nd May 1860.

So far, very Jane Austen. But this was not a marriage that ended happily ever after. First there was the issue that their firstborn, Ellen, known as Nettie, was a girl:

Poor mother: often has her face looked wistful when she told me how his first child being born a daughter instead of a son infuriated my grandfather, and I am afraid that she, poor dear, started life under an unfair handicap on that account.

The couple settled in Barnes and John Rogers resumed travelling into London to work as a solicitor. Five other children were born to John and Ellen: John [Jack], Louise, Charles, Alice and Charlotte [Lotty]. But the children [even two precious sons] did not cement the marriage, and Ellen's fancy was taken by the son of one of their neighbours. Willie Hall was a consumptive; when he was ordered to Australia for his health, Ellen shocked everyone: she left her husband and six children to join Willie Hall there.

This was a professional calamity for John Rogers, a respectable solicitor. It was a personal blow for all the children, especially the sixteen-year-old Nettie, who was taken out of her school in Tunbridge Wells to keep house for her father, while her siblings remained in boarding school or were farmed out to relatives.

Ellen eventually left Willie Hall and returned to England. After some heated recrimination, reconciliation was agreed, and the family was reunited. They settled in Bedford Park, *'a small private colony of well-to-do London businessmen who preferred to live outside the bustle of the city'*. But not for long: when Ellen received news that Willie Hall was dying she abandoned her family again to travel out to Australia. This time there was to be no reconciliation, because while Ellen was in Australia John Rogers had *'accidentally made the acquaintance'* of Connie Forrester, a young circus equestrienne in Lord George Sanger's Circus. This had major consequences for the family:

Attachment followed and he became involved with her to such an extent that his partners, his father and Jull, dissolved partnership and he started on his own at 53 Conduit Street as solicitor, also holding the appointment of High Bailiff of Brompton. With a large family on his hands, a responsible position in the city and worries of his home, it is small wonder that my grandfather became reckless.

John didn't just lose his reputation and business partners – he lost his first family. His wife Ellen returned from Australia after Willie Hall's death, and was legally separated from John. His second daughter Louise became a house-keeper in Devon. His two youngest daughters were in a convent in Belgium. He had already lost his two sons:

Unable to stand the erratic temper of his father, eventually Jack Rogers went to Canada to take up farming and to endeavour to carve out his fortune in the new land which was then offering such great promise to settlers. With him went his brother, the only other son, Charles Rogers.

This left Nettie, now aged 27 and with no prospects, in London with a destitute mother who was grieving over Willie Hall. Her father was starting a new family with a circus equestrienne who was three years younger than Nettie. It's not surprising that she jumped at any prospect of escape, however unappealing it might seem. The escape route was provided by her brother:

My Uncle Jack made a splendid fight in Canada against all sorts of odds, but eventually wrote home to my mother that he could not run a homestead and farm at one and the same time, and so would be reluctantly obliged to chuck up farming and go as a platelayer on the railroad that was even then pushing its iron way west'ard .... my mother received the news that my uncle Jack couldn't carry on alone on his farm, and straightaway she wrote out and offered to go and housekeep for him.

In the year 1887, my mother, a young and none too strong woman, left the comforts and safety of civilization and plunged into the wild desolation of a Canadian winter. To anyone who has not intimate knowledge of the mushroom growth of the huge towns that today exist in the north-west, the utter desolation of that land thirty odd years ago would never be credited by them. The railroad had not yet got through, and no proper scheme for settlers had been organised.

For eighteen months my mother kept home for my uncle and during this time she led a life which would have broken most women of her age and training. But she lived it out and despite the hardest of set-backs, she made good and never failed in her part. During the winter of 1887 the whole of my uncle's place was destroyed by fire, and my mother lost her every cherished possession, but they didn't give in, and ere next summer was over, they were installed in a new house which was better than the old one.

When Nettie met Hilton Keith, she was vulnerable and ready to be married to the first person who asked her. But Hilton Keith was not perfect husband material, despite his impeccably respectable family.

Hilton was born on 14th September 1856 in 19, Fellowes Road, Hampstead, London, the fourth of eight children of Thomas William Keith and Mary Baddeley [pictured below]. Thomas

Keith was at that time on his way to becoming Accountant General of the India Office. He was a friend and colleague of the philosopher John Stuart Mill, his grandfather had been tutor to the royal family and an author of key mathematics and navigation textbooks, his father had been a friend of Coleridge and Wordsworth, and he himself was the epitome of Victorian respectability. Hilton's seven siblings were similarly

respectable: three daughters married professionals while the other stayed at home to support her parents, two sons became solicitors and one followed his father into the India Office. Hilton was very much the black sheep of the family.

From an early age Hilton was an unruly child in an orderly household. It didn't help that he was an epileptic in an era when there was a taboo about such things. His father was described by his eldest son as having a dominating personality, *'in many respects much to be admired, clever in an eminently practical way – but above all, no dreamer'.* His father's stern pronouncements were like *'water off a duck's back'* to Hilton. Clashes were inevitable.

Hilton was sent to Kensington Grammar School, where his father was a governor, but he got into trouble [for fighting older boys, getting out of detention by climbing down a drainpipe] and was asked to leave. He was enrolled as a cadet in the Royal Navy, but he was involved in a conspiracy to set fire to the training ship HMS Worcester [allegedly it was older boys who were going to do the act, but Hilton was caught with the matches]. It was agreed that the open air life would be better for his health, so he was sent to Scotland and to Somerset to learn farming, but neither led to a permanent solution. At the height of the British Empire, one solution for wayward sons was to send them to a far away colony, and in 1875 Hilton was given a first class ticket on the SS Strathmore to New Zealand.

Above: Hilton's shipwreck involved privations and adventures that caught the imagination of the national press

The Strathmore's maiden voyage ended in disaster – a shipwreck on the Isles of the Apostles, lonely rocks quite near the Crozet Islands in the southern ocean. Hilton was one of 49 survivors who clung onto life for six months before they were picked up by an American whaling ship. He returned to Hampstead, jumping out of a seaman's chest to announce himself. Within months he left again for New Zealand's gold rush. He failed to prosper, joined the Freemasons, returned to England destitute, and then left for Saskatchewan, Canada, where he became an Indian Agent in the aftermath of the Sioux nation's expulsion after Little Big Horn. Claude takes up his story:

He had some little while before received an offer of a post which was only open to married men. Apparently he had laughed and jumped at the offer of the government to take three months

leave in England and see if he could find a wife to his liking. My aunt, Ellen Keith, or, Aunt Nell as I know her, has since told me how sore put to it she was to introduce him to suitable English girls who did not immediately lose favour in his eyes after he had put them under the searching rays of his naturally critical nature. Then he met my mother and her sister, my Aunt Louise, and vowed that he liked them better than any others. For a whole day did Aunt Nell conduct the quartet about Richmond Park, leaving Hilton with first one then the other sister. At the end of the day, worn out, she anxiously enquired, "Well Hilton dear, which one is it?" but he just laughed and replied, "Oh, I don't fizz about either of them." This seems to have killed the fond hopes of Aunt Nell to find him a bride, for very soon afterwards he returned to Canada and took up the appointment of a single man on one of the Indian Reserves in the then wild North-West.

Above: Hilton, the frontiersman, and Nettie, the London girl

So Hilton and Nettie had already met in England before Nettie went to Canada to be with her brother, and he had already rejected the idea of marrying her. But the pressure from his employers was on him to marry – to be in charge of an Indian Reserve [a vast area with complex responsibilities], the Agent had to be respectably married as there were too temptations for a young unmarried man with so much power over so many vulnerable people.

Then one fateful day came a buggy with a prospecting party, bent on picking land for a new Indian reserve, and with that party came Hilton Keith, Indian Agent, North-West Territories, of Canada.

I never knew what by what wiles he won her woman's heart, though I doubt not that it was through the easily opened door of pity. Be that as it may, in the year 1889 Hilton Keith and Ellen Mary Katherine Rogers were made man and wife, for better or for worse, in a little wooden house, miles and miles away from a church by a clergyman whose name I have forgotten. Yes: in the heart of the wild north-west they were married: he that had rolled up and down and *round the world, and she, a delicate slip of a girl who had been fighting nature in its wildest form on the great unfenced prairies of Canada. An ideal match it should have been, shouldn't it?*

Claude, who never met his father and who was brought up by his mother, takes his mother's side over what happened next, and implies that Hilton swept away a vulnerable young girl. His Aunt Nell, Hilton's sister, gives a contrasting account, suggesting that Nettie had pursued Hilton out to Canada and had entered the marriage with her eyes open, and that Canada was not as impossibly bleak as painted by the Rogers family:

He liked all four Rogers girls, but not one in particular, and therefore he was quite right, even if perhaps, on his return to Canada, he might have to give up his appointment, it were better than to dishonour himself by pretending to bestow love which he <u>did not</u> feel. His father agreed that this was right. …… After these, he returned to Touchwood Hills ……. One of the 4 sisters called on me, and said she had lost her heart to my Brother, and was distressed at his departure without a word. She said she was so unhappy, and intended to go out to visit her brother in Canada! It was a painful interview, especially as I considered Hilton had acted right. I shall never forget her parting words – she said: "If my happy days were not to come, I would not wish to love"!

Two years after, Hilton announced his engagement to her! He told his fiancée about his health – my father had insisted on it. A consultation with doctors declared, <u>provided</u> the lady was aware of the fact, it was the best thing that could happen – his marriage. The Bride elect wrote sweetly to my father, to say dear Hilton's health or suffering could only endear him to her, and she should do her best to make him happy. So they married, and he took his wife to a lovely home, on Touchwood hills, with a lake in the grounds, and a boat on the lake christened "<u>Nell</u>". All opened happily and promised well, and the silence of long months which followed was put down at home to the natural selfishness of a happy couple. "Where ignorance is bliss 'tis folly to be wise".

The marriage was not a happy one, probably right from the start. Claude's account attempts neutrality, but his sympathies lie with his mother:

Well, in 1889, as I have said, my parents were married, and my father took his young wife to live in his little official residence near the Sioux Indian Reserve. Tucked away somewhere I have moccasins made by Indians of the Touchwood Reserve, and in my first days of life I have been cradled in the arms of a squaw. I still treasure a small watercolour painting – devoid of artistic merit – which shows that little prairie shack which was the first home my parents ever had. Set down anyhow in the midst of that vast expanse, it seemed to court disaster. Ere long they moved to another reserve to the south of the Touchwood Hills, and their new home 'Kutawa'.

Early, all too early, in their married life it became evident that my parents did not pull well together. The responsibility for having a wife and the lack of his former freedom seems to have jarred on my father and made him resent my mother's smallest wish. I think that they must have understood each other very ill. All her unselfish efforts to please and humour him seem to have only had the effects of annoying him. He had been such a thorough man's man that the presence of a woman was strange and worrying to him. It is not for me to judge my parents, therefore don't think that I defend him. Anyhow, their married time before my birth which should have been happy as a May Day dream, was a time of sorrow of being out of sympathy with the man she had married and having no one to whom she might turn. She was miles away from any other woman.

Hilton and Nettie in 1889

By the time Claude was born in October 1890, the marriage was in serious crisis. Nettie moved to Qu'appelle to give birth, and Hilton did not accompany her. Ominously, Nettie's mother Ellen, who had form when it came to leaving husbands, was there to support her daughter.

As time drew on and the day of my birth drew nearer, she journeyed down to stay with some friends, the Cassells, who lived at Qu'appelle Station. He, Mr. Cassell, was the manager of the Dominion Bank and it was in the Bank buildings, Qu'appelle Station, Saskatchewan that I first saw the light of day. Mercifully, and English doctor was available, a Dr. Carthew, otherwise it is certain that my poor mother would not have lived to see my face. As it was her sufferings at the time of my birth undoubtedly brought on that cursed Graves Disease which eventually led to her death. It was blowing a blizzard when I was born and the glass stood at 60 degrees below zero! The winter had broken early, for it was only October 21st when I was born, but snow had already fallen in plenty. My grandmother, Ellen Rogers, had journeyed to Canada to be with my mother during my birth, and it was she who held me in her arms when my poor mother was yet too ill to take me to her own breast.

The unsympathetic attitude of my father decided my grandmother to take mother and myself back to England. My mother lay at death's door for weeks, and when eventually she became strong enough to undertake the journey, her mind was not normal. Journeying by easy stages – for the railway was just through to Qu'appelle – we reached Quebec and stayed there a while. We embarked on the Allan Liner 'Parisian' and arrived in Liverpool in January 1891.

Claude gives the Rogers side of the story. His Aunt Nell puts the Keith side:

One sweet letter at first came from the bride [<u>which I have read</u>] then months after, <u>one</u> other from her, the contents of which came like a bombshell to me and Father and us all. It was written before she left Touchwood to go into a town, to stay in the house of friends, and near to a doctor, a little while before you were born.

You, dear fellow, know both the details of both shipwrecks of Hilton's life. I spare you.

Stanley [Hilton's brother] *obtained 6 months leave, and went out to his brother in his trouble, and found staying with him in his house, a clergyman, and also the Bishop of Qu'appelle, son of Lord Anson – who went to show the world that there was no cause <u>morally</u> for the blow received. These and other friends and family and Stanley rallied round him, but soon after their departure, Hilton threw up his appointment, and for years became restless and a wanderer...*

Whoever was to blame, the story of Claude's birth was to have a profound influence on his life. He never knew his father [Nell alleges that Hilton was told that his son died at birth, but this is very dubious], and he was brought up in households devoid of men. The rift between the Keiths and the Rogers endured his whole life, colouring even the christening of his own son in 1926. Claude's later obsessive research of his family roots and maybe his craving for love and acceptance mirrored the insecurities that stemmed from the events on a snow-swept prairie in 1890.

Chapter 2 A nomadic childhood

Nettie and her mother arrived in England with Claude aged three months in January 1891, but this did not bring resolution with the Keith family. The two families of solicitors took their dispute to court. The Rogers family successfully sued Hilton, forcing him to return the dowry money that had come with Nettie. In turn, the Keith family demanded custody of the baby son. Nettie remained in poor mental and physical health, terrified that she would lose Claude.

Nettie's mother Ellen rented a house in St. Mawes, Cornwall, and later in Falmouth, where Claude's first memories were set. He was surrounded by women, because as well as his mother and grandmother, Nettie's sisters, Alice and Charlotte [Lotty or Tatts], were often living with them. Claude comments that he was dreadfully spoiled as a small child, but adds that the memory of such affection had to last him through the dark years that were to come.

In August of 1894 my mother heard that the Keith solicitors were trying to trace me, and that so thoroughly unnerved her, that against all advice, she fled off into the wilds of Wales and left her address only with a Mr. Wright, her solicitor. This was an awful blow to my grandmother and Aunt Charlotte, as they didn't feel my mother was strong enough to be alone, she had a paltry £60 a year to live on, and of course the Keiths could have found her just as easily in Wales as in Falmouth. My mother said goodbye to her sister, Charlotte, at Plymouth, and despite vain pleadings fled off to Wales without any fixed plans. We moved on from place to place, visiting Shrewsbury, Chester, Conway, Port-y-llyn, and many other places, finally reaching Llandudno where we spent Christmas of that year. My recollections of my mother at Llandudno are very vivid. She wore a heavy dark brown cape, a hard felt hat and was a little energetic figure with great startled eyes and a sad haunted expression. Brave little soul: how often have I not wished that God would have spared her to me to give me the chance of repaying in some small way part of all the sacrifices she made for me. We had rooms over a shop in the main street of Llandudno and I was great friends with a little girl there.

Out of her slender purse, my mother contrived to give me a Christmas replete with all seasonable good things, and there I remember my first Christmas tree. The winter was a very hard one, and the streets were all covered with ice and the town looked more foreign than I have ever known any town in this country to look. Gladys and I had great times leaning out of the window and screaming "Happy Christmas" to everyone that passed, and she it was, I think, who initiated me into the usages of mistletoe. Conway Castle bridge I remember, and also one incident at Chester when the Duke of Fife came there to open or inspect something. Well I remember the Highland pipers, the first I had set eyes on.

In February we moved on to Aberystwyth and my mother decided to look for a house, as living in rooms was beyond her slender means. Staying in a dingy little apartment house my mother was scared to death when an old man went down with typhoid fever. Straight away we cleared out to other rooms at Borth, a small village to the north of Aberystwyth, but the damage had been done, and I sickened with the fever. As a matter of fact, I got over it well, but the anxiety nearly killed my mother. I remember that they fed me on a filthy purplish mixture of rice pudding and port wine. Never to this day have I been able to eat even plain rice pudding.

In Borth Claude first attended school, recording that he got whacked many times when learning to read, and that he was already fascinated by mechanical things. They were visited in Borth by his Aunt Lotty, with whom he formed a great bond that was to last through her life. In March 1896 he witnessed the great flood of Borth, in which five houses were swept away:

The sea started rising and rising and rising, and then the wind got up! The water in our cellar came up to the level of the hall, and as the tide came in the whole street was submerged. Just when there were about four feet above street level, a gale sprang up, and then the houses that were opposite to us and on the sea side of the road came in for the full benefit of the high sea that ran. In my nightdress, for it was early, I stood and breathed on the panes of my bedroom window, frightfully bored with life in that I wasn't allowed to go out and help in what was going

on. It was a wild scene: great boulders were sent flying through the passageways of the houses opposite, and very soon they started to collapse. Retreat to the rear was cut off by the bog, and anyway, it was possibly as safe to stay as to try to make the high land which lay between us and Aberystwyth. All that

morning havoc was wrought by the sea, and then, as the ebb set in, it all calmed down and nothing like it has been known since. We cleared off to Aberystwyth for the night, but we had no need: the storm had come, done its damage and gone its way.

Nettie's mother moved back to London, and in June 1896 Nettie took rooms in London, too. Claude had his hair cut for the first time, developed a life-long love of the stories of Hans Christian Andersen, and got first chicken-pox and then measles. They then moved down to Southsea, where Nettie's brother Charles had settled with his wife, but they had an unsettling experience:

Xmas of 1896 was a rollicking affair at my uncle's place with my cousins Nell, Dot and Gwen. In February whilst I and mother were walking along a street in Southsea, an elderly woman [presumably Mary Keith, Hilton's mother] rushed up and bent down and kissed me, saying as she did so, *"My darling Hilton's son."* My mother drew herself up and demanded in icy tones, *"And have you nothing to say to his mother?"* I forget what the reply was, but mother cleared off and was very upset about it.

They returned to London for a while, then back to Borth to pack up their few possessions, before moving to Tunbridge Wells, where Nettie thought that Claude could be schooled, while she took in paying guests.

I was sent to a dame's school in Tunbridge Wells and had quite a good time, as boys always do at dame's schools. I was a veritable vagabond out of school, and used to take delight in doing odd jobs on unfinished buildings, of which there were many near us. I actually learned to lay bricks and today I wouldn't mind setting out to lay my 200 bricks a day with any union man. I also investigated a good deal of the negotiable sewer pipes in the town. My poor mother: she nearly got grey hairs at times.

In June my Uncle Jack and his family went back to Canada , and then I began to think about Canada and realize that I wasn't just a common Englishman as were my confreres: I was Canadian, and I rose immensely in my own estimation.

The doctors then said that the air in Tunbridge Wells wasn't bracing enough for me, and Littlehampton was recommended. At once my darling mother panicked to get there: I think they had said I needed the moon, she would have made an almighty effort to get it for me. Oh God, why couldn't she live that I might try and do as much for her?

They moved to a maisonette above a greengrocer's shop in Littlehampton, but they were soon on the move again, to Helford, Cornwall, where Lotty had retired after the man she loved had married another woman for an inheritance. However in August 1899 Nettie became seriously ill, and they moved to be with her brother Charles in Southsea. The doctors recommended complete rest, so they went to St Helens on the Isle of Wight. When Nettie's teeth became a problem, they went to stay in Cornwall again, via a short stay in Newton Abbott, because Nettie's sister Alice had married an American , Fred Spaight, who was training to be a dentist, and his teacher practiced there. Claude had a lovely time running wild in each of these places.

In January 1900 Nettie and Claude moved to Broadstairs in Kent, partly because the air was good there, and partly because there was a good school for Claude, Pierremont College. Claude records that his interests had broadened: keeping animals [rabbits, a dog, a cat, a canary and even a billy-goat for a while], football [but not rugby], with a passion for geography and maps.

Nettie's siblings started to disperse: Alice and her husband moved back to Massachusetts, Jack returned to Canada, and Charles migrated to South Africa. Nettie and Claude were soon on the move again. Nettie failed to find enough paying guests or music pupils, and so in 1902 they had to move to a cheaper smaller house in Ramsgate, where Claude joined St Lawrence School in May 1902. Due to Nettie's lack of money, they got a small hardship grant towards the fees, and Claude attended as a day boy.

Public schools were often brutal places at this time, and predictably Claude had to fight his way to acceptance, to overcome the stigma of being *'a mere day bug'* and receiving a grant. At this time he also had his adenoids removed – the process so was so fearsome at Middlesex Hospital that he fled the place and walked back to his grandmother's house in Bedford Park, only to find that he had been the subject of a police search. Later he was forcibly administered chloroform in the Children's Hospital in Paddington so that the operation could take place.

Aged thirteen, Claude was already confident, independent and a confirmed smoker [a habit he kept all his life]:

During the summer [1903] I determined to have an adventure, and when the holidays came suggested to my mother that I should bike to London – a distance of 89 miles!

"Oh all right, are you going to start this morning?" she laughingly said, and start I did. I had but sixpence in my pocket and no lamp. The sixpence I spent on cigarettes and when I had got as far as Woolwich it was lighting up time, and I had a deuce of a time dodging policemen, who were out for my blood. Having left Ramsgate at about 11 am, I eventually got to my grandmother's place in Bedford Park at 2 the next morning! I decided not to wake her, but I had to burgle the house as I was famished, having gone the day without food. I had no matches, and could find none. I broached a window and after a wild hunt located a big pot of blackberry jam – this I promptly woofled! How good it tasted: I can remember it to this day. In the morning I nearly gave the servant a fit, as I was dust and dirt begrimed and clad in an old blue jersey.

Life in the Junior School at St. Lawrence was uneventful. He loved French, Geography and Carpentry [*'How I blessed my knowledge of wood-working in after life and what a contempt I have for a man who cannot do his own wood-working.'*], but hated Latin and Maths. Then:

Next term held a surprise for me: I was suddenly moved up to the Upper School – a dreaded happening in the mind of us juniors. True, Hill i and Bowden had gone up last summer term, but when I met them they seemed changed. It was all so frighteningly rough and brutal. One had to fight for an existence at all hours of the day. You fought to get near the tuck shop, you fought to retain your games clothes from someone who had forgotten theirs. I was at once bagged by a monitor as his fag, and he roughly outlined how my leisure hours should be spent for his benefit. I then asked him when it would be likely that I could get home. "Oh, you're a filthy day-bug," he cried. "Why didn't you tell me that before?" He proceeded to give me a thorough walloping on that account. God! How it hurt my pride. I took a few more wallopings like that, and then the worm turned and I never had another. God, what tyrants boys are to each other, if you don't sit up and take notice and assert yourself! On the whole I suppose it's as well, and is a goodly lesson for another life.

I have always seemed to have a comic specie of walk, for at the junior school I was promptly nicknamed 'My Lord' or 'Lord Keith', and this followed me to the Col, where all sorts of senior boys were pleased to do obeisance and then turn and mock. However, even then I was growing thick skinned and they soon found that they didn't get enough change out of it to make it worthwhile.

In 1904, while staying with his Uncle Jack in Highcliffe, Claude took his mother out for a ride in a cycle sidecar. He went round a corner too fast, and Nettie was thrown from the vehicle, receiving a bad gash on her head. Claude felt over-powering guilt waves of guilt, and was sent off alone on a coastal ship to Cornwall to spend the rest of his summer holiday with his Aunt Lotty, while his mother recuperated. Next term his school report stated that Claude had to 'cultivate a more cheerful spirit'. But cheer was in short supply: the event that everyone in the family was dreading happened sooner rather than later.

[Autumn term 1904] ... This term I was playing for the Dark Blues in a particularly strenuous game we called 'sixes' – that is a soccer team of six, playing the ordinary game 20 minutes each way. We had won the first two games and imagine my disgust when mother begged me not to go back to school on the afternoon of the third game. She said that she was feeling ill, but I put her off by telling her it was imperative that I should play, but that I would bike home straight away without staying to change.

When I got back I noticed that she seemed very curious and I was rather surprised when she told me she had telegraphed for Uncle Jack and Aunt Lotty. Uncle Jack arrived that night, and bundled me off to bed right away. Aunt Lotty with Uncle Fred – my Aunt Alice's husband, who had just arrived from the USA – turned up early the next morning, having travelled all night. They had all realised what I had not: my mother felt a reoccurrence coming on of what had nearly taken her life in 1889. I suppose the strain of trying to make ends meet on the pittance we had, had proved too much for her. I shall never forget that morning: her reason completely went, and whilst we were all sorrowing, she was elated and happy, saying that everything would come right. I was bundled off to school as usual.

As is usual in these cases, my mother suddenly took a violent dislike and mistrust to Fred, whom she declared had been sent by my father to take me away from her. She became so violent when he was near that everyone deemed it better that he should leave the house, and so he went into rooms farther down the street and my  *grandmother came and joined him there. That night my mother turned against Aunt Lotty and eventually she had to leave her. By this time she had become utterly exhausted and her nerves were thoroughly out of control. Worse was to come: next morning she failed to recognize me and said I was a stranger, an imposter who had been substituted for her son. This made her so violent that it became obvious that she could not stay where we were. The advice of a medical man was taken and she was taken to – I hate to set it down – the County Asylum at Chartham. The opinion was that they would be able to calm her and probably set her right quicker than her own people could. All the agony of it is ever fresh with me: what I would not give to this day to have it different – to re-live it under different conditions!*

I stayed on with Gran in lodgings for the rest of that term and then went down, by myself, by railway to Aunt Lotty in Helford. Mother was very weak, they had said, but they were feeding her up and had every hope of her recovery.

Next term, that is the Lent term of 1905, I was sent to board in the private house of the Science Master, the Rev. G. E Battle ..... he was a typical parson of the type I loathe: sanctimonious, self-righteous, mean, hypocritical and bullying. God, how I hated him! .... Living with him as I did gave me a very thorough training in fitting myself in undesirable conditions....

During my last holidays I had determined to go into upright collars, as I was big for my age and felt that Eton collars were very derogatory to my prestige in life. Lotty had promised me some, but at the last moment she recanted, as I had offended her in some way. However, I wasn't to be denied, for I bought six with some pocket money I had, at a little store in Paddington. I still smile at my own importance as I walked into that shop in 1905 and demanded the collars of a man! Also, about this time, it seems I smoked pretty freely during the holidays.

From the Battle's I journeyed every fortnight to Chartham to see my sainted mother. It is not possible for me to tell you in so many words what my sensations were. You will never know unless you make a similar pilgrimage and please God, you will never have that sorrow. It is a nightmare to me to this day, and seldom do I allow myself to cast my thoughts back to it. Poor darling little mother: in a way, if I had never come into the world, she would have been spared all that, as it was due to the Graves Disease which had started at my birth. The appallingly sad part of it was that this cursed disease only causes periods of violent insanity, punctuated by periods of comparative normality. Imagine what you'd feel to suddenly find yourself among mad people, and be treated as mad? Wouldn't it send you off into high-strikes?

That Xmas was a sad one – naturally. I went all the way to Helford, via London and Falmouth. I was getting quite a good education in travelling, and soon knew my way about London very well, as I always had nearly a whole day's wait between arriving from Ramsgate and catching the midnight express from Paddington to Falmouth. I had no money to speak of during my London meanderings, so I used to tramp about just picking up street knowledge of the great city. It has since held me in good stead.

Returning from Helford, I was met by my Uncle Fred. Fred is an American out-and-out, and he was never tired of cramming American ways and ideas down my young throat. I owe Fred very much in life, for he had extraordinarily high principles and practical ideas for carrying them out. He taught me much in respect to chivalry and courtesy generally, and for that I shall ever be grateful.

I had been told that they had decided to move my mother from Chartham to a more expert place at St. Andrews at Northampton, and there she was moved by Lotty and Fred during the Lent term.

I was still living with Battle, and I hated him as much as ever. He had moved me from a top floor room to a room in a sort of annexe, which led out into the garden. Out of sheer devilment I used to creep out into that garden at night and clear off over the fence, and wander round Ramsgate by night – a thing no boy was allowed to do even by day! Clad in my ordinary clothes, but disguised under a 'cadger' cap, I used to wander about with a cigarette between my lips, and drink in that glorious sensation of freedom. I became a specie of outlaw against every order Battle might make.

My Easter holidays were spent at Helford. On my return to London, on my way back to school – no, I am wrong. I was sent up from Helford to London about halfway through the holidays, as mother was worse, and they wanted me to go up to St. Andrews to see her. In London Fred met me and as we were sitting side by side on the top of a London bus he said to me "Have you ever thought that your mother might die, for she is very ill?" My heart froze but I said nothing, so he continued, "Would you be very surprised if you received news that she had died before we could get there?" Again I said nothing: I couldn't. Then he let fall the bombshell: "Your mother died the evening before last."

I remember it was a cold and windy day and dust was whirling up from the streets. The bus swayed to and fro and I was physically uncomfortable. I idly watched the traffic as we approached Piccadilly Circus, but I never said a word, and I kept my head turned from him. So she was dead, dead – gone forever. I repeated this to myself idly: my brain seemed numbed. I felt that I lost some part of myself, and through all these years I never feel that I have regained that essential intangible indefinable something .....

It was decided that my mother should be buried by the side of her godfather – a Belgian gentleman named Alexandre Demaret, who was buried at Margate Cemetery. To Margate we all went, and lodged ourselves at Lilly's Hotel on the Fort Hill. What a miserable affair it was. I wanted the luxury of private grief, but that is always denied one. My mother's end had been so peaceful, such a fading away that we were half afraid she might have slipped into a coma, so it was arranged that her ceratoid vein be opened – sealing her fate! When this was done and over her dear dead face was arranged a window in her coffin.

The day she was buried was one when God seemed out of temper with the world. Rain, cold unsympathetic rain teemed down and blew in great gusts. The service was taken by an unpleasant flaccid parson who has set me against his kind forever and aye. When he had had his say, the coffin bearers removed the shield from the glass window and I was led behind the bier to take my last look at the woman who had given her life, her daily care, her everything, that I might prosper. Swathed in the cold white of grave clothes I saw the peaceful face of my sainted mother, her eyes closed as It In peaceful sleep. It didn't seem a bit awful – this was the first dead face I had seen. Gran followed me and burst out crying. Then they moved me on, and I saw them screwing down the cover plate. Out through the rain they carried her and slowly down, down into the pure white chalk grave they lowered her .... my mother.

SELF AT
St LAWRENCE
1006

When I turned away I had locked up all that part of my life and turned my face to the future. I refused to mope and moan, and probably they thought me heartless to want to go and forget everything in a music hall show that night – which I did. I don't know what would have happened if I hadn't done so. I dread to think.

Claude returned to finish his schooling at St. Lawrence. He made friends with a boy called Rackstraw, and together they would manufacture keys for the schools locks in metal work classes, and then roam the grounds at night, doing no worse than smoking cigarettes. Claude notes that he was never made a prefect, and never got on with the Rev Battle, with whom he continued to lodge. Given the distress and the personal guilt that Claude felt about his mother's death, it's unsurprising that he went through a difficult time in the era before counselling.

It must have been about this time that I was very distressed about the scheme of things in general, as I read and re-read many theological books, and, finally, being dissatisfied with them all, proceeded to write a scientific explanation of God and the universe. I laugh to think of my appalling presumption, yet it had more than a few grains of truth in it. I also became terribly keen on the study of the mind and waded through several of Prune's [a teacher] books on psychology. I even précised that weighty book, Sully's 'Outlines of Psychology' and this I have by me today.

In July 1907 Claude went up to London to take his Matriculation Exams. He failed them, doing worst in the subjects he was most confident in. He had planned to take the Inter Science course before doing a Bachelor of Science degree at London University, but his exam failure ended such plans. He had no back-up plan. He had no parents, almost no money, and nowhere to live. His guardian was his young Aunt Lotty, who was holed up nursing a broken heart in an ancient cottage in Helford, Cornwall. She too had very little money, no experience of parenthood, and no experience or contacts in the world of work. It must have been a dismal situation for a young lad aged seventeen.

And so ended my schooldays – happy vagabond days, when responsibility was unknown and everything was thought out and made easy for one. I admit that I was far too unruly, but I could never stifle that longing for adventure which has so often led me into the most awful scrapes, both in school and in after life. I left school in a very embryo stage: I was an impractical idealist. I had never kissed a girl properly – had never wanted to! It was a secret hope that I might travel and see something of the world, as my father had done, and I was incredibly proud that I was Canadian born. How my hopes were realized! Within five years I had journeyed up and down and round the whole wide world and found very useful my schoolboy's knowledge of geography.

This is an extraordinarily positive assessment of what must have been a miserable, lonely and worrying time, but it was written twenty years later when Claude had made a success of himself, and had a son of his own. His harsh schooling and the early death of his mother were to prove vital formative influences on his subsequent life.

Chapter 3   Starting at the bottom: life as an electrical engineer 1907-1909

Claude became an electrical engineer because he had nothing else, and nowhere to go. Having failed his exams, he could not go to university. He had almost no money. There was no careers advice service, no unemployment benefits. His guardian was a maiden aunt who lived in the remotest corner of Cornwall and had no idea about careers for young men.

So Aunt Lotty wrote to the parents of Claude's school-friend, Norman Rackstraw. He had been taken on as a pupil at Marconi Wireless Telegraph Company, the pioneering engineers who were making the first radios at Tysen Street, Dalston, North-east London. Rackstraw's sister was engaged to Monty-Herring, the secretary of the manager of the factory. Lotty obtained a place at the factory for Claude, but not with the same advantages as Rackstraw: he started as an ordinary learner in the machine shops, in the status as an ordinary mechanic and to receive the ordinary learner's pay of one penny an hour. If he did well, he would become a pupil to the firm and to go through the other departments and finally join their engineering staff. *'In other words, I had to justify my existence'.*

Claude was found lodgings at 154, Dalston Lane with four *'Dickensian'* old ladies, the Misses Atkins, who also kept a small school, and often treated Claude as a schoolboy. His life was one of long hours, stressful work and intense loneliness. He had to be at the works by six in the morning, had half an hour for breakfast and an hour for lunch, finished work at five in the afternoon. His work involved standing all day at a lathe doing strenuous work in a very noisy workroom where he was judged constantly on the speed and accuracy of his work. When he returned to his lodgings he had no energy to do anything beyond getting himself clean and then *'slacking'* before the evening meal. After the meal he often attended electrical engineering classes at the Hackney Institute nearby. He never met other people of his age: Rackstraw was working in the offices, not the factory, and went home to his sister's in Chiswick, and Claude says of the working class area he lived in: *'no one knowable lived near Dalston.'* He was also very shy: he fancied a girl called Ada at the works, but found it too hard to ask her out until it was too late.

Claude gives an account of his daily working life that was probably just like thousands of other boys of his age, but the difference is that he was totally alone in this world, and totally unprepared for it:

How I hated early morning rising. It was October 1907 when I started with Marconi's, and when I went out into the cold morning air to walk to the works, it was quite dark and often drizzling. The huge flaring arc lights that lit the streets made everything appear weird and ghostly. As I shuffled along the cold deserted streets, I used to hear the alarm clocks of people more fortunate than I, in that they evidently hadn't to be up so early, and I often met the man whose living was calling people. For a few pence each week you can hire him to come and rap at your door at any unearthly hour that necessity causes you to rise and leave your bed. At five minutes to six the works hooter went, and five minutes later the gates were closed until seven, and thus you'd lose a whole hour's pay. Arrived at the works, you fell in with the queue that was filing to the entrance of the shop you worked in, and as you passed the time clock, you took out your time card and punched it in the time-clock, thus recording the time and day when you started work. Every time you entered or left the works, you thus recorded your time of arrival or departure, and your weekly wages were made up from these entries. It was all mechanical: you were but a number and you were treated as such.

Above: two pictures of the Marconi works at Dalston, in approximately 1905, two years before Claude arrived.

Once in the strange silence of the machine shop you exchanged good mornings with those near you, slipped on your overalls, carefully extinguishing your half finished cigarette and set it aside for the breakfast hour, turned on your lamp and waited until, precisely at six, the shop foreman walked over and set the driving motors going. The peaceful dead air of the place was at once transformed into a deafening mechanical din, as the great lines of shining shafting took up their motion and transmitted it through a thousand whirling leather belts to the machines that were dotted about all over the place. In a few minutes everybody, encouraged by the ever watchful foreman, would be busy at their jobs and the work of the day would be started. At breakfast time I had a hurried rush and at lunchtime I just had time to catch a glimpse at the daily paper before I again took my stand behind my lathe.

My metal working training at St. Lawrence stood me in good stead, but I very soon learnt that speed was an added requirement to the accuracy of work. Every 'job' I was given carried a job ticket on which was entered the rough material that I was issued with, the amount I returned after completing the job and a record of the hours I spent on the work. The costing department then got busy on the job ticket and worked out exactly how much each of the articles had cost, and if my cost was too high, I was taken off those articles and given something easier, and vice versa. Thus they sort out the good from the bad workmen, and when you can produce work at *prices below normal, it was an argument for a rise of pay. My first job was by no means an easy one: it was usually done by a workman earning five pence an hour – which of course meant that I could take five times as long without increasing the manufacturing cost. I got away with it, but I scrapped an excessive amount of material and it was some time before I was again given such a job – turning and polishing ebonite. Another thing hampered me very much at first: one had to make almost every tool one used. Now tool making is no easy matter until you have had lots of practice, and I had many sad failures before I could with certainty forge up, temper and grind my lathe tools or drills, etc. However, it all came in time, and although the wretched firm would never increase my paltry penny an hour wages on account of it being my step to becoming a pupil, at the end of my time I was regularly entrusted with jobs usually done by men getting as much as nine pence an hour. In those days, eleven pence was the maximum wage, and there were not many who drew that.*

Our working week was of fifty hours, so I drew a dollar every Saturday. This was my pocket money, as Aunt Lotty paid up for my living and washing and bought me such clothes as I needed. I never had many, as any old thing did by day, and I never went anywhere much at other times. Out of my weekly four shillings and two pence I had to pay for cigarettes, stamps, note paper, transport fares, library subscription, daily paper, any special tools I required, and technical books. It didn't leave much margin, as you can imagine.

His first break from the factory was unpaid holiday to go to his Grandmother Rogers' funeral in Portsmouth, and then to spend Christmas with Lotty in Cornwall. He was very proud to buy his aunt a present using his own money. Lotty accompanied him back to London, and having seen his lodgings, decided to move him to new lodgings, run by *'a dear motherly old soul'* called Mrs. Dennis. Life improved:

She fed me, provided me with a furnished room, fires and washing. I revelled in the luxury of being absolutely free after my work was done, and I think that the time I was there was one of the happiest in my life. A very pronounced stepping stone between boyhood and manhood. I was only just turned 17 years of age, but the life I led aged me. I used to belong to a paper covered library, and for 2d a week I could get almost any classic. I read much and deeply in those days. At the Hackney Institute I was engaged on a course of advance Electrostatics, and the value of this somewhat obscure branch of electricity was very manifest when I came to grapple with the problems of wireless telegraphy.

Claude looked forward to Sundays. He would set his alarm for the usual work day time, and when he was awoken he would turn off the alarm and fall back into luxurious sleep. He spent much time just walking the streets of London, exploring with a map, and he tried several denomination of church without finding one that satisfied him.

In the summer of 1908 there was a slump in radio orders, and many were laid off before the Dalston factory was closed, and production moved to Chelmsford, Essex in July. Claude was moved there, still working for a penny per hour in the machine shop. Trade perked up, and he found himself working 13 hour days.

In October 1908 he had satisfactorily served his year and he was formally articled as a premium pupil. This now meant that instead of getting paid a penny an hour, his guardian Lotty had to pay him an allowance and his grandfather paid the 200 hundred guineas to the firm to teach him! His friend Norman Rackstraw graduated away from pupilage at the same time, so he still had no friends at work. However, the work was now less onerous and much more interesting, and soon Claude was moved to the firm's London offices in the Strand, where he and Norman worked on mechanical drawing in the same room as the desks of the Chief Engineer and the Managing Director. Claude admired both of these men and said he learned a lot from them. He also attended a special course of lectures by Dr. J. Erskine-Murray at the Northampton Institute on the then almost unknown subject of wireless telegraphy.

The work became more varied: he and Norman were often sent down to Millwall docks to repair installations on ships, and he manned a stall at the Northampton Institute, both of which improved his confidence. They both took an exam on wireless telegraphy [probably the first one of its kind anywhere in the world], which Claude passed with the top mark of 97%. He was given the job of installing a wireless on a theatre stage, which gave him the great thrill of seeing the actresses backstage, and led him to a *'tawdry little theatre restaurant in Mornington Crescent! There I think I drunk my first champagne – supped it from a loving cup of a spritely little 'soubrette' with a peroxide coiffure and a handmade complexion'*.

Claude moved into a boarding house *'as I had found rooms alone endangered one of falling into the recluse habit, and I realized the absolute necessity of a young man's mixing with all sorts and conditions of his fellow beings.'* His increasing confidence extended *'to the recklessness of a box [price 3 shillings] at the 'Queen's Music Hall, Poplar'* – a practice he had previously considered too vulgar.

In April 1909 he landed his first real construction job, being sent to Southampton to equip five of the largest liners of the Royal Mail Steam Packet Co with wirelesses. The work to equip the 'Avon' [pictured], the Aragon, the Araguaya, the Amazon and the Asturias took five months, during which time Marconi's paid Claude's board and lodging, helping his finances. He was also helped by his Grandfather John Rogers dying in June and leaving him a legacy. *'This was entirely unexpected, as during nearly all my life he had never been able to forgive me for being a Keith!'*

Claude spent some of this money on an eight day Cooks holiday in Paris, which he bought for himself and his Aunt Lotty – he only told her after he had bought the tickets. They had a wonderful time, visiting the places they had read about.

Back in London, Claude and Norman taught themselves Morse telegraphy and typewriting, but Claude was soon sent off again, this time to fit channel ferries with wirelesses. He stayed in the imposing Hotel Metropole in Dover: *'It was to me a very swagger place and though the bills were booked to the firm, it took me all my time to live up to that standard. I couldn't dress for dinner, as it had never been possible to buy any dress clothes up to then – they were too expensive!'*

Whilst in Dover in 1909 he witnessed Bleriot's first crossing of the English Channel by plane. One might have thought that he would make a great thing of this, given his subsequent life in aeroplanes, but he doesn't give many details, which makes one wonder if he didn't actually miss the event. Claude and his boss moved on to Folkestone, fitting many other channel ferries, crossing the Channel repeatedly to test their equipment.

Towards the end of September the job was done and I was back in London, keen for another outside job. I got more than I bargained for! In those days there was an awful dearth of engineers. Bradfield, the Managing Director, leant over and told Gray he'd have to find someone at to fit Gordon Bennett's yacht in Cannes in the south of France. "Can't be done," said Gray. "I haven't anyone available." Then Bradfield caught my eye. "What about you, young fellow? Can you speak any French?" Forgetful of my Matric failure, I glibly murmured "Yes, sir. I was in Paris for my holiday in August." "Right," he said. "Get all ready to leave for Cannes in three days." I could have kissed him!

This was the start of Claude's life of world travel. At last he was going to experience the places in his atlas that had pored over.

Chapter 4   Women, wirelesses and world travel 1909 – 1914

So Claude was loosed upon the world, courtesy of Marconi's missions. It changed his life, giving him confidence and heightening the sense of adventure that had always run through him. Putting experiences to the places he'd studied in an atlas, meeting exotic foreign women, meeting up with relatives, staying in the comparative luxury of hotels, wrestling with difficult engineering and technical problems – Claude loved them all; he grabbed at everything life had to offer, and he grew up in the process. It also gave him the illness that probably led to his eventual death.

In October 1909 he set out for Cannes with a radio operator called Stapleton, who was to stay and operate the radio once Claude had installed it on the Lysistrata. They met two girls in the train from Calais to Paris. Claude was thrilled that his chat-up lines worked, for the Danish girl ['*a dream in gold and white*'], who was on her way to a convent near Paris, allowed him to escort her across Paris, to take her out for a meal, and to write to him afterwards. He commented: '*I was certainly growing up*'.

He was still excited when he reached Marseilles:

Arriving at Marseilles at dawn, the sight of the waking sun breaking through the blue mists of night and striking the golden figure of Natore Dame de la Garde was a sight I shall never forget. Then I went down to the town and smelt it, and that almost wiped out the pleasure of the street. The Avenue de la Gare is a wonderful street. I there came across the first automatic bar that I had seen, and nearly got sick through drinking a horrible mixture of liqueurs for the sheer joy of seeing the automatic part of it work!

Claude and Stapleton stayed at the Hotel Royal in Cannes, where the officers of the Lysistrata were also based. The boat was a marvel of its time. Gordon Bennett was the most flamboyant media mogul of his age, and his yacht cost $635,000 [$225 million today]. It featured Turkish baths, theatres, and a specially padded stall for an Alderney cow to ensure an adequate supply of fresh milk at sea. It changed the world of yachting in that it opened up new realms of luxury and paved the way for a future world of super-yachts as status symbols for the mega-rich.

Claude had to hassle the customs to release his radio gear, and the French could not believe that anyone so young had been sent to do the job, so he changed his age from nineteen to twenty-one. He was struck down by '*a dose of enteric*' but used Dubonnet, '*the good old French quinine wine*', to pull through. He observed the casinos in Monte Carlo, visited Menton, San Raphael, Nice and had a good time, as well as going with the Lysistrata on a trial run to Genoa.

He was back in London by the end of the month, and received a bonus cheque – he regarded this as fair since he was still technically an unpaid learner for Marconi. As soon as he had unpacked, he was off again, this time to Lisbon, sailing in the Amazon, which he had already installed with radio. The mission was to fit the arsenal and three warships with radio, and Claude was under the command of an engineer called Leary who took his Newfoundlander wife and small child with him. They stayed in the famous but expensive Hotel Avenida, but then downgraded twice to cheaper hotels. The work went well and he enjoyed working with the friendly Portuguese naval personnel.

I hadn't much money, so I filled in time wandering around the lovely old city, and I don't think I missed seeing much of it. I was growing up all the time, but was still free of vices, except for the occasional cherry brandy or glass of wine, and cigarette smoking. I found Mrs. Leary a very typical 'rubber-necker', and she and I dragged Leary to visit all the sites worth seeing. I have no feminine memories of Lisbon, except it be the violet blue eyes of the hotel proprietor's wife at the Avenida. I was young, and she scared me – had I been older, I might have found trouble! She was an adorable looking Swede and he was a fat Spaniard. The circus and the bull ring are the chief amusements in Lisbon, and these we visited often.

Claude returned to London on 5th January, 1910. Having been hampered by his rudimentary Morse Code skills, he applied to go on a telegraphy course, and was sent to the operators' school near at Seaforth, near Liverpool. He stayed with the manager, Cross, who gave him personal lessons in exchange for Claude lecturing the students on the technology of the equipment. His Morse speeds and teaching techniques were to stand him in very good stead in his RAF career.

Cross promised Claude a trip as an operator on a transatlantic liner to practice his new skills, but Claude received a telegram from Marconi ordering him to travel to Durban, Natal, to install a new radio station there. He set sail in the RMS 'Balmoral', from Southampton, and had a great time on the trip. He was starting to enjoy the power of his good looks.

We called at Madeira and Tenerife, and then straight to Cape Town. The trip was an ideal one with a good crowd of passengers. I entered into shipboard life with zest. On this trip I sported my first outfit of dress clothes – the ones I still have! On board was a Pole, Berta Atkin, and under her spell I gradually fell, although I was too shy to admit it. Pretty dark eyed Berta! I wonder where she is now. She left the ship at Cape Town to join a man whom her father wanted her to marry. Poor Berta. I never saw her again although she wrote me piteous letters of her misery after her marriage.

Life in Durban continued the party. His Uncle Charles had emigrated there and Claude fell in love with his cousin Dot:

At Durban were my Aunt Mabel and cousins Dot and Gwen. Cousin Nell was up at Johannesburg. Dot is six months younger than me and Gwen four years younger. Kos [Claude's boss] and I put up at the Federal Buildings in Beach Road. The station site was over near the lighthouse on the bluff and across the bay. We went to and fro on the ferry each day. The life was a typical care-free colonial existence, where one is too happy to worry about the petty dictates of English social life. I learned to dance at Durban, and Miss Fenton taught me to dance in a way that earned me much praise in those day .... The work of clearing the jungle from the site with black convict labour, the erecting of the mast, the troubles and the trials of the work aged both Kos and I. In between times, though, we had an excellent time as picnics and drinks were the rule every day or night. The Natal government were awfully nice to us, especially Mr. Weightman, the Chief Engineer of the colony. We went up to Pietermaritzburg and visited him at his home. When we turned over the station they gave us a dinner and it was there that I had to give my first public speech.

It was out in Natal that Claude found out that he had become an orphan. His reaction – to get on with things in the short term, and then to ponder things more deeply – is understandable, considering he had never met his father:

Curiously enough it was over a telephone wire in Durban that Aunt Mabel told me that she had received news from a sister of hers in Victoria, British Columbia, that my father had been killed in a fall down stairs. I could do nothing from Natal, so I just waited until I should be back in England. The work completed, Kos and I sailed back in RMS 'Saxon' in September of 1910. On my return voyage I again found a Polish lady crossing the way of my life: this time I took safety in flight!

I went on holiday when I got back, down to Helford. From there I went over and visited the huge Trans-Atlantic Wireless Station of the company at Poldhu, and was terribly impressed by the size of it all. Little did I think that in two years it would fall to my lot to install an equally big modern plant alongside the old one!

In order that I might get in touch with the executors of my father's will, I applied to go on a job that the firm were to do in the Fiji Islands, as I could travel there via Canada, and call of en route and transact my own business. It was useless to try to do it from London, and naturally my Rogers relations were against my seeking the Keith family at a time when it would certainly have looked as though all I was after was gain. My father dying was a contingency I had never counted on. In a dim way, I had felt sure that I should meet him some day. Until I was of age I could do nothing in the matter, as Lotty, being my guardian and having control of my finances, had complete control in the matter. In any case, it would have been grossly ungrateful to cut myself off from the family who had done so much for me, and so I had to just wait without worrying to take any steps, until I came of age.

So the rift between the Rogers and Keith family was still active twenty years after it started, and it prevented Claude from getting in touch directly with his father's family and executors. If he had done so he would have risked 'cutting himself off' from his mother's family.

As Lotty had seemed very lonely in England when I was away in South Africa, I decided to get her to come with me to Fiji. This we arranged, and both of us set sail from Tilbury in the RMS Minnehaha on 9th November of 1910. On board I lost my heart to a curious little American. She handled me very kindly, and taught me much. I have always kept up the friendship thus begun.

Mrs. Charlyne Courtland had recently been widowed in 1910, and had been appearing in a West End play. She was seen off at Tilbury by the actor Lawrence Irving. She was actually a minor film star in the silent films, and she appeared on Broadway in 1926. She is the subject of Chapter 2 of Claude's book 'My Rosery', in which Claude describes how she seduced the innocent young 'self' [but not 'all the way']. Curiously, in the

Minnehaha list of that voyage, she is listed as a member of the crew, and Claude mentions that she played the piano very well, so maybe she was working her passage.

Lotty [pictured left] and Claude travelled across America and Canada, visiting his Uncle Fred and Aunt Alice in Ludlow, Massachusetts, then going back to New York to visit Charlyne, before travelling to Banff via the frozen Niagara Falls and Claude's birthplace, Qu'Appelle, Saskatchewan. They travelled to Vancouver, where he met the woman who had helped his mother when he was born, before travelling to Victoria, where his father had died. At this point his pupilage with Marconi's finally expired, and they started paying him a proper salary.

In Victoria, he met a number of his father's friends who told him what they knew of his father. These heroic tales, including ones about his father rescuing soldiers from rebel Indians, no doubt first told by Hilton himself, gave Claude a new rosy tinted view of his father, and probably hardened his ambition for adventures of his own.

At Victoria I felt my name was known as my father's son, and so we went and put up at the palatial Empress Hotel. I had done all I could to probe the matter of my father's will and estate, but could get no satisfaction. They seemed a parcel of rogues. My father had been buried by a man he had once befriended and a monument erected over his grave. It is at the cemetery near Colonist's Park, Victoria.

Claude met up with his Marconi 'team', Strickland and Nicholls, in Victoria, and they set sail across the Pacific in a 'wretched little tub' called Moana. They encountered rough seas, but enjoyed calls at Honolulu and Fanning Island en route to Fiji.

At Suva on Fiji they met up with his boss Leary [but not his 'rubber-necking' wife this time]. They stayed in Athestone Lodge, a boarding house run by *'a lady in reduced circumstances, a Mrs. Rowlands'*, while Leary stayed in a smart hotel. They had a long wait for their gear to arrive, and in the meantime they became involved in local life:

Suva is a sociable little community and we rapidly made friends on all sides. Dances and picnics came our way very frequently, and we all entered into the zest of it. I was at an age when one enjoys life whole-heartedly and without conscience for tomorrow. My heart was well under control, and so I entered wholeheartedly into as many harmless flirtations as seemed to promise interest. I took up riding and also got in a fair amount of tennis.

In Suva I met nearly all the whites. I brought a letter of introduction to one family from a former partner of my father – to some people called Land. We saw much of the Lands, and after beginning by violently disliking the eldest unmarried daughter, I ended up by getting too fond of her! However, the work ended abruptly, and it never got into the danger zone.

This is completely untrue, and it perhaps indicates his unhappiness or even shame at the incident. He ended up proposing marriage to Ada Land [pictured right] by post two years later, and paying for her fare to England. This saga came to intrude on his later life and career. From his account, she sounds manipulative, capricious and maybe cruel, but despite this Claude was characteristically generous about her. Lotty obviously took a dislike to Ada in Fiji, and was horrified by the subsequent attachment. It's possible that Ada was very bored out in Fiji, and saw Claude as her ticket off the island.

BEACH NEAR VATAWARA, WHERE WE PICNICED.

Claude's photo of the Grand Hotel, Suva

The Marconi contract was to provide for three radio stations. One was to go up near Suva, the site being chosen at Vatawaqa, and another at Wieyevo, on the island of Taveuni, and the third at Labasa on the island of Vanua Levue. Once the gear arrived, they went to live out at Vatawaqa, while Lotty stayed at Athestone Lodge. When the first station was complete, the others went to Taveuni and left Claude at Suva. Then, when the second station was done, they all went on to Labasa and got that erected and tested.

On Labasa, Claude lost his virginity in an affair which seems shocking to modern readers. It is the subject of a chapter in 'My Rosery', and is reproduced in full as chapter 6 of this book.

The contract fulfilled, Lotty and Claude set sail for England on 22nd October 1911, the day after Claude's 'coming of age' party. They visited Aukland, Sydney, travelled overland to Melbourne, then by sea to Adelaide, Fremantle, Colombo, Suez, Port Said, Naples, Marseilles, and Gibraltar en route to London.

Now he was over twenty-one, Claude was free to get in touch with his Keith relations:

On my return from Fiji I got in touch with one of my Keith uncles – Graham [left] – and had an interview with him. He treated me both kindly and sensibly, and having got to know him it was only natural that I should make the acquaintance of my Grandmother, the surviving head of the Keith family. I called upon her and there met several more of my Keith relatives. I suppose that, having knocked about as I had, I did not feel very strange in meeting them for the first time. I had had to stand on my own merits and let them justify my existence too often to feel any qualms about doing it amongst my own family, even though they had never seen me before! I knew what to expect as to what they would be, as I knew their status in life, and of course I was but confirmed in my anticipations: I found them a typical English family of the same status as my mother's. They now tell me that I appeared painfully Americanized; this was due to my daily contact with Leary, and having just come back from New York. Anyway, they were, one and all, very kind to me.

31

Claude's account above omits a couple of the steps in his reconciliation with the Keiths. It would seem to have been a bit more complicated and took longer than he admits. He had actually approached them in 1910, before he went on his trip around the world. His visit to his father's executors in Victoria would seem to be an attempt to bypass the Keiths en route to his inheritance, but he was obviously thwarted. This is the account by Claude's Aunt Nell in the Keith family yearbook:

1910. Graham told me that Hilton's son had walked into the office and wished to be known to his father's family! We had for years ceased to look for him! We thought he had died in childhood!!!

23rd October 1910. Hilton Claude Keith 20 today [sic – actually 2 days previously]. *When he was 6 weeks old his mother stole away from Hilton with the boy and tho' <u>every effort</u> has been made to trace her whereabouts and to gain possession of the boy, <u>all has been in vain</u> – lately <u>we hear the mother is dead</u> & on 5th October a firm of solicitors wrote to Graham to claim on behalf of Claude all his Father has left him in his will! Graham of course at once asked for an interview with Claude at his office & for proof of his identification. <u>This he refuses</u>! He has a post in the E.I Co & is to start for Fiji – says he will go to Victoria B.C. and claim from the Executor there his father's effects etc. On the next page I have copied the marriage certificate of Claude's parents, the certificate of his birth, the originals of both are before me. They settle for good the <u>untrue and unkind rumours</u> of certain relations as to the legitimacy of Hilton's son!*

December 1911. At Xmas time Claude Hilton Keith called on his Uncle Graham at his office and made himself known to him. It appears that he has been to Victoria B.C., and seen his father's friends, and <u>heard the truth at last about his father</u>, and visited his grave! He has claimed his effects, and wishes to be received into the Keith family. His mother became mentally ill when he was young. Her relations in Cornwall seem to have brought him up. He was trained there in the Wireless Marconi Co. Works, in whose firm he is earning £200 a year. Until his 21st birthday he could do nothing in making himself known, as <u>according to his story</u> he was dependent on his aunts. He wishes no reference to the past! A very sad memory for him, but he spoke of his poor father, and is anxious to know his history. He is a good sort of fellow, 6 feet high, fair, <u>not the least like the family,</u> of an independent character. Graham liked him. When Claude returns from a business trip to New York we hope to welcome him into this huge family.

Claude had been brought up by the Rogers family, who had given him a very different slant on the bitterness between his parents and their family, and Ellen Keith [later known as his adored Aunt Nell] only hints in the passages above at some of the issues that divided the two families. The Rogers had accused Hilton of some very bad things that are not recorded, but had deeply wounded the Keiths. Since both families had London solicitors in their ranks, they belonged to a small world where respectability and reputation were vital. Simply rolling up and asking for his inheritance was unlikely to be simple. However, the Keiths were open to reconciliation. Ellen and her mother Mary had been depressed since the deaths of the family patriarch, Thomas, and his eldest son, Herbert, and they were ready to be charmed by this handsome adventurous new addition, miraculously restored from the ranks of the presumed dead.

Nell recorded that Claude had told them that he was off on a business trip to New York. Again, that wasn't strictly true: he was working his passage on a transatlantic liner as a telegrapher to meet Charlyne Courtland in New York. He was disappointed to find her *'older and wiser'*, but they spent time amiably and remained friends. At least he didn't get this trip on a liner that was just being finished – the Titanic! On the return trip he was thrilled to take tea with another American film star, Gaby Delys [pictured right].

Claude's next job was within biking distance of his Aunt Lotty in Helford: Leary,

Strickland, Claude and a bright young man were to put in all the electrical plant of an up-to-date and duplicated installation at the original Transatlantic Marconi Station at Poldhu in Cornwall near the Lizard. The picture below shows the hotel that Leary stayed in, but the rest of the team were in cheaper lodgings. The other picture shows Strickland chatting up a local girl outside the Old Inn at Poldhu. Claude himself *'fell under the spell of a local girl'* called Mary Downing [pictured]: *Others had done so before, men older and wiser than me, so why should I fear to admit it?*

Poldhu Hotel & Marconi Station.

My job at Poldhu was no sinecure. I have seldom worked harder, nor for more hours per day. The wretched firm was now under a Jew Managing Director, and his idea was to cut down working expenses. He expected us to do the construction work at Poldhu on the same pay as we should get on running and maintenance work. This we kicked at, and eventually got that pay plus all our expenses. It was but the first trouble over salary, as the firm became a skinflint organization from the time that Godfrey Isaacs took over the Managing Directorship. Certainly he forced the market value of the shares up to dizzy heights, but we were some of the unfortunates who helped this.

[An unfortunate case of anti-Semitism, and not the only instance of it in Claude's writings.]

GANG AT POLDHU 1912

SELF 1912

Chile was to be Claude's next destination, but the disillusion with Marconi and its boss was not over:

The firm had now managed to get a big contract in Chile to erect three small and two huge stations for the Chilean navy. Leary was given the job and he of course asked for Strickland and myself to go with him. Strickland and I were to go ahead, but trouble arose as neither of us would go under the other, and one had to be sent in charge. Strickland was older than I; I had considerably more engineering qualifications than he. The matter was finally decided by their sending out a third fellow – Dockray – in charge of both of us. Then we had a row about the offered salary and refused to sign our contracts for the sum they mentioned. They sacked all three of us but within twenty-four hours Isaacs had to climb down and we got the pay we had stuck out for. We were bound for two years, to do work anywhere in South America.

BIG WIRELESS STATION WE ERECTED AT PUERTO MONTT

In October the three of us sailed from Liverpool in the Pacific Steam navigation Company's liner 'Oriana'. We went right round to Valparaiso, the seaport capital of Chile, calling at La Rochelle, Lisbon, Madeira, St. Vincent, Fernando Noronha, Pernambuco, Bahia, Rio de Janeiro, Santos, Punta Arenas, and Coronel. It was a wonderful trip and we had a more than ordinarily good time.

The stations were to link up one end of Chile with the other, right from Arica in the north to Punta Arenas, which is nearly three thousand miles to the south. The sites were near the towns of Arica, Antofagasta, Coquimbo for the small stations, and for the large stations near Puerto Montt and Punta Arenas. The northern stations were tropical, the southern ones Antarctic! The difficulties and delays and disappointments on this contract would fill a book, but suffice it to say that bit by bit we fought them down, and completed the work. The delays in receipt of the instruments necessitated our dodging to and fro from station to station, doing what we could in any one of them.

Leary came out towards the end of 1912 with Nicholls and Benning, but had a row with the latter soon after arriving, and sent him back. The three of us had got Arica well under way when Leary arrived, and by stages we pushed on with the three smaller stations, finally completing them by the middle of 1913, when we all collected at Punta Arenas. Here delays were sickening, but the station was practically finished in April of 1914, when I was ordered back to England, having had a bad dose of lung inflammation brought on by the terrible climate in that wild part of the world.

These pictures by Claude are all of the station built in Punta Arenas in 1914, showing what a complex undertaking it was in such hostile an environment. Below: Tierra del Fuego

Tierra Del Fuego by Claude

I set sail for England in the new PSNC liner 'Orduna' on the return half of her maiden voyage. It was a wonderful ship and I was mighty glad to get away from Chile and Leary, the latter having made himself very disagreeable at my leaving.

At Rio who should get aboard but an old pal of mine, Leo Ransome-Jones, who was an engineer with the cable company. He and I used to stay at 17, Newton Road together in 1909 when we were both learning our professions. His mater and sister also stayed there. On board there was a blonde dream of a Parisienne, and dancing together soon made Germaine Lachaux and I firm friends.

Arrived back in England I went to see a Harley Street specialist and he said that serious trouble might set in if I were not careful, and that I would have to lie up for a long time in a sanatorium. Imagine my feelings: I had no money for this and though I certainly had three months leave due on full pay, I had other ideas as to the spending of that! Eventually it was decided that I should go to Linford Sanatorium, near Ringwood in the New Forest, but I stuck out for a few days in Paris first.

Lotty and I accordingly went over and there I renewed my acquaintance with the fair Germaine who had left the 'Orduna' at La Rochelle. I was thoroughly reckless during the time I was there. Had I not got to enter 'la vie morte' as soon as I got back? Well, why not make sure of a good time while the chance still existed? And I did! Races, dinners, theatres, operas followed one another in such quick succession that I fear that I nearly did for poor Lotty! We were staying at the Hotel Louvre and the weather was as divine as only a Parisian summer can be. It was good to be alive, even if I had the sword of Linford hanging over my head.

In May I entered Linford and proceeded to lead a 'medical life', during which the doctors got me as fat as a poisoned bull pup. I was a good patient and they expressed no fears for my complete recovery. In July my leave was up, and at my request the firm agreed that I might be sent to a quiet job on the Running and Maintenance Staff at the Poldhu station, which I had re-constructed in 1912. It was handling the daily news service to the Atlantic liners and also a service to Spain. On August 4th, 1914, of course, the whole world was in turmoil. On August 8th I reported at Poldhu, which I found was already surrounded by miles of barbed wire, guarded by soldiers and under Admiralty control. Three naval officers were there as censors – A.S. Chambers, W. O'Brien and the Marine, Major Wylde. I lived at the Poldhu Hotel and led an easy open air life. Even as it was I had one bad relapse in February 1915, but eventually I got over it all right.

As you can imagine, I wasn't too comfortable to be at Poldhu when my fellow men were offering themselves as fodder for the Hun guns, but it was impossible for me to do anything, firstly because I was a 'starred' man, and secondly in those days I could never have passed the medical examination.

Claude's employment with Marconi came to a sour conclusion in 1915:

In July 1915, the Marconi Company wanted me to go up to Stonehaven and put in the electrical plant of a station they had erected for the British Post Office. The contract was for £21,000 and yet they had the nerve to expect me to do it for a notional salary, which was little more than half what the Post Office inspector was to be paid for watching me do it. I was so disgusted that I straightway offered my services to the Air Department of the Navy, and they gave me a temporary commission as Lieutenant in the RNVR.

I wrote telling the firm, and they promptly wrote to the Admiralty and had my commission cancelled, saying that they couldn't spare me. This made me so furious that I collected all the power to my elbow that I could and proceeded to 'have at them'. I laid my case before Sir John Snell, the President of the Institute of Electrical Engineers, and I went to Commander F. Loring,

whom I had met in 1909 when he inspected my work on the Royal Mail ships. He was Inspector of the wireless for the Post Office and he went clean off the deep end when he learned of the salary I was to get for doing the £21,000 Post Office station. I went to my second cousin Vincent Baddeley [left], the Assistant Financial Secretary of the Admiralty. Between them they hit the Marconi Company pretty hard, and on their advice I wrote and resigned. My resignation was accepted and Bradfield and Gray were furious. It didn't matter: on 17th August 1915 I was gazetted as Lieutenant RNVR attached to RNAS for wireless duties, appointed to HMS President II, and reported for duty to the RNAS depot at the old White City Exhibition.

So ended my days of commercial engineering. It was an excellent experience. I saw the world. I learned lessons which the youngster who starts in a cadet college never learns. I had gained experience which enabled me to eventually gain a permanent commission with the newly forming Royal Air Force in their first small gazette of but 700 commissions. In my tussle to get clear of Marconi's no one was more kind or more helpful than dear old Lt-Commander Chambers, the Chief Censor at Poldhu. Both he and his wife have proved the truest friends I have ever had.

Above: Claude and Lotty in Helford

Chapter 5   The Mango Tree By Moonlight – Labasa, Vanua Levu, Fiji Isles, July 1911

Extracts from 'My Rosery' 1:

There are twenty-two chapters in this book, each one telling the story of an encounter with a woman. Some of them are little more than flirtations, while others are deeply passionate. I am including just three in this biography; the chosen ones aren't representative – most of the tales are of consensual affairs with English girls or women [see the previous chapter], but the three chosen are the most interesting for their exotic locations and for what they tell us about Claude. The first, set in Fiji, may shock the reader, and while it is important not to judge Claude by today's morality and standards, it is easy to be horrified by the colonial attitudes that are revealed.

Have you ever laboured the livelong drudgery of a tropic day, and then stood, stripped to the waist, washing in a mountain stream – stood and watched the sky fade from lemon to indigo, and then the pall of night cover up everything? It is as though someone had drawn a curtain of black velvet across the sky, and dotted it with sparkling diamonds for stars. As the sun goes down the usual nightly concert begins, and ten million insects burst into their own particular songs, and sing that life is yet good to live. Little fire-flies come out and wander to and fro, flashing their little lamps as they go. By the time you are changed you have taken on a new spell of vigour and are full of vim once more, ready for anything and anyone. It is so delightful to feel clean and fresh and cool, dressed in loose white clothes, white socks and white shoes. Each such evening I feel as if I have put the clock back several years; my step becomes springy, whereas it has been dragging sadly towards the hours of daily labours.

Then one feeds and how good is the food of the evening meal. Noiseless bare-footed Indian houseboys hurry to and fro with efforts of their wrangling, which has gone on all afternoon.

After the cook has prepared the dinner he is silent, but whilst he is cooking it he is arguing with everyone, scolds everything, and when he is not doing either he sings. Having cooked the dinner I suppose that he is committed to it, and words can no longer avail him either way. To come out on the verandah after a good dinner with a sweet cigar well under way and find a smiling white moon climbing into the sky usually stirs me into almost as much energy as that acquired by a wild bull that has run amok.

And so it was on that evening of July in the long ago of 1911 in the far away of the sunny South Sea Isles. The scene, as I stood on the verandah of our bungalow, was utterly charming. Away to the south-east, across the dark fields of waving sugar cane and thick undergrowth of tairi, one could just see the little silver thread which marked the course of the river as it wended its way to the sea, which was just visible as a silver streak across the horizon. The night was still, so that weird sounds came to my ears from all sides. Insects, birds, owls and the monotonous roar of the sugar mill machinery blended with the tom-toms from the coolies' huts. Like a ravenous monster that sugar mill devours cane, night and day without stopping, for four months every year.

I was musing that I should have hated to work on such a night as that, to have to tend to the mad rush and race of machinery, when Mathe strolled over to me and spat solemnly far out into the gloom. Had I not respect for his shooting, I would have gibbed.

"I've promised King that we will go and pick him up and go and see the maramas do their war dance up at Weiylasa village. It will while away the time and amuse you heaps."

"Right, I'll come," said I. "Are you pushing off now?"

We sauntered away down the wide grass path between the cane fields, stopping to collect King. The village of Weiylasa is an exceptionally pretty one as it is almost entirely built under huge trees, and there is no attempt at organizing them into rows or streets. As we entered it, the effect of the heavy shadows thrown by the moon through the trees made it look weird and ghostly. Silent black figures were hurrying to and fro. We wended our way to the chief's place and made our salaams. It was early, he said, and we must drink with him. We did!

The forthcoming dance was a source of much merriment amongst the men. It transpired that the women of the village were ranged round in a semi-circle, laughing and chattering. As the old chief approached on a sort of dais which was prepared for him, they all took up their pre-arranged places and in a moment had started that weird song-song tune which these people always sing as they dance. Most of them were decked out with leaves and strips of colour over their ordinary clothes, which some had substituted for their old barbaric costumes, which don't leave much to the imagination – but then it wasn't daylight.

Then they all started to move – 'dance' – if you will. To and fro, here and there they darted, skipped, rolled and leapt. Viewed as we saw it, it reminded me of the surface of boiling liquid.

Faster and faster they went, their faces getting shiny with exertions, till suddenly they all stopped, fell flat and the whole place was heavy with a dead silence. The men lifted up their voices and clapped and roared and laughed. The old chief was best pleased of all, I believe. He turned and told us that kava was waiting for us at his large burri, towards which he led us. Kava drinking is a nasty business until you have been thoroughly broken in to it. The root of a tropic shrub is dried thoroughly in the sun. A piece of it is then taken away by a virgin of the tribe and chewed in her mouth until her mouth is filled with a mass of pulp. This she spits into a huge bowl, made out of a tree trunk, and fashioned with three legs. Her effort is then mixed water and then strained through coconut fibre. Sitting behind the bowl, the chief ladles the liquid into half coconut shells which the virgin holds out. When the shell is filled, she crawls and presents it to each person in turn. They drink it in one long gulp and then spin the shell back, whilst everyone else claps their hands. Kava tastes like peppery bath water, but it is an excellent thirst quencher and possesses many good medical qualities.

Well, that is what we had to face and make the best show we could of liking it. Soon after we bade the old boy good night, thanked him and wended our way, by common consent, to Fenton's store, there to cadge some whiskey to drown the flavour of the kava.

Poor old Fenton was in bed, but he got out and gave us his square bottle with quite good grace. It didn't last long. Just as we were moving off, we heard someone ride up, and young Champion came in.

"What glad sight do I see?" said he, his eyes glued to the square bottle and his tongue beginning to bulge.

"Your luck is out," said I. "Have a loving cup, for the bottle is run dry." I handed him the remains of mine.

"Thanks'" he said, and drained every blessed drop of it.

"Now, what's on, Champion?" said Fenton. "What devilry have you got on the go tonight? I thought you were on night shift at the mill tonight."

"So I am. The fact is that we have just very successfully cut up a perfectly good black gentleman, and as the said black gentleman has a dutiful wife waiting for him near here, it is but decent that I should call and say that her lord and sahib won't want any breakfast with tomorrow's sun. There you have it all – you know all. Voila tout, as we say in dear old Paris." He executed a sweeping bow.

He went on. "It's a nasty job – who'll come with me and help me out? I'll give 'em a drink when we get back – don't all speak at once."

No one said a word, so finally I said "I'll come along with you, Champs."

"Good-oh, my stout fellow," he replied. "Let's be getting on straight away." We bade the others goodnight and shoved off right away.

I hate riding behind anyone else on horseback, but there was no alternative. I was greatly pleased when he hauled in and said "We'll stop here. The place is over there, across that rice field and under that mango tree."

We tethered the old brown horse at the side of the grassy road and started out along the little path by the side of the rice field. Growing rice always fascinates me. In the tropic heat where one meets it, its pale green swaying blades seems so cool and restful. That night a soft breeze was rustling it into low whispers and its surface was shimmering like the surface of water. As we neared the mango tree a low howl greeted us, and a lank disreputable pyiah dog slunk towards us, growling yet wagging its tail. The lowest of the canine kingdom, they are: if they dared bite you they would, but they fawn on anyone they fear. The heavy scent of the ripe mangoes came to our nostrils – a pleasant pungent smell of sweet turpentine. In the shade of the tree I made out the outline of an Indian hut, built of boughs and leaves.

Champion stood still and hailed the place in Hindustani, and in a moment a low cry came back in answer. The rickety door opened and out came the diminutive figure of an Indian woman, wrapped in flowing white clothes, and jangling with bracelets and anklets. She was very small, and she came towards us in the moonlight, and by the way she hid her eyes with the back of her hand, I guessed that she had been wakened from sleep. She walked with that divine grace which is unknown in white women. Her small black head was uncovered, but she hastily wound a dark sari round her neck and over her head as she approached us. With one hand holding the sari together over her throat, she stood before us, looking into our faces and asking us what we wanted. Champion started in and told her in her own lingo, which I knew only very lightly and couldn't follow.

I watched her face, which was turned towards the moon. She had beautiful regular and very small features, and the dark lustre of her eyes was enhanced by charcoal smeared round her eyelashes, which is a common habit among her class. Scarcely a muscle did she move, but I saw her forehead contracting between her eyes, and she seemed to shrink together as though with cold. As Champs finished speaking, she pulled a sari over her head, waved her arms in the air, and let out a long moan, like that of an animal in pain. Her cry brought up the dog, which had been prowling round us. He cowered up to her and licked the hand which she had let fall.

I felt rather in the way. I was sorry, but my knowledge of her lingo didn't enable me to say so. Then came the sound of a crying picaninny from within the hut, and as the mother heard it, she turned towards the door. As she approached it, a tiny black figure emerged, dressed in nature's costume except for a string of shining golden sovereigns hung about its neck.

"It's rotten luck to leave her like this," said Champs. "I will ask her if she hasn't a father or mother nearby."

Yes, it seemed that her brother lived not far away, so Champs offered to go and fetch him. "Stay – let her weep on your shoulder," he called to me as he moved off.

I pulled out my cigarette case, and as I stood knocking the tobacco tight, she came to me, and by signs, begged for a cigarette. I held a match for her, and she eagerly sucked in the smoke, letting it come back through her nostrils. With a sigh, almost of content, she readjusted the sari over her head and shoulders. Clinging to the sides of her skirt and looking at me with suspicious black eyes, stood her small babe. I made a dive at him, and he ran shrieking and laughing to the other side of his mother. She looked first at him, and then at me, and smiled. Then I suppose that she remembered, for she moaned softly and drew her clothes more closely about her. Poor little soul: she wasn't more than a girl herself. I patted her on the shoulder, and in my best Pidgin English, told her to buck up for the kiddie's sake.

I suppose that the touch of my hand released something inside her, for she caught my arm, bowed her head on it, and let forth a mournful string of Hindustani, whilst I again patted her shoulder with my hand. It looked as if she'd understood Champs' injunction to me about letting her cry on my shoulder, only I don't know how she'd have reached to it, unless I'd knelt down! The kiddie soon felt he was being neglected, and started to howl. This broke in on his mother's sorrow, and she gave him something to howl for, which sent him flying into the hut, there to bemoan his cruel fate in fortissimo tones.

"Again she turned to me. "Sahib, sahib ..." and then followed more gibberish. I was very distressed, but I didn't feel I could do much until, remembering that she was a specie of woman, I decided to do what one would do to most women under the circumstances: I held my arms open to her. In a second she had gratefully flung her tiny self against me, bowed her head, and it had all started again. I was most distressed for besides feeling a bit of a fool, I didn't want Champs to find me taking his parting instructions so literally.

Her little body swayed its weight on to my arms, and I could feel she was shaking from head to foot. Loosening one arm, I stroked the hair from her forehead and over her eyes. Then I heard

Champs' voice hailing us and "Ship ahoy" came from along the path. Gently I pushed her away and yelled an answer.

He had brought back the brother, who talked far quicker than I had ever imagined it was possible for anyone to talk, and he took charge of the whole situation. We turned to go, and then she ran to my side and, hanging on my arm, said something to me. I thought she was thanking me, and mumbled some suitable reply.

"She says to come again and see her in a few days: she has something to give you," said Champion. "It seems to me you've made a hit," he continued, smiling.

I turned to her and nodded my head and salaamed her goodnight.

"A regular black lily," mused Champs, "as pretty a piece of black velvet as I've seen. What eyes and features! If only one could bleach her skin to white, how London would rave over such a face.

I happened to have been thinking the same thing, so I replied "Oh, they're all the same at her age. She can't be more than fourteen. At twenty she'll be a hag of skin and bones."

But she wasn't twenty yet!

&&&

A month went past and then one night, after dinner, I made some excuse, took a hurricane lamp in my hand and strode off towards the mill. It was a goodish walk and part of the way I had to go along the railway track, walking on the sleepers. The moon had not yet risen and it was a tiresome business, as every once in a while I had to step aside to let the fussy little engine pass me, dragging its train of trucks laden with sugar for the mill. Beyond the mill the road was wide and grass covered, and the going was easy and pleasant. Twice I thought that I had missed my way, but no, there to my right lay the rice field, and as I trudged along its side, I was greeted by a low long drawn howl from the dog.

Looking at the mango tree's darkness, I saw that a fire must be alight underneath its spreading branches, as they were occasionally lit up by a dull red flicker. Then, as I came nearer, I saw a miniature figure in white bending over a fire, cooking something. I hailed her, and when she caught sight of me she burst into a rapid string of Hundustani, which I judged to be a hymn of welcome. As I had not the slightest idea of her name and could not enquire it, I gave her one, and dubbed her 'Yasmini' after Lawrence Hope's poems.

She busied about whilst I stood looking on, stirring a pot every few seconds. My curiosity was kindled and I lifted my lantern to look at the seething interior. It was evidently mainly composed of rice and ghee [a very unpleasant specie of rancid butter]. I must have made a face, for she threw back her head and laughed, pointed to the pot and sucked her lips. Going inside the hut, she returned dragging her funny little black baby with one hand and a coconut mat with the other. She flung the mat down by the fire, motioned me to sit on it and again busied herself with her cooking, which was now viewed by the kiddie with evident interest.

44

I lit a cigarette to keep off some of the mosquitoes, and was presently glad that I had done so for when she offered me some of her culinary efforts, I pointed to my cigarette and shook my head. Her cheeks bulging, she gaily chattered away, waving her arms to and fro. It didn't last long, or I would have got up and gone. Perhaps my twice looking at my watch spurred her to activity. Anyway, she soon got up, bundled the kiddie into the hut and shut the door on him, stoked the dying embers of the fire and then, lowering her head coyly on one side, she stretched out her hand to me.

She led the way and guided me into a narrow twisty path which penetrated a thick undergrowth. She led me to her brother's place, and there fitted on my finger one of the four piece puzzle rings, which Indians beat out so cleverly. It wasn't of great intrinsic value, being of silver, but I could see that the giving of it seemed a big event in her eyes, so I made a low salaam and thanked her as best I could.

Then we turned to retrace our steps and to pick up my lantern, which I had left near her fire. I remember seeing a giant yellow moon peeping over the edge of some trees as we started back, and thinking that a lantern wouldn't be much use now that the moon had risen. She walked just ahead of me, as the path was narrow – a little stately figure, lithe and dressed in flowing white, jangling with bracelets and anklets.

I studied her carefully as she walked ahead of me, and I suppose the Devil laughed, for I began to think of her as woman! Remember that I was very young and wholly inexperienced at the time. It was a tropic night and the blood in my veins was young and full.

I remember whistling and as she turned, I slid my arms under hers and clasped my hands across her soft young bosom. I could feel it swell as she gasped in surprise. The feel of it soft warmth under my hands intoxicated me, for her raiment was thin as shadow, and her waist was innocent of corset curses.

I think that she must have hoped or expected me to do this, for God knows she made the fulfilment of my every wish easy. In the heavy scented gloom of that tropical night, with only the moon to see, I felt the hurried pitter-pat of her little heart beating against mine, and was thrilled by the passionate sob of her breath as it came and went whistling through her tightly clenched teeth.

&&&

Time must have flown, for I remember starting up feeling deadly cold and noticing that the moon now rode high above us. A powerful longing to get up and away seized hold of me, and I sprang to my feet and plunged off towards the mango tree. In my feverish haste I picked up my lantern and literally ran off to the road, leaving her standing by the ashes of the fire.

A surge of muddled thoughts filled my brain as I ran until it was finally pulled up through want of breath, the blood throbbing through the veins at my temples as though they would burst. I sat and rested. And I then wandered home slowly, solemnly, and perhaps sadly. As I got into bed I adjusted the mosquito netting and lay back for sleep, but I felt indescribably older. The world and life seemed to have changed. And so I suppose it is for every man.

&&&

I never went down to see her again. I guess I was too scared to do so. In due course we finished our work and loaded our gear on a dhow, ready for paddling down the river to the sea, there to load it aboard a ship. All our gang of native boys stood on the quayside as we shoved off into the stream, and sang us that mournful chant, which I think some Wesleyan missionary must have taught them –'Oh I shall never forget you'. Their voices are naturally wonderfully melodious and they sing in seconds with the power of an organ. 'Samoce [goodbye]' they yelled as we neared the bend, and 'Samoce' we cried in reply. "Levu loloma maramas [much love to the women]," called out Strickland, and a high pitched giggle told us that his message had been heard. Then the bend brought us a mass of tairi across our view, and we had seen the last of them.

ON THE LABASA RIVER, FIJI

Lower down the river a bend brought us near the mango tree I had come to know so well, and I succumbed to the temptation of saying goodbye to her. Jumping ashore, I told the boys to wait and off I ran across the fields. There she was, pottering about her housework duties. As she recognized me she ran towards me with wide opened arms, and as I came near, she took a flying leap at me and embraced me with arms and legs at the same time. It took me several minutes to explain to her that I was not going to stay. She couldn't or wouldn't understand it and followed me as I turned to go. As we neared the boat she guessed, I suppose, that I was going away for good for she let out a low despairing cry which drew several long whistles from the boys. I felt a fool and half angrily bade her stand where she was. She obeyed me, but still went on saying something which sounded like "Ni jao, sahib" – which I believe means "Don't go".

And that is the last I saw of her. The river ran in a long straight line from where we left her, and as we paddled downstream along it, she still stood there, a little white pathetic figure, murmuring "Ni jao, ni jao". And thus she passed out of my life, and never since have I been within ten thousand miles of that spot in the far away sunny South Seas Isles. Somewhere I have a crumpled and wizened hibiscus flower which fell from her hair on that fateful night of long ago. The ring I lost while bathing within a year. Poor little dark eyed Yasmini – where are you now?

Chapter 6   The Story of Blanca Aguilera, Antofagasta, Chile 1913.

Extracts from 'My Rosery': 2.

We were seated playing bridge, when someone came into the smoke room and shouted "We're almost there", so we chucked in our hands and wandered to the ship's side to see what manner of a place it was. We had been lazing along through a giant oily swell, the sea being blended into the sky by a tropic mist. The coastline was dull – a long irregular drab streak. The town as I first saw it looked dead. I was reminded of a card town built by a child, in the lee of a sandbank, and which the wind had blown about and covered in a rubbishy dust. Stretching up towards the hills at the back of the town I spied a big collection of little white objects like dominoes, and then I remembered that Antofagasta was famed as having the largest cemetery on the west coast of South America! 'A city of sin, corrugated iron and cemeteries," a woman American journalist had once dubbed it, and her view seemed justified.

Antofagasta, Muelle de Carga, 1910

These pictures might be close to Claude's first view of Antofagasta.

Ere long we let go our anchor and lay rolling in the trough of the swell, which was crashing itself into a white fury on some villainous rocks inshore. The roar of the surf just reached us – otherwise everything seemed dead and drab and dusty.

We had the usual haggle with customs officials, but eventually made our way to a hotel in the plaza. At close quarters the town was even more disreputable looking than it had seemed from the steamer. The streets were lanes of drab dust. It never rained, it was said, and nothing green ever grew there. Ten years ago it had once rained for a few hours and the roads had been reduced to mud channels, the stench of which had been too much for most people, and a fever epidemic had followed. There is no attempt at drainage: two huge refuse destructor parks cope more or less efficiently with the filth accumulating from 70,000 souls. Converting it into ashes and foul smelling gases and smoke, most of which blows back onto the town! Inland, the 'hills' gradually rise to some 6,000 feet and form an effective barrier. The refuse destructor parks act as sentinels at either extremity of the town precincts, so you can't escape it anyway!

The hotel was built in a hollow square with galleries running round inside the courtyard at each floor. It didn't pretend to cope with the requirements of visitors with sensitive nostrils or pander to hygienic maniacs, but otherwise we found that we could live in comparative comfort there, and do as we wished.

In the centre of the plaza stands a virile little clock tower. The tower was made by Doulton's in Lambeth of faraway London town, and every quarter of an hour the clock chimes forth the comforting notes of the Cambridge chimes. It is the gift of the British residents there. Round the plaza are small ornamental lakes which harbour a few decrepit bullfrogs. To wake in the middle of the night and hear the croak of the bullfrogs mingling with the crystal clarity of the chimes struck me for a long time as incongruous, but I soon got used to it – one can get used to anything, and therein lies the danger ...

Above: Claude's hotel, and the clock-tower on the Plaza Colon, with a general view.

Before we could start our work across the bay we had much to settle, and each day saw us closeted with the captain of the port – fine looking old blackguard whose interests did not go much further than women and wine. From him we learned a little of the government's requirements, and much of his own escapades in the heyday of his youth. And so we dallied on, taking a week to do a day's work.

The new year festival was beginning to absorb everyone's interest, and round the plaza weird and wonderful firework stands were making their appearance. It was as though preparations were being made for a children's fete. "Wait," said the old Chanceaulme, "you will not be disappointed."

One night we took a box at the local circus, where it was rumoured that there would be every chance of thrills, as the lion tamer was due to enter the cage of a new beast 'positively for the first time'. The arena was dirty and ill lit, and the whole show looked as if it was falling to bits, having been bought from some other country, second hand. In another box I spotted little Miller who had come out from England in the Oriana. He was such a nice kid – a babe! I always had admired the staunch way that he had refused to drink anything stronger than ginger ale, and how he'd blushed and walked away when anyone had started in on some yarn of questionable taste. A Scottish minister's son he was, out on a six year contract at what seemed to him like a princely salary.

"Hulloa, C.H., come and let's get a drink," he called to me.

"I'm with you," said I, and he came round and piloted me off to one of the drinking dens of which the town is full.

"Yours?"

"A whiskey," said I.

"Two whiskeys," he told the waiter.

"Oh-ho," said I. "You're off the T-T racket?"

"Yes, I'm growing up," he said with a smile.

"You're prone to grow a damned fool," I told him, as I watched him gulp it down, almost neat. "Let's be getting back."

As we re-entered the circus, we brushed against a couple that at once held my interest. The man was obviously English. He was slight, baked a dusty brown, and was thin and wiry, his jaw being extraordinarily wide, which brought his lips together in a thin line. His eyes were large and piercing brown. His companion, who stood waiting for him to get the tickets, was as perfect a specimen of womanly beauty as I had seen for ages, and, unlike all the other women of that country, she had glorious golden hair. Masses of it, with fascinating little curls clustered round her ears and across her forehead. I must have gazed too ardently, for she smiled – and turned her back, that time-worn habit among pretty women!

Miller couldn't enlighten me as to whom she was, but said that he was a surveyor who was very much a freebooter, here today and gone tomorrow.

The circus bored us. The lion obviously wasn't very hungry, and so Dockray and I wended our way back to the hotel and sat ourselves in the lounge, sipping tonic water and blowing smoke rings. Ten minutes later my surveyor of the piercing brown eyes swaggered in, looked around, and then came up and begged a match. He seemed in no hurry, so we asked him to sit and have a drink. His flow of language was facile and he kept us amused as he rattled off anecdote after anecdote of his rambles over the pampa and up in the nitrate fields.

"When you fellows get fixed up over the bay, I'll ride over and see you, if I may," he announced. "And now I must get going, for I have to ride to Caldera to register a claim there before tomorrow's sun is very high." With a click of his spurs, a long sweeping bow, he turned and left us.

"A queer cuss," said Dockray.

"Very," said I. "Too much to say. I have never cultivated a like for the scent of verbal bouquets. However, he will amuse us if we ever get to see him when we get over to Caleta Vieja."

That night we had an object lesson in Spanish jealousy. The lion tamer, who had the room above us, came home late, and was probably 'well oiled'. It was unfortunate that he should find a strange pipe in his wife's dressing table. Of course she protested her innocence, and so he got out his lion taming whip and proceeded to do a lion taming stunt on her. Screaming seven kinds of murder and calling on every saint of her church, she fled, clad in only a thin night garment, round the balcony. I, standing below, saw the whole show and was much amused, but it got a bit too thick after the infuriated husband caught her and proceeded to lay into her with his whip, so Dockray and I were just going up to put our spoke in, when the manager came up and said that he wouldn't have his hotel disturbed and he didn't care how the senor beat his wife, but he'd have to clear out there and then, and then he could beat her all round the plaza, and we'd all be most interested etc, etc – all in a fortissimo voice!

Then came the famous celebrations of Neuvo Annio. In the afternoon we were fools enough to attend a blessed bazaar for some charity, where all the youth and beauty of the place were to minister to our wants and bring us tea or whiskey or cigarettes or chocolate or ... anything that could cloak for highway robbery and help them divest us of our money. I certainly derived a pleasant time bandying words in my atrocious Spanish with Mariquetta, the charming daughter of the old captain of the port – a Spaniard in her prime and a damn pretty one at that. Several times her old blackguard father cast longing eyes at her lithe body and murmured "Ah, had she been anyone else's daughter!"

On the night of the feast, we dined lazily and luxuriously. I satiated my desire for caviar at God-knows-how-much a tin! We were a happy rowdy crowd. At eleven we mingled with the jostling crowd that had gathered in the plaza. There seemed too many more women than men. I watched the people with interest. I was struck with the simplicity of the women's dress. The flaunting vulgarity of the lower class English women always depresses me. The Spanish wear a quiet black dress with its becoming black lace mantilla.

Suddenly the clock tower began to solemnly strike midnight and that was the signal for pandemonium to break loose! At first I was honestly scared, and cannot clearly recollect all that happened. Afterwards, I suppose I must have got infected with the general madness and taken part in it. Firstly the band, which up till then had been playing a lazy Viennese waltz, stood up and played the national anthem of Chile. A crowd of comic old monks or priests appeared in the belfry gallery of the old cathedral in the plaza, and set the bells swinging into merry chime. Everyone shouted a song or whistled, and everybody danced or jumped or waved their hats in the air. On the distant hills, giant nitrate flares were lit, and soon the place was as light as day. And last, but by no means least, the fireworks! Have you ever stood and let an amiable lunatic let off a rocket at you? Well, dozens of rockets were being loosed among the crowd, and giant Catherine wheels were whirling showers of sparks over a shouting mob.

Then gradually a stream of carriages started to drive round the plaza, people pelting the occupants with confetti as they passed. Most were occupied by more or less beautiful women, dressed in plumes and satins that reminded me of Longchamps or Auteil. Faster and faster they drove, round and round and round. Holding hands round the clock tower, the English element were singing Auld Lang Syne, while the Germans had taken possession of the bandstand and were playing Deutschland Uber Alles.

"Who are the pretty ladies in the procession?" I asked a brawny Scot whose hand I had been waving whilst we sang.

"They? Auch, man, they're anybody's who'll hire them."

I stood and scanned their faces after I had received this somewhat sordid intelligence. For all their smiles I thought I could detect that hungry hard avaricious look in their eyes that so inevitably stamps these women. Then as I stood looking I saw ... my God, I saw the woman who had smiled and turned her back on me at the circus! I felt physically sick when I saw her. I felt like I wanted to shout to everyone to stop her – that his tomfoolery had gone far enough and that tragedy had happened!

Again I turned to the Scot. "Who is that in the coach with the light coloured mudguards?"

"That? That's Blanca, Blanca Aquillera, the Queen of the Harlots. Never seen her before? Pretty she is, I'll allow, but proud as hell – she, who's lost all right to pride. To hell wi' her, say I."

Fascinated and horrified, I crossed the plaza – fought and elbowed my way across it – to gain a nearer view of her. My heart was beating heavily against my ribs and my lips were dry and sticky. Yes, it was her beyond a doubt, for catching my eye as she turned, she smiled. As she came nearer she stopped her carriage, and the creature who sat opposite her climbed on to the box, leaving vacant the seat by her side.

"Venga mechito," she cried to me, and without hesitation I took the hand she held out and entered her carriage. Quickly she turned her coachman away from the Plaza and down a backstreet.

"Senor, tonight is young and the world is happy: come with me and dance." I replied that I gladly would if she would resign herself to my wretched Spanish. "Calle Esmeralda 549," she called to the driver, and sank back into her seat. I suppose I looked scared, or as though I half repented what I'd done, for she smiled again, moved to one side and motioned for me to sit beside her.

"You tremble," she said, as though I was unaware of doing so. "Oh, is it already that you tremble for love of me?", and she laughed me a little mocking laugh.

Arrived at the house she sought, she dismissed the carriage and opening the door, waited for me to enter. I couldn't form much of an opinion about the place. It was a low tin building in a dark road at the base of the town, as I could see the bay shining in the pale moonlight of a waning moon. From within came the racket of music, the clinking of glasses and the bust hum of conversation – a typical Chilean drinking saloon! Going first she piloted me through the saloon where a murky crowd stood or lounged, smoking and drinking, to the dancing hall. The garish lights and the row and bustle rather bewildered me, but I followed her round to a settee in one of the corners and there she motioned me to sit. A noisy ceuca was in progress, everybody joining in the clapping of hands and stamping, whilst a weird old soul banged away at a tinkling piano and an anaemic youth beat a tambourine; just the sort of scene that I had seen so often down south, but tonight it affected me differently. I was dull and sat wondering, till fair Blanca jogged my elbow and pointed to two tiny glasses of some yellow liquid. Rather against my will, I lifted mine, and drained its contents, murmuring the conventional 'nuevo ano felicidades'. Then the dance ended and as the music stopped the buzz of conversation became more intense. We couldn't talk and I fancy both of us felt rather awkward. She evidently divined this for she rose and, taking my wrist, led me out of the room by another door and into a dark room, the air of which was heavily scented.

"Tiene phosforo, senor?" she asked, and in answer I struck a match and handed it to her. I was rather afraid that she had brought me to her own apartment, but no, we were in a small sitting room which had a sewing machine stowed away in one corner and a pile of fancy work on the table. An anaemic canary cheeped as she lit the lamp.

With a laugh she flung herself into a chair, and I also sat down and looked at her long and carefully. She was so slender and dainty; her dress of simple black and white striping was so perfect in taste – so quiet. Could this woman with those solemn amber brown eyes and happy smile be as McM said, the 'Queen of the Harlots'? It didn't seem right.

In our broken lingo we talked and she asked me of myself and what we were there to do. I felt strangely at home with her – the sweet understanding look in her eyes made talking easy. Then a waltz started and she laid her hand on my arm and I felt her little fingers tighten around my forearm. Instinctively we both rose.

"Come, let me dance into your heart," she murmured.

"I'll let you <u>try</u>," I replied, "but quien sabe?", and together we went and waltzed.

With a good partner, a good tune and a smooth floor, a waltz may be the most sensuous movement on earth. So I found it. With her lips parted just enough to show her gleaming white teeth, eyes half closed, she lay in my arms light as a feather and danced whither and how I wished. Her golden head lay on my shoulder and the soft scent of her hair was in my nostrils. It all seemed utterly unreal. I only know that I wanted it to go on and never stop.

And so the first hours of 1913 found me occupied. Ere I left I became so weary that life seemed a dream. I remember stepping out into the night with 'Calle Esmeralda 549' ringing in my head and a dull recollection of having promised to go and dance there again.

As I lurched out on the dusty street towards the town, I remember hearing the clock chime a quarter past – "Quarter past what?" I idly wondered. I saw no one, though the streets were full of the usual crowds of mongrel dogs tearing over the rubbish bins in a vain search for food.

Across the bay I could see the gaunt form of Morro Moreno rise up against the sky. Its upper heights were already becoming faintly lit by some stray rays of the sun which was hurrying towards us from hundreds of miles east of the Andes. It had begun to get quite light ere I laid my head on my pillow and sought the sweet relief of sleep.

Late in the afternoon of the next day I sought out McM, and made him tell me all he knew of Blanca. We were having a drink together at the end of his working day, and he spared neither time nor words to embellish her story. This is what I learned:

"I'd have you know," he began, "that Blanca is a mystery. She's a dual personality. As a woman I'm told that she is clever and proud and idealistic – I can't say. I have never known her as a woman. As a prostitute she is hard and dreadfully versed in all the sordid vagaries of her trade. She keeps her two natures utterly separate. As a woman she is so proud that few have ever known her. As a harlot – why, I suppose that everyone has at one time or another known Blanca. It's a species of baptism in this hell that everyone passes through, and Antofagasta wouldn't be the same if Blanca wasn't here. Her father was an officer, a German from Hanover, on one of the Kosmos boats, her mother a Peruvian. For years her father called and saw her mother every time he passed through these parts. Then came the cholera plague of eight years ago. That carried off the mother and when the steamer called again, her father had been shifted to another run, or had retired, or died or something. Blanca was stranded and it is not surprising that she found her way uptown – I suppose it had to be that or the convent and she didn't choose the convent. Years later young A came out here and met her. He was young and enthusiastic and everything else, so he needs must feel it his duty to 'save' her.

He took a shack for her. He furnished it and then he got her to go and live there. As often as he was in from the pampa she lived there and she looked after him. I guess she loved him after a degree. Well, he'd made his gilded cage and he'd got his bird there but he couldn't make the other birds friendly. I suppose that bit by bit the other women got on Blanca's nerves for one time when A was on a long jaunt to Sucre, she beat it back to her old life. It was what we all expected. Once a woman's gone that way, she's gone for good and aye.

Well, she went back to the old life and all A's pleadings and promises couldn't shift her – and there she is! If ever A is around she has eyes for no other, but at other times she tucks away her inner self and plies her trade as cold-bloodedly as any of 'em. A queer cuss is Blanca. Don't you go and get enamoured of her, as many men have done, for she's as hard as rock. She'll be yours as long as you pay her, and then ...? Then she'll be bought by someone else."

He spoke so easily and earnestly, giving, as he thought, sound advice, that I felt helplessly depressed at his words. It seemed so sad. She was so young and sweet, and what could her present life lead her to?

&&&

Next day we left the town and with all our worldly possessions set out across the bay in a little ramshackle steam launch. We landed on a surf beaten shore under the shadow of the gaunt Morro Moreno. A vast pile of packing cases marked the site of what we had come to do, but otherwise there was nothing to break the monotony of the vast unbroken plane of sand stretching away to the foothills of the Andes. Myriads of seabirds were the only sign of life; not a green blade of grass was to be seen. The town we had left lay hull down across the bay.

"I think that God must have forgotten to finish this place," murmured Dockray.

Weeks rolled into months and we made good progress. The house was up and we were living in it. Our days were flooded in golden sunshine, so we lived in comfort clad in nothing but shorts, but the nights came in cold and heavy, due to the sea breezes that howled round the great mountain. At sunrise and sunset the sun lit up the mountain long before it came to us, and we had the most wonderful rosy twilight in consequence, when all the world went red – a most weird sensation.

When the day's work was done I would sometimes tramp along the beach, sending up shrieking flocks of sea birds, and look at the glare on the horizon which marked the town. Then I'd think of Blanca and feel again her arms round me and her soft, warm, young body pressed to mine, as we danced together. In that solitude, memories of her bred desire, and small wonder it was that when some weeks later I had occasion to visit the city, I should find myself toddling up the hill to Calle Esmeralda, with burning forehead and thumping heart.

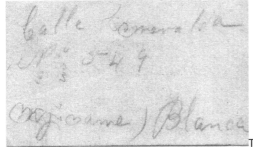The card Blanca gave Claude

Would she have forgotten me? Would she be alone? I banged at the door as she had done – twice quickly and then twice slowly. It was eventually opened a few inches by a horrible looking hag. Without waiting to argue, I put my shoulder to it, and went down the passage followed by a foul protest from the hag.

Blanca was there. Blanca was alone. Blanca was so glad to see me. I forgot everything else but her amber eyes and her glorious golden hair. She sat and played for me – played little scraps of Richard Strauss' famous 'Chocolate Soldier' waltz, which had just got to Chile.

"Blanca, let me be your chocolate soldier," said I, but she didn't know the words of the song, and I had to tell her.

The light in her eyes unnerved me. She was so intense. I felt that no word, no action, no thought of mine escaped her. I felt like an Eton boy making love to a Leicester lounge barmaid! Her face was folded in little lines round her eyes and mouth, which, without being wrinkles, enabled her to change the whole expression of her face in the twinkling of an eye. But I can never do her justice in a word picture. Blanca was Blanca and she was deliberately making herself charming to me – and that was more than enough.

I stayed and danced and danced, but soon after midnight she anticipated any suggestion on my part by saying that she was going to bed – she was tired and she had a headache.

Many times did I go to see her, and always she was the same. Sometimes I found her doing fancy work, sometimes playing, but always happy and sometimes smiling. Every evening when I stayed to dance she pleaded a headache and saw me to the door and bid me 'Buenos noche', until it was more than plain to me that she didn't wish me to regard her as, well, other women, women whose smiles and lips were purchasable for the coin of the country. And Blanca became a habit to me. Little by little she came to know my ways, and my hopes and my cares. I suppose she drew me out, as a pretty woman who has sufficient strength of character to keep silent always can.

Then again I had to go across the bay and plunge into the wilds, completely cut off from the outside world. What a hell of a place it was – how often every possible thing and impossible thing went wrong! At times I nearly lost hope, but, looking back, I now regard it as a priceless education for today it has enabled me to smile at things which formerly would have driven me grey with worry.

 Slowly we fought out every difficulty and gradually [oh how gradually] the work neared completion. Then came the day when I had to 'take up my bed and walk'. As I stood on the shore and saw my gear put aboard the launch, I looked back and felt half sorry to quit. There had been so many days of sweat and toil, and so many difficulties to overcome, that now it was time to leave it all – leave it all in perfect working order for some newcomer, who had never known the pains of its birth – I was in many ways sad. Then they managed to drop one of my suitcases overboard and that changed my mood of sorrow to one of white hot anger!

The steamer I was leaving by sailed in the morning, but I got all my gear aboard that night, all settled so that I could be free to spend my last hours with Blanca. I felt very light of heart as I stepped out towards Calle Esmeralda, my own black moon shadow dodging just ahead of me. I must have gone at a great rate for I was soon out of breath and turned to cool in the breeze. In the bay lay my steamer. A fresh cold sea breeze met my face and gave me new strength and vigour.

For the first time I was disappointed in not finding Blanca there. She had gone out to a cinema show. I had not dined, so I asked a comic old Irishman whom I met there to come and break a festive crust with me. We dined slowly and cracked a good bottle of the country's very excellent red wine. There was no hurry as Blanca would be late. We yarned of many things and many places. He had travelled a lot and we found many places we both knew. We were in a funny little Austrian 'boliche' in a little private cubicle.

At eleven I again called for Blanca. She had not yet returned, so I decided to wait. Sitting at one of the little round tables in the saloon, I was persuaded by my Irish acquaintance to drink a glass of that liquid poison, pisco. It tastes like an infusion of raisins, but it is actually distilled port wine, and once drunk it runs through your veins like liquid fire.

A motley crowd adorned the place. We had but finished our drinks when a great commotion arose at the other end of the room. I afterwards learned that where the senora dispensed the drinks a nasty Arab had asked for a beer. He was given a glass and charged, as he contended, for a bottle. He demanded the rest of the bottle, and finally the senora banged it down on the table so hard that she spilled some of the contents of his glass. This set fire to the Arab's temper, I suppose, for he raised a huge glass 'giraffe' full of water and crashed it down in front of her, smashing it to smithereens and covering her and himself with water. She screamed and, turning, picked up a revolver and deliberately fired a shot over his head which ripped through the tin roof. For a moment he was cowed, but then he picked up a beer bottle and raised it over his head.

"Down, down!" yelled my old Irishman, and dragged me to the floor. As I subsided I overturned the marble topped table and spilt the remainder of the pisco down my neck. We manoeuvred the table as a screen and squatted down there amongst the sawdust and expectorations of God knows whom! Everyone was making a big noise by this time, calling on their pet saints by name. Eventually a friend managed to get the Arab to move away, and just them the door opened, and in walked Blanca.

Seeing me she grabbed me by the shoulder, and scurried me along the passage without delay or ceremony. Opening a door she pushed me through, and then slammed it to. It was very dark.

"Where are you, nino?" she cried. I was so close that I felt her warm breath on my ear. It sent the blood racing through my pulses, even as the pisco had done. I groped in the darkness until I felt her. Almost roughly I threw my arms around her and pressed her to my chest – pressed so hard that I heard her gasp for breath. She had turned her head away, for her hair filled my mouth and the scent of it maddened me. I could hear the hubbub from the saloon, I could hear the tick of a clock somewhere nearby in the darkness, and I could hear my own heart banging inside my ribs with hammer blows. As I held her we swayed – I felt drunk. Freeing one arm, I forced round her head and wildly kissed her half open mouth. I could hear the quick breath come and go through her nostrils. We stayed thus through what seemed an eternity. My brain seemed to be bursting.

Suddenly with a weird little cry her head fell back and she murmured "Madre de dios!". I released my tight hold on her and as I did so I felt her arms flung round my neck, her soft white warm naked arms, and she sealed my mouth with hers.

I have never yet fainted, but I think that I must have been very near to fainting then. My memory fails me until Blanca leaned back and fumbled for the electric light switch. As I had instinctively felt, I was her in her own room!

Hurriedly she explained that the shot might bring the police and anyone might become involved. I was safer with her, I was to say nothing, but leave her to deal with them.

What did I care for police? I blessed them that night! When again wouldn't I risk the police for the joy of holding Blanca in my arms? I switched off the light. We sat in the dark and I let her fill my world. At first she was torn between conflicting interests, but as time passed and no police came, her fears quieted. Once she weakly suggested that I should go – go back to my hotel, but I stubbornly refused.

"Tomorrow I go for always, Blanca," said I. "Let tonight be ours." At long last she agreed. I stayed .... and in the cold morning air tramped to the quayside.

I hailed a waterman and was put aboard. I cursed him for no reason, and then flung him triple fare, also for no reason! I wanted the ship to weigh anchor and be gone. I paced the cold wet decks in a frenzy, and cursed the deck hands who were washing them down and making them still more wet. Then I went below and tried to eat some breakfast. It felt like drinking champagne after a funeral.

As I came on deck we were swinging to sea. Over the stern I gazed at what I thought to be the house of the ten thousand others – 549 Calle Esmeralda. I tried to penetrate the ugly tin walls and see a slender white form, gowned in a flimsy blue nightdress, tousled head half buried under bedclothes, and the clock monotonously ticking out the passage of another day. Ticking as it was when I left it, but three hours ago!

&&&

And I have never written. Blanca said it would be idle to do so, and made me promise not to. I sent her a copy of the 'Chocolate Soldier' from London when I got back, and I got a card with just 'Gracias' scrawled across it – nothing more. And so I know that Blanca was alive in early 1914, but since then ...? Whither can her dainty little footsteps lead her but to one of those all too well filled cemeteries. As she has sewn [sic], so I suppose shall she reap. Perhaps one day I shall have news of her from someone who has seen her there, but I fear that they will only tell of the hard hateful side of Blanca – the Blanca which, thank God, I never knew!

Chapter 7 Prangs, women and uniforms: World War I

For most of Claude's generation, World War I was a time of unimaginable horror, and many young men suffered life-changing trauma, serious injury or death. Although Claude was close to losing his life on a couple of occasions, his life during the Great War was generally comfortable, and if he suffered any traumas, they weren't inflicted by the war. Claude actually enjoyed much of it, and found his true vocation in the RAF that emerged from the war. He seems to have expressed a small amount of guilt in 1914-15, when he couldn't join in with the war, but he pointed out that his medical problems contracted in Tierra del Fuego would have prevented him passing a medical for the army. Also, he was a 'starred' man, which meant that he had knowledge and skills that were too valuable to risk in the front lines.

Claude started in the RNVR [Royal Navy Volunteer Reserve] on August 5th, 1915 – the day before the allies lost so many men landing at Suvla Bay on Gallipoli – reporting to Flight-Lieutenant N. B. Tomlinson, who was in charge of a camp of boy mechanics training at the Roehampton Kite Balloon Station, of the Airship Wireless Stores Section at the RNAS Depot on Wormwood Scrubs, and of a small wireless section at the White City Exhibition. Claude was in plain clothes because his commission did not come through until the 17th, but his services were needed immediately. His first duties were to draft explanatory pamphlets on the various service instruments, inspect and test instruments at makers' factories, and deliver a series of lectures to the Boy Mechanics at Roehampton.

Soon Claude was crossing southern England testing equipment being made for the war effort. This included returning to the Marconi works in Chelmsford, where he was very rigorous in his tests! He also went to Kingsnorth to test the new type of airship called the Coastal Patrol. He moved on to the Isle of Grain to test the equipment of old B.E.2c seaplanes. This involved his second ever flight in an aeroplane – something that thrilled him. Next he went to Felixstowe to test Flying Boat equipment, but the weather was too bad for him to get into the air again. Claude found the life exciting:

The life was new to me, and I was very keen on it. Everybody was keen in those days – the war made one so. My days were very full: I used to tear to and fro on my FN motorcycle, and I had my full share of night duties.

His nights were exciting in another way: his landlady in Roehampton, Gladys Tatham [pictured left], had seduced him, and they embarked upon an affair. When Claude was transferred to the navy experimental wireless centre at HMS Vernon, Portsmouth, to carry out research work for the RNAS under the direction of the navy, Gladys gave up her house in Roehampton, and took up residence at the Rising Sun Hotel in Warsash. Claude moved out of his '*deadly dull*' rooms and moved to the hotel.

Claude's main duties on the Solent were to measure up all the electrical constants of a service seaplane. To do this he would cross by service launch from Warsash to Calshot every day. His work was to pave the way for the design of an aircraft wireless transmitter for use between seaplanes and the Grand Fleet. It involved many theoretical and practical problems, and Claude was fortunate to be assisted by the brilliant Lieutenant Harold Morris-Airey. Their commanding officer at Calshot was Squadron-Leader A.W. Bigsworth, DSO, RN, the pilot who had earned fame by being the first to bomb an enemy submarine.

Claude and Airey continued their work through early 1916. Claude visited Eastchurch, on the Isle of Sheppey, because he suspected that their development programme was overlapping, and there he had long conversations about airplane design and about Chile with Horace Short, the famous aeroplane designer. He also took a trip to the Vickers Works in Barrow-in-Furnace to see the new rigid Airship No. 9, which impressed him hugely.

Calshot gym class

Gladys Tatham returned to London, and Claude took *'the worst imaginable'* digs in Calshot, before moving to Fawley. These circumstances led to what later proved to be a serious mistake in his life. His account shows that he understood why he made this mistake:

The life was a busy one, but at times lonesome, as most of the pilots were empty headed schoolboys. I suppose I also suffered from the force of example by Strong – a Flight-Lieutenant who was set to marry what he seemed to think was the only girl in the world. He has since married her and is, I hear, very happy. Good luck to him. Well, it made me jealous – his anticipation of so much joy – and so I began to feel like I'd like to get married. I had kept up a fairly regular and intimate correspondence with Ada Land, the girl whom I had met in the Fiji Isles. I now collected any photo I had of her: I had them copied and framed. People admired them. I began to gild her memory, and in the end I wrote and asked her to become engaged to me. In June her reply came – by cable. I hopped on my

motorcycle and rode hell-for-leather for Bournemouth and bought her a diamond engagement ring that cost me a couple of months pay. I was very pleased with her, myself and all the world. My days seemed to have ceased being empty and my leisure hours were filled in writing her volumes of letters.

Calshot, photographed by Claude in 1916

In fact Claude didn't pine for his fiancée – he tells of a wild weekend of drinking, dining and sex spent in Seaview on the Isle of Wight, when he and a fellow officer, Cooper, met up with two rich women called Dot and Gracie, driving a smart red Lancia. Dot was the Countess Conelli, whose husband was in Greece; she later took a house at Bitterne Park for further intimate evenings with Claude and 'Coops'. Gracie later went into film acting, and left for America. Claude wrote of her: *'I have never met any woman who was so casually intimate. One had no sense of conquest with her for she seemed to expect anything that happened to her as a matter of course.'*

Cooper had another influence on Claude: 'air fever'. Claude was determined to become a pilot, and Cooper pulled strings for his friend to get Claude an interview and examination for entry into the Royal Navy Air Service.

The medical examination was a farce – anyway I got through it all right. Wing-Captain Edwards was the President of the examination board, and he was not inclined to transfer me. "You are over age," he told me. In truth I was nearly 26, but I told him that I had first applied to fly before I was 25, so eventually he agreed, but added, "You will have to drop all seniority and start at the bottom. If you do very well I shall probably give you back your second stripe three months after

60

you graduate as a pilot." His promise never materialized, as the poor old chap died suddenly in his bath from heart failure, and though I graduated with a first class pass in every subject and gained an average of over 90% of marks, I had to go my first full year before I got my second stripe, so I am nearly 320 places down the list from the position I ought to have been entitled to.

This resentment was not an isolated one in Claude's varied career – he had left Marconi's with a grudge, and he also wanted to transfer from the RNVR to the RNAS because he believed that the RNAS treated the RNVR officers as *'dogsbodies'*. In World War II there were to be running battles with the Air Ministry as he fought for more privileges and rights for the men under his command. Claude had a strong sense of entitlement and personal pride in his worth, which wasn't always attractive.

In August 1916 he transferred to the RNAS and left Calshot, but not before he got into another romance, this time with a girl with whom he had a road accident. He collided with Dolly in the New Forest – she was on a bicycle and he was on a motorbike. Claude wrote that he nearly broke his back, but his mind seemed to be on other things as they lay on the road:

I was on my knees in an instant. Her dress was badly torn and an adorable silk-stockinged knee peeped out. I suppose I admired it too ardently, for its owner put out a protecting hand to cover it, and when I looked to catch her eye again I saw a divine pink blush had dyed her cheeks.

Apparently the blush was not one of rage, because later when Claude went to visit her to enquire after her health, it was the start of an affair. Dolly had escaped a 'wicked stepmother' and was unhappily married to a man away at the Western Front. Later Dolly became an actress, before dying young. From Claude's account, it's clear the she was a very capable woman who was in control of her life, and did not play the part of a vulnerable victim to Claude's predator.

After a month's holiday in Cornwall, partly spent with his Aunt Lotty, Claude reported for a drill course the RNAS depot at the Crystal Palace in London. There were seven thousand air mechanics under training there, and five hundred officers. Claude admired the fanatical attention to smartness and rigid discipline. On October 29th, he transferred to the newly opened Cadet Training School at Cranwell near Sleaford in Lincolnshire. Claude regarded it as a *'wonderful place'* with a terrific teaching staff.

— SELF AFTER FIRST TRIP IN THE WHAIF. —

I started to learn to fly almost at once, my instructor being none other than Flight –Commander Bernard Fowler, the famous 'circuit of Britain' pilot. On the second day I got to Cranwell, who should turn up but young Benning, my former assistant at Poldhu! He had enjoyed a meteoric career in the RNAS, joining as a Flight-sub-Lieutenant under Tomlinson, and had taken up kite balloon work, had got a second stripe through good work in Canning out in the Mediterranean. We both had our baptism in the air in zoggy old Maurice Farman 'Long-horns'. After ten thrilling hours tree scraping in Long-horns, we went on to Munday's flight which was of the American designed Curtiss tractor biplane. My anxiety when up on my first flight with Munday was comic, as they seemed too quick and difficult to fly, so that I thought that I would never learn to fly them. However, a couple of weeks later I went on to Cox and started to fly Avros. These were very easy money after the Curtiss, and I soon made up my mind to loop. Very quietly I flew away from the station, and when safely out of sight, I executed my first loop. It gave me immense confidence and I had no qualms when I went on to fly Scouts under Gerrard. My Scout flying was got through in one busy day, when I did four and a half hours in the air, flying Bristol Bullets, Sopwith 'One-and –a- half strutters', and Nieuport Fighters. They were very keen that I should stick to aeroplanes, but I was determined to at least learn to fly seaplanes, as it seemed to me that to wear naval uniform and not to fly marine aircraft would be absurd.

Claude worked extremely hard for the exams, and passed them all with first class passes in all five groups of subjects. This earned him an instant rank of Flight-sub-Lieutenant RN with three months seniority. He was also promised that within three months he would get back his 'second stripe' that he had relinquished to transfer to the RNAS.

In January 1917 Claude returned to Calshot to take a course in seaplane flying. For someone so conscious of hierarchy, he found it difficult to be of lower rank than he had been there previously, and to have to salute officers who had previously saluted him. He also went off sick for a fortnight with ophthalmia, a painful eye complaint which he had originally caught in a blizzard on HMS Baltic in 1912. However, he found learning to fly seaplanes and the exams easy compared to those at Cranwell.

Before Claude had left Cranwell, he had been offered a staff job there, as they had wanted a pilot to fly for the experimental wireless section. As Claude had hopes of his fiancée Ada Land coming to England, and therefore wanted a steady job, he took it and went back to Cranwell on February 15th. He was assistant to an officer called Simpson, and soon found that as the new boy he had to do the lion's share of the work.

— Self in the one & only Beardmore Bomber! —

Above: Claude in his own Sopwith Pup.

However, his happy marriage to Ada never happened, and the fall-out threatened his good name and career, and could have resulted in his death.

In May I arranged for Ada to come to England, and hoped to get married. I had had to supply her with the passage money, as the journey was too great a cost for her none too well off family. She was to travel via New Zealand. She got as far as Wellington, and there she was held up indefinitely. I made her an allowance and she did the best she could.

In August I was at Helford on leave, when I got a wire from Ada from Kingston, Jamaica, and she arrived at London in September. Without entering into the sordid details, I have no hesitation in saying that she behaved in a pretty outrageous manner with a man she met in Wellington, and with whom she travelled to England.

She obviously regarded me as a foregone conclusion, and I soon became aware of a side of her character which I had never dreamed of before. Aunt Lotty and I realised that marriage was out of the question, and so I persuaded Ada to go and live with friends until I could arrange a return passage for her. She eventually agreed to do this, and I made her an allowance.

The general worry of all this had an unpleasant effect on me: I, who had never grazed paint off a machine before had five minor crashes in succession and ended up with one that that ought by all the laws of probability to have ended my career in one short sharp moment. However it didn't, and after five weeks in hospitals – first in Lincoln and then in Haslar, I was back on flying duties at Cranwell.

— CRASHED AVRO. —

With the perceived disgrace of his broken engagement, Claude now 'fought tooth and nail' to get out on active service in the war. He claimed that he was nearly court-martialled for his insistence. Instead on December 14th 1917 he was sent back to Calshot to fly seaplanes. His CO Bigsworth – now a Wing-Commander and the possessor of a bar to his DSO – sent him over to Lee-on-Solent to be a seaplane instructor under the splendidly-named Squadron-Commander D.C.S. Evill. It's clear that the RNAS handled Claude sensitively: they knew that a man torn up by personal issues would be a danger to himself and a liability to others if put on active service. Even Claude admitted that his duties at Lee-on-Solent 'kept me from unpleasant thoughts of my own affairs by providing me with a volume of work.'

— 'PUP' ON ITS NOSE. —

Ada Land wrote to say that she refused to return to Fiji, and Claude replied to say that he would pay her return fare as soon as she wanted, but that he wasn't going to pay for her maintenance in the meantime. As she didn't reply to his offer, he assumed that she agreed, and it all went quiet – for the time being.

However, in February 1918 Bigsworth transferred Claude to be Senior Patrol Officer at the Cherbourg Seaplane Station. Claude was revived: *'Life at such a full out station as Cherbourg [pictured below] came as a joy.'*

Claude liked his Commanding Officer and enjoyed the work, the camaraderie, and the banter at Cherbourg. He spent a blissful spring there. This is when he had his affair with Helene, Vicomtesse d'Esparbes [see chapter 8] in Paris. But it was another affair, with the Corsican

Lotty Aureilly [pictured], which got him into trouble. It's clear that she seduced him rather than vice versa, but he did know that she had previously been the amour of his station Commanding Officer, so when Lotty started publicly pursuing Claude [even standing plaintively against the barbed wire of the Cherbourg Station], he shouldn't have been surprised when he was suddenly transferred back to England:

Life was delightful, so imagine my disgust when Bigsworth signalled that I was to take up a staff billet on the newly established Group Headquarters at Warsash, opposite Calshot! I had no choice, scarcely any time to pack, for a flying boat came for me and I and my belongings were dumped down at Warsash almost before I realised it. I started there on May 5th.

Lotty followed him to England, taking rooms in Southampton, but it wasn't the same for Claude once back in England, and the affair ended quickly and amicably. Lotty got married to an American soldier who owned a Kentucky tobacco farm.

Despite having what was predominantly desk-bound work, Claude found his new job important and very rewarding. He was responsible for all the air operations against the enemy submarines in the English Channel. They had five seaplane stations, three small airship stations and one large one, four aeroplane squadrons and the kite balloon base. Claude had a staff of six very capable officers under him, and his job was to co-ordinate all these stations, and to translate and distribute all the available intelligence on enemy submarines to them. Claude's work resulted in him being gazetted in the newly formed Royal Air Force as a Staff-Major.

This work against submarines kept up at full pressure until 11th November 1918, when the Great War was finally ended. Unlike so many, Claude didn't record his feelings about the end of the war, merely calling it *'fateful'*, but his war had been very different from the war of most of his generation. Several of his Keith cousins lost their lives on active service, but he never recorded their deaths, and he probably had never met any of them. None of his Rogers relatives and none of his friends or colleagues lost their lives, so he wasn't touched in a way that most people were. He probably had a degree of 'survivor's guilt' in common with others in the armed forces who came through unscathed, but he never expressed it in writing. Claude was a man who would have adored military glory, and he certainly came to enjoy yarns of his subsequent exploits, so it may have been galling that many of his Great War stories involve affairs with women and rifts with Marconi and his fiancée. It may explain why he continued to take an adventurous path after the 1918, and why he recorded those adventures in such detail for his son.

Daddy, what did *YOU* do in the Great War?

Chapter 8   Helene of Paris, 1918

Extracts from 'My Rosery': 3.

"Over the sea to France!
Needles astern, Barfleur to port
Hague on my starboard bow"

I sang a snatch of my old squadron song at the top of my voice, but all was swallowed up by the dull savage roar of my engine. I had just left 'Needles astern' and somewhere in the mist was 'Barfleur to port and 'Hague on my starboard bow'. It wasn't particularly interesting, flying in this mist. I was at a thousand feet, and the sea looked calm and lazy. The sun was up and blazing on the haze, so that to my left I was blinded by a beautiful golden glow. There wasn't much wind, so I thought I ought to make Cherbourg in an hour. I was starting my long earned leave from the time I landed in France, and with great anxiety I scanned the various pressure gauges, and listened to my engine.

The seaplane I was flying was a new one, and well rigged, for I could fly her 'hands off'. I stuck my two thumbs up to my observer, to show him all was well. I was allowing for about a 10 knot wind on my port quarter and holding a compass course of 205 degrees. I grew bored and wanted to get up and do something. There was no sign of life below – not a bird and not a ship, not even a cloud above, just a monotony of grey-blue shaded into gold.

Time passed, and I thought we were flying well, and I was beginning to think it was high time we saw something, when quite suddenly Cap Levi lighthouse loomed up right ahead, and I at once swung off to starboard and glided down towards the harbour. An excellent crossing without a hitch: a new seaplane for good old 243 squadron, and there was I, free to collect my suitcase and shove off on leave.

That night found dear old Peach and Coates and I jammed together en route for Paris. They had each scrounged 48 hours leave, and I had promised to at least attempt to show them something of the French capital. A comic trio we must have looked: I in the gilded glory of a newly acquired 'brass hat' and wearing a light blue Air Force uniform, Peach in faded khaki and Jack Coates in our old RNAS naval rig. My brass hat proved very useful, as it opened all doors, and I have since learned that golden oak leaves round a cap peak are only worn in France by generals!

I had taken them to the usual run of cafes, and we had just quit the Casino de Paris, when Jack said, "Now let's see a bit of the wicked side of Paris. What about the ravishing little grisettes and mannequins I've heard about?"

Just then a nasty sly looking creature sidled up and in broken English offered his services as a guide. I stood trying to remember; I had done the round myself in 1909 when I was on my way to Cannes, but that was a long time ago. Anyway, I didn't like the look of the guide, so I said that I'd try to pilot them, and we started off. I located the famous, or infamous, Palais de

Crystal near the public library, and we visited it and one or two other hells, but I could see that the fellows weren't impressed.

"What about all the beauty and delicacy of Paris?" demanded solid old New Zealand Coates, and turning, he asked one of the loiterers, who chanced to understand his curious French.

"Let me take you to the Rue Hombourg," that worthy replied. "You will see the mostest splendid womens of all Europe there. Go for to see, with no obligations."

And so it was agreed. I wasn't feeling a bit like it, and said that I'd quit for bed, but as Peach pointed out, I might as well stick to the ship, as if they found a spot of bother, they couldn't talk French. We got into a fiacre and were soon clattering up the cobbled hill past St Lazare Station.

Inside the place we were shown into a pleasant drawing room, and were given cigarettes by a maidservant.

Then in sailed Madame. She went right to the point. "Three young ladies will be presented to you. You may talk to them on strictly conventional subjects, and I hope that your conduct will be beyond reproach. After three minutes they will retire. You will make any arrangement with me, after they have left. If you are not satisfied, three other ladies will meet you. We understand, eh?"

The comic side struck me, and I nearly laughed, but old Coates warmed to it and cried, "Let's see all they've got," and Peach replied in a whisper, "You might wish you hadn't."

In a moment three young ladies entered. They were quite different from the ordinary run, I could see at a glance. Madame presented them. We bowed, they bowed, and we started to talk on general subjects in an entirely conventional manner. In three minutes Madame re-entered and they rose and departed.

"You have decided, any of you?"

"Not yet. Let's see others," said Coates, who was full out by now. "It's going to cost two hundred francs a time, and I'm too poor to decide in a hurry," he whispered to me.

The whole affair was too cut-and-dried, too damnably cold blooded and smugly respectable for me. I was taking merely an impersonal interest. These two blighters went on and on, until they'd seen every blessed woman in the place, and I was bored and Madame was wringing her hands and inclined to be rude. Finally they recalled two very charming young Parisiennes.

"You do as you wish," said I. "I'm beating it back to the hotel. It has left me cold. If these are the best women Paris can boast of, I'll turn celibate for the future."

They packed off, a deux, and I stood chaffing Madame.

"I will tempt you yet, my goodness, I will," she assured me, and bustled away. She was back in a minute or so. "Will you come to my boudoir, monsieur? I have a most charming lady there, who is very, very shy."

I followed her into a seductive little room flooded with soft rose pink light. A slight figure was standing on one side, wearing a plain tailor made costume with a wide brimmed velour hat, which hung so low over her head that I could not see her face. She was young, I judged from the slightness of her figure, and her legs would have rejoiced Kirschner whilst her tiny feet were shod as only a Parisienne can be shod.

I was presented, and bowed formally. She held out a small white gloved hand and slowly – very slowly – raised her eyes to mine. As I looked into the rich red-brown depths of her lovely eyes, a glorious blush mounted her cheeks and dyed her face an adorable pink. She was faultlessly pretty, of her type: dark ruddy brown hair, delicately pencilled black eyebrows and heavy eyelashes, full moist red lips that curved in a slightly imperious pout, a peachy skin and high cheek bones that spoke of hauteur and temper. She was, I felt, a 'thoroughbred' if ever I had seen one.

She raised her eyebrows in surprised question, as I had said nothing, so I quickly begged her to give me the honour of supping with her. And so it was decided, and as we walked out I bade Madame my adieu and gave her the prescribed 200 francs. There was a smiling gleam of triumph in her eyes!

Once outside in the still dark damp air, I felt a fool and quite at a loss. Eventually I hailed a taxi and we bundled into it. I had told the taxi driver to go to Laroux's, but she laid a small hand on my forearm and said, "Monsieur, I will not sup. Where are we to go?"

That rather flummoxed me, as I hadn't thought of it, but I yelled to the driver to take us to my hotel – the Louvre at the bottom of the Avenue de l'Opera. In a very distressed voice and with averted head, she whispered that she had nothing with her, and in an equally distressed voice I offered her a pair of pyjamas.

Her nervousness seemed infectious, I took her direct to my room, and as I switched on the light she again blushed and hung her head. "If M'sieur would leave me to prepare for sleep..."

"Why, of course," said I. "Here is the bathroom, and use whatever you like of mine. I'll return in half an hour."

I tapped carefully at my own door when I returned, and entered in response to a low "Entrez". I tried to switch on the light but no light came.

"I have removed the bulb, M'sieur. I beg you will pardon me. It will be more discreet," she said in explanation.

I felt as I suppose a husband must feel with his newly married wife, and yet her arms embraced me and her half open lips burned passionately on my mouth.

69

Little by little, talking in the darkness, we got to know each other better.

"M'sieur, would you say that I am a madame or a mademoiselle?" I hadn't thought of her being married. "I am but 23 years old and I have a little boy of 3 years old. I was married when I came from a convent in Orleans. My husband was killed when the Germans took Liege, and I retired into mourning in my mother's house. I have been in the country seeing no one, going nowhere, ever since the first week of the war, until a month ago. Then I revolted. My young blood could stand it no more. I came to Paris alone, except for my maid, Yvonne. I know many people here in Paris, and all were kind, but my Spanish blood – I am half Spanish – demanded more than kindness, and I could not deny it. Yvonne it was who told me of that dreadful Maison Rendez-vous in the Rue Hombourg. I went there dreading who I might meet. I think that I could never have dared to meet you, had I not been assured that you were English and a stranger to Paris. But that is past; I am here, here with you, and together we may help each other forget yesterday and tomorrow."

Her name was Helene, she told me, and the way she said it made it sound as soft as music. She asked me mine, and repeated it over and over again to herself, when I had told her.

&&&

She insisted on departing very early, and said that she would go alone and on foot.

"But it can't all end like this," said I. "Let me take you somewhere quiet for dejeuner."

She hesitated for a long while, and at length opened a dainty little bag and drew out a visiting card which she toyed with, hitting her bag with it after the manner of a woman in thought. With almost a snap, she made up her mind. She stood up erect.

"You will call for me, mon cher, and I will give you an aperitif and then we will go and dejeuner somewhere in the open air." She moved towards the door, which I opened. She turned, held out the card to me, and was gone.

In the excitement I dropped the card and it fell face downward. Turning it over as I picked it up, I read: [see left]

"Ye gods and little fishes!" I ejaculated *[sic!]*, and straight way ran off to tell the others. Peach was too sleepy to get excited, but when Coates had grasped the situation he grumbled, "I suppose that's the reward of patience and being so damned hard to please. If I'd stuck it out I ought to have collected a princess at that rate." The conceit of some men!

Her house was as sumptuous as its address had led me to suppose. I was ushered into a Louis XV room by a dream maid – Yvonne, no doubt. Then one of the mirrored doors was flung open and there was Helene holding out her two shapely hands in welcome to her home. Yvonne brought sherry, and whilst I drank it, Helene told her to bring in M'sieur Robert. Robert was a cherub and I liked him from the start. His mother had never spoken one word of English to me, but she evidently warned him, for he greeted me in pure childish English, and his great solemn eyes looked at me sadly. He was in sailor rig, and looked very delicate.

We lunched at the Cafe de l'Orient under the limes of the Champs Elysees, and a most delightful meal it was, over which I lingered as long as prudence allowed me, for I had to catch the train back to Cherbourg that afternoon. Helene came to see me off at St Lazare. I so well remember her standing on the platform, wrapped in huge biscuit coloured blanket coat, as perfectly formed specimen of womanhood as I have ever seen. The journey back was hateful. A hundred times I cursed myself for quitting Paris, as I need not have done so, for I still had eight days leave to run.

&&&

Above left: A photo taken of Coates, Claude and Peach on their return from Paris
Above right: Helene and Robert

In but two days I was back at St Lazare, pushing my way through the crowd towards the barrier, beyond which I could see Helene waiting for me. I was tired and hot and dirty, and wanted to shove off to my hotel at once, but she would not hear of this. "M'ami, time is precious and I refuse to waste a minute of your time. A hot bath awaits you at my home. Come." She directed the taxi driver.

Yvonne carried my bag unblushingly into a room of green and gold, which was obviously Helene's, and despite my momentary confusion, I remember mentally thanking my lucky stars that I had brought green and not pink silk pyjamas! From the opposite side of the room, a delightful bathroom opened. There I found a luxurious crystal glass bath, filled with sweet scented hot water, ready waiting for me. The delightful delicacy of every item of decoration surprised and delighted me. Everything in the bathroom was of palest green, and all the metal fitting were gilt, whilst under the transparent bath were fitted long tubes of golden electric lights, which shone up through the water. I must have lazed longer than I had intended, for Helene came rattling on the door to tell me that dinner would spoil if I didn't hurry.

We dined alone, as Robert had already gone off to bed. The salon was delightful – very plain but in perfect taste. Rose pink was the predominant colour, the palest shade, and it harmonized perfectly with the rich ruddy brown of the mahogany furniture. After dinner we smoked in the Louis XV room and with coffee came a visitor. It was none other than M. Malvis, who has been described as the 'evil genius of France' on account of the misfortunes that took place during his tenure of the office of foreign affairs. I was presented and we talked awhile, but Helene declined his invitation to motor to Melun next afternoon with his wife and daughters, and soon after he took his departure. **[There has never been a Minister for Foreign Affairs called Malvis, or anything near to that name.]**

With a smile Helene rose and left me. "I'll be back in five minutes," she called back.

She was back in less time, and I saw that she had discarded her evening gown and changed into a wonderful flimsy negligee.

"Helene," said I, "that wrap was made to tempt. I shall re-christen you Eve."

"Ah well, if it will tempt you, mon cher, it will serve me well. I will tempt you tonight as you have never been tempted before. I will sip life from your lips and I will crush your head to my breast. You shall become my 'enfant doré'."

&&&

For a week I lived a happy dream. The sun shone and glinted in Helene's hair, the birds sang gladly on the trees round the house and my every want was tended. Then came the time for me to go. As Yvonne carried my bag to the waiting taxi, I noticed that she had already put in another – Helene's! Nothing could dissuade her from making that dreary journey with me to Cherbourg. "Your last moments in France shall be mine," was her only answer. I smiled as I tried to picture dear old Scott's face as I rolled up with a perfectly good French Vicomtesse at Querqueville. However it did come about, and Scott's face certainly was delightful.

Coates and Peach met the train with our motor boat and after the long dusty train journey the trip across that famous harbour was like drinking iced champagne. It was cold as we shot across the calm water at a good 8 knots, cutting our way along the lane of liquid gold shed by the setting sun. Half the town turned out to see us embark from the town quay, as no one like Helene had been seen in Cherbourg since the war began. Wonderful Holly, the mess corporal who before the war was a section waiter in the Picadilly Hotel Grill, arranged a wonderful supper, and we sat and yarned. Then the two of us went back to the town by road and got accommodation at the Estrella Hotel, and early next day I leapt into the air and headed for England, whilst I suppose that poor Helene had to endure the dreary discomfort of that vile train journey to Paris, alone.

&&&

Leave was scarce: the war was occupying everyone's every effort, but a wonderful chance actually sent me from the Group Headquarters at Warsash direct to Paris! I had to go and confer with the French admiralty about the use and training of carrier pigeons. It seemed too providential to be true. This time I had to cart over several baskets of the wretched pigeons so I had to cross in a troopship to Cherbourg, and I had the most vile journey. However, in due course I arrived in Paris and set out to find Helene, who had now given up her house and was living in a suite in the Mercedes Hotel near the Arc de Triomphe.

I had but three days in Paris, days which were not wholly my own, but I wasted no time. One day we had a heavenly picnic on one of the islands in the Vincennes woods, and took Robert with us. He and I had become great friends, and he used to pester me to give him pig-a-back rides whenever we went out. [Helene pictured in the Vincennes woods, left]

By this time Helene had decided that we would marry, and I was rather shaken one night when she took me out to a private dinner party and introduced me as her future husband. She told me she was going away into the country to settle some affairs of her estate, and after that had

been completed she would come to England. Her mother's family was the old French family of Chateaubriand, and their estate was at Segre, where I believe they had one of the lovely old French chateaux [pictured right].

Before she got to England though, I managed to scrounge a few days leave, and was again in Paris. She hurried up from Segre to join me. Her mind was more fully made up by now, but she had also decided certain details in her own mind, in the matter-of-fact way which French women always adopt before they tie themselves to matrimony. It exposed a hard calculating side to her nature, which rather scared me. We had long talks. My future was doubtful, as was the future of anyone in the war, but even if I got through it all, what should I do? I could scarcely go whining to the Marconi Company to give me back the billet which I had so raised heaven and earth to get clear of in 1915. She had arranged it all, it seemed, but the one essential condition to its fulfilment meant that I should have to naturalize as a French subject, and this I stubbornly refused to contemplate.

My last day had dawned and we had yet to come to an agreement, and I'm afraid that her persistence had very much altered my attitude towards her. Undoubtedly she recognized this. That afternoon we had decided to go to the Pere Lachaise Cemetery to see Berthelot's famous sculpture group 'Aux Morts' [pictured left]. As we neared the gates Helene left me and came back with a huge bunch of glorious Gloire de Dijon roses. I supposed they were for the tomb of someone she had known.

Pere Lachaise always holds a weird fascination for me: it is such a veritable 'city of the dead', with its long avenues of closely packed tomb-houses [see below] each with its tiny altar and cross and candles. We wandered here and there, and as the afternoon grew late a great sullen red sun sunk down into the purple mist that hung over Paris, and the air grew chill. All the leaves had fallen and the wind was scurrying them mercilessly to and fro.

Helene wound her way, still bearing the lovely yellow-gold blooms, and finally stood before the tomb which I instantly recognized: it was the "Shrine of Unrequited Love'. She turned a sad and solemn face to me and dropped the flowers on the breast of the stone figure which adorns the tomb. I felt very sad myself. She made a charming picture, standing there dressed in simple black and swathed in heavy furs, her lovely 'Kirschener' legs rising out of a dainty pair of wickedly high heeled shoes. Neither of us said anything. The only sound was the rustling of the dead leaves and the faint moaning of the wind in the bare branches overhead. Then she turned to me.

"You understand, m'adore?" she asked. "It is not for you that I do this."

I said nothing – what was there to say?

In silence we turned and wended our way back to the city.

In the taxi, as she sat by my side with crossed legs, I remember thinking what adorable legs she had, clad in black silk stockings. Then, as we turned a corner suddenly, she swayed and her skirt jerked up above her knee and she showed me a dainty black silk garter embroidered with little pink rose buds. That almost made me change my mind – but not quite. I escaped its lure, and I left Paris and I left Helene, and to this day I do not know where she is.

Sometimes I amuse myself by trying to picture the life I might have led and which prudence caused me to renounce. I should, in time, have become 'sieur of that old French chateau, I should have become step-father to Robert, I should have – oh but what is the use of building idle castles in the air? It must have been written and that is all about it, but as the years roll on the memory of Helene – Helene of Paris, as I call her – remains quite fresh. A closed chapter but one that I can re-read with interest but no regrets.

Chapter 9   After the Great War

The end of the war did not bring great joy to Europe. Too many had died or been crippled physically or mentally. It was a time of famine, economic depression, international insecurity and humiliation, epidemics and unemployment.

Some of this sense of insecurity was felt by Claude. Although he had been gazetted as a Staff-Major in the fledgling RAF, it was not a permanent commission. He could see the thousands of servicemen being demobbed, scrambling for rare jobs. Claude was a specialist electrical engineer who had left Marconi in acrimonious circumstances, and he had come to the RAF older than normal, so his anxiety about securing a permanent commission in the RAF or finding a new civilian job was palpable. At this time, the last thing he needed was a scandal about his private life, but that's what happened:

Early in 1919 I got the nasty shock of having a summons served on me for a breach of promise action brought by Ada Land. In view of my promise to pay her return passage and expenses, I was surprised, but I am pretty sure that there was a grasping influence behind her action on the part of someone else. About this time I had been interviewed for a permanent commission with the RAF. I didn't much expect to get one, but I knew that it meant starting out in a new firm if I didn't.

Ada Land and the 'grasping influence' had picked their moment shrewdly. Claude was in no position to risk fighting them.

Anyway, I decided that I couldn't afford to fight the case in court, partly because of the bias it might give to my chances of getting a permanent commission and partly because I didn't like the idea of the Keith family name getting into the undesirable columns of the Sunday papers. To be on the safe side I engaged Schiller and a junior counsel to work up the case, and both seemed to think that I would win it. It came as far as being called, but I settled out of court for the reasons I have stated. Naturally it galled me to have to do so as she could not have made a black case against me not brought up anything dishonourable. I lunched with her counsel, and his sympathy was balm to my soreness.

There is no record of the nature of the settlement, but Claude's soreness was further relieved when on 5th August he was one of the few officers to be gazetted in the new permanent RAF, with the rank of Flight-Lieutenant.

When the war ended, so did the campaign against German submarines, so Claude had become engaged in producing a service training manual for marine aviation navigation. He found it hard but very interesting work, even though it kept him seated at a desk, and the end product proved important. There were other compensations, as well:

The place was choc-a-bloc with all types of women – WRAFs. I had them working in my office, they cooked our food, waited on us at table and scoured our rooms. There one could study women at leisure. It was peculiar how each had her own favourite amongst the officers and would do much for him and as little as she needed for the others. But war was on and women, as women, had no place at Warsash until the memorable 11th November, when the jollifications of the armistice broke down all barriers. Gradually supper parties with two of the WRAF officers became the fashion. Time was freer for outside engagements.

There were also dances: he met his future wife, Angel, at one – see Chapter 9. Other women he met more furtively: Marjorie [left, below] did typing for Claude, and confided to Claude her hopeless love for another officer. Claude found himself comforting her *'too well'*. Mildred [below centre left] was a subtle seductress who told Claude that her husband had been killed in the war out in India, but suddenly broke off their affair to return to her miraculously recovered husband! Agnes [below centre right] was a sweet young ingénue whom Claude merely watched from afar. May [below right] was different: she was a friend of the family whom Claude only saw as a sister, but it's easy to infer that she was greatly liked by his aunts, who nudged her into the matrimonial frame. Claude liked and admired her, and after his marriage broke up, he had many 'what if' musings about May.

In August 1919 Claude had another bust-up with a superior officer, and again it was over a woman. This time the woman in question was to become his wife, but in the meantime he thought it better to get away from his commander, Bigsworth, and so he applied for a job in the Air Ministry. All officers in the new RAF had been asked to choose a specialism in one of five subjects: Engineering, Navigation, Signals, Armament or Photography. Claude had chosen Navigation because he thought it would give him the greatest chance of remaining an active flying officer, and because his time hunting submarines had shown him how important accurate navigation was. When he applied for his job in the Ministry, he was asked to rough out the lines of how aerial navigation should be taught.

His application was successful, and he was sent to Andover to be one of a navigation soviet being formed by the Deputy Director of Training to work out how to teach air navigation. Claude called the station *'thoroughly rag-time'* but said that they got through a lot of good work. The term 'soviet' referred to the practice whereby the pupil of one lecture would be the instructor of the next lecture – they taught each other because at the birth of this new service there was no one with the knowledge to teach multiple aspects. Whilst at Andover, Claude also developed an interest in working out how to drop bombs accurately.

In February 1920 Claude was off again, this time back to Calshot on the Solent, where he was appointed Flight Commander of a Flying Boat flight. At this point, Claude, normally so methodical about writing about his career, leaves a two year gap in the narrative, except in telling the story of his wooing of Angel. All we have of Calshot 1920 to 1922 are some photographs – a few are set out below.

— F.B.A. IN CLOUDS. —

— WHEN KING GEORGE VISITED CALSHOT. —

— SELF & OLD W/T GANG AT CALSHOT. —

In 1922 Claude moved to 230 Squadron. In 1923 he took a short two month practical Air Gunnery and Bombing course at Eastchurch on the Isle of Sheppey in Kent. Six of the twenty pupils, including Claude, were selected to take a further two month course to qualify them as Squadron Armament Officers. Claude became very interested in armaments during this course. This was a time when the force was analysing the lessons learned in the First World War, and arguing about what could be done to improve effectiveness should another war happen. Claude, with his pioneering electrical engineering background, was the sort of man who wasn't satisfied with the status quo – he was always questioning and experimenting.

At the end of the course at Eastchurch, the CO told Claude that he would be back. Claude laughed at the suggestion: he wanted to get back into a flying job and then stay there. But in 1925 he was posted back to Eastchurch as Chief Armaments Officer.

I complained that I was not an Armament specialist [he was a Navigation specialist], *was not qualified 'A', and had not done the long armament course. The official answer was to print an 'A' against my name in the RAF list, and I was left to get on with the job.*

For the next two years Claude was at Eastchurch, in charge of all the RAF armament training for pilots, observers, gunners, telegraphers, armourers and fitter-armourers. Claude comments that although he never would have chosen the job, it did interest him greatly, and he gathered around him a team of outstandingly clever mathematicians and teachers who worked out solutions to the many problems that arose. His team *'had a lot to say'* about the institution of annual bombing and firing practices, and they standardized the system whereby the bombing results of one squadron could be compared with those of another squadron. Thus efficiency could be improved, not by logging how long airmen had flown or how many practice bombs they had dropped, but by the actual results of their bombing.

Then in 1926, Claude got the release he had been waiting for: he was sent to No. 70 Squadron, who flew heavy bomber-transporter planes out of Baghdad, Iraq. Now a married man with a small son, he was going to be back in active service, fully immersed in the adventure he craved. It was a boost to his career, but it wasn't to be so good for his marriage.

Chapter 10 Why did he do it? Claude's first marriage

It's not hard to see why Claude wished to get married. By 1919 he was twenty-nine years old, and many of his friends were settling down with wives and married pay allowances. Claude was naturally sociable, and although he had adoring aunts, he had no close family of his own. He had suffered the debacle of Ada Land, and was keen to put things right. He was a man who was fascinated by family trees, and at present his own branch wasn't bearing fruit.

What is much harder to understand is why he chose Mary Angel Constance Montgomery to be his wife. They were totally unsuited to each other; Claude was very attractive and could have had a pick of a wide selection of brides, but he chose one whom he didn't even like, and who was probably disliked by most of his relations. He ignored several warnings from colleagues, relatives and even from his own heart. Predictably, the marriage turned out to be the central disaster and sadness of his life. Why did he do it?

In the autumn of 1919, while on the staff group of No.10 group at Warsash, he accepted an invitation to a dance being given by a Mrs Montgomery, the widow of a naval officer, in the Forest Hall at Warsash. He didn't know the family, but it was quite routine for officers to be invited to such functions. Claude recalls the evening as being *'very ordinary'* and *'the crowd left no impressions'*. A few days later he received an invitation from the Montgomery family to play tennis, which he declined, but a few days later he received on the telephone another invitation, this time from the eldest daughter [whom he didn't remember from the dance], and this time he accepted.

When I got to their house, Jesmond, which was about a couple of miles from the RAF Headquarters, I at once recognized their daughter as the dark girl of the dance with the huge brown eyes. My tennis was indifferent, but I enjoyed the change and was glad to be asked again. Angel, the daughter, didn't thrill me. She had a peculiar, somewhat distinguished voice – in fact the whole family had it, but it sounded somewhat as though they were trying to talk with a plum stone in their mouths. She was very slight, quite young and thoroughly inexperienced, but very keen to discuss deep questions.

One day after playing a set or two, she suggested that we should go to look for pears in the orchard. We did and conversation turned on various deep subjects. Gradually our intimacy deepened. I told her of my unhappy experience with Ada Land and how that had killed my interest in women.

Claude's account above suggests that he had played tennis several times before the *'deep subjects'* came up. By this time Claude had learned of Angel's family. Her father had been a naval commander, who had retired through ill health as a Captain and died some few years before. She had a sister of about eleven, Josseline, who was under a governess who also looked after Roger, the brother who was then about six. The eldest brother John was a Sub-Lieutenant in the navy, the second, Jaimie, was a cadet at Dartmouth, and the third, Alick, was at Wellington. The mother's name was Hudson, and her father was an old retired naval captain. Angel had been educated at Cheltenham Ladies College, and had worked in the Chart Issue

Branch of the Admiralty, but had given this up when the war was over. She was twenty-one years old in 1919. This large family with service tradition and respectability may have attracted

Claude, but at this point he certainly wasn't thinking of Angel as a potential bride.

'Angel and I saw one another fairly often, and she came and had tea with me and our WRAF officers. We planned outings and gradually our intimacy developed along harmless and conventional lines. I thought nothing of this acquaintanceship, I meant less. I always called her Miss Montgomery and was entirely conventional in my conduct.'

Pictured above: [front] Josseline, Roger, Mary, Alick, and back, Jamie, John.

Claude was off to Andover for a course on aerial navigation, and Angel was going to take up a secretarial post with the Officer's Family Fund in London, so that should have been the end of it. However, some external meddling from Claude's commanding officer at Warsash changed things.

Then one morning Bigsworth [pictured on the right, with Claude on the left] came to me and warned me that I should get into serious trouble if I was not careful. How the mother was determined to get Angel married, was herself somewhat mad and how I should have to be very careful or I would get landed with a breach of promise case. The whole thing seemed to me to be so absurd that I laughed and said that I hadn't a guilty conscience.

That evening I met Angel in response to a note from her, and she told me that Bigsworth had been to see her mother and had said that I was the most undesirable person for her daughter to associate with, etc, etc, and that her mother had forbidden her to see me again, and was taking her away to stay with an uncle in the Channel Isles.

Then I told her what Bigsworth had said, and we agreed that Bigsworth was fearful for his own safety, as he probably guessed that Angel and I had probably discussed his behaviour with Josseline – which we actually had. Angel had to return quickly, as she had sneaked out of Jesmond secretly, but before she went we had fixed up a method of writing with invisible ink, and sworn to see one another again when she returned. The very attempt to separate us actually brought us much closer together.

We don't know what Bigsworth's behaviour was with the eleven-year-old Josseline, but he obviously had some previous dealings with the family – when Claude had mentioned to him that Angel was looking for a job in the WRAF at Warsash, he had apparently *'hit the roof'*.

Certainly his behaviour with Claude went far beyond the normal duties towards an officer under his command. Presumably he told Mrs Montgomery about the Ada Land saga, probably the Lotty Aureilly episode in Cherbourg, as well as maybe other dalliances in Warsash. Whatever Bigsworth's intentions, his actions had the opposite effect.

Claude went to Andover and met Angel a few times in London. When he transferred back to Calshot, Angel, unknown to her mother, came down for a big dance at Beaulieu Abbey. Claude and a brother officer shared one room at the Balmer Lawn Hotel in Brokenhurst, while Angel shared another with Claude's cousin Brownie. The dance didn't go quite how Claude had hoped:

We dined comfortably before setting off for the dance. The dance was held in the old Domus, where a modern dance-floor had been laid and where dances were regularly given by a dance club to which I belonged. That dance was excellent, but so were all of them. There was a waning moon that night, as between dances Angel and I stood in the ruined cloisters, I remarked "The moon is south, it must be three o'clock." I was full of my nearly acquired astronomical knowledge. "What a remark to make," said she, and I realized that her thoughts were far more human than mine. I linked my arm in hers – a thing that I had never yet done – and we sauntered into the shadows. We found ourselves in a ruined cemetery, and she shuddered. I put my arm around her waist, and with my right hand caught hold of her chin, and turned her face towards me. She smiled and in a flash I realized what she expected, and before she could have detected my hesitation, I kissed her mouth.

She did not move, and as the first kiss had not been a brilliant success, I kissed her again. The second was no better: she evidently didn't know how to kiss. "I didn't want this to happen," said I, and she moved off, and we walked back. "But since it has happened, may I have another?" I concluded. But she hurried me back and wouldn't let me kiss her again. She was quite unwarrantably piqued. After that I called her by her name, Angel, but it was quite a long time before she let me kiss her again. How wise she was – how very wise!

Above: Balmer Lawn Hotel and Beaulieu Abbey cloisters.

It was actually years before Angel allowed Claude to kiss her again – he had to wait until the spring of 1921! During the intervening time they met sporadically, either in hotels in the

New Forest, or up in London, and Claude was allowed to hold her in his arms, but not to kiss her. It wasn't until the night that he had been installed in the Chair as the Master of his Masonic Lodge, and then later he and Angel had been locked into Hyde Park and had been forced to climb the Albert Gate, that she allowed him a kiss.

Angel attracted me by reason of her very coldness. Her kisses were not easily won. She was impersonal even when she kissed me. I was pretty sure that her sex experience was nil, but I was not quite sure, and it riled me to think that she was making a fool of me. I determined to break down her cold reserve. She seemed perfectly under control as she was quite confident that she could dominate any situation.

I tried oh so hard, and eventually she allowed me to sleep in her bed, but she coldly told me that she had no intention of letting me do more. To lie and hold her in my arms when she wore but a thin flimsy silk nightdress was maddening enough, but to think that I could awake no response was ten times worse. I think she liked my being there with her: it was a new experience and she thrilled at the knowledge that she was doing something unconventional and was playing with fire. What we did was risky: this staying at Miss Hogan's [her landlady] and, late at night, my creeping to her room and sneaking away whilst it was yet early dawn.

About the middle of 1921 I told her that I loved her, and was shaken to the core to be told that she had never thought of me in the light of a lover, and could not love me, though she liked me well enough as a platonic friend. Nothing daunted, I patiently persisted, until one night as she lay in my arms, I must have awakened some faint response, for she turned to me and said "Now I must tell you what I had meant not to tell you – that I do care."

It is clear that one significant reason why Claude pursued Angel was because she was a challenge. First he wanted to prove Bigsworth wrong, and show that he was not an untrustworthy cad. Then he needed to break through Angel's cold defences. Whether Angel was playing a clever game, or whether she was genuinely frightened or revolted by the idea of kissing and sex is harder to tell – she left no story of her own.

In the summer of 1921 Claude took Angel to stay with his Aunt Lotty in Cornwall. They bathed, boated and cycled together. They spent one uncomfortable night sleeping under the stars at Kynance Cove. Aunt Lotty was clearly unhappy with the relationship, but Claude wasn't listening – maybe it just added to the challenge.

It was idyllic in many ways. I often call to mind Angel, as she sat in the early summer's sun, on the edge of the stream, combing her long black hair, and smiling to me.

Idyllic summer romance soon slid into an inevitable engagement and marriage. Claude, backed by Lotty, tried to apply the brakes, but Angel was suddenly adamant and her mother also had her foot on the accelerator:

Having told each other we loved, I had tried an engagement ring on Angel's finger as she was flying with me one day when we visited Hendon – tried it on and taken it away, but she hadn't forgotten it. I told Aunt Lotty, and she was opposed to me hurrying, but Angel eventually gave

me an ultimatum. We were in Helston, and while we lunched at the Angel Hotel – appropriate name – she made me promise that I would write to her mother, and she said that she would like to do likewise, to announce our engagement. In vain I had begged for a postponement, but she was adamant: either I did it then, or she left me forever. We went and wrote those momentous letters in the post office, and the deed was done.

I visited her home to face the storm which our letters had created. I found all calm. Her mother received me with open arms, and the usual feeling of 'meeting the relatives' set in. It must have been in September of 1921 that we announced our engagement. I wanted it to last for at least two years, but Angel would not hear of it. Eventually I agreed to have the wedding as soon as my long aerial navigation course was over, and it was fixed for 22nd December.

Claude made Angel promise not to get a job before their marriage so that he could visit her. *'This she very reluctantly did, as she hated being under the same roof as her mother.'* The wedding arrangements were all made by Claude: he chose St Mary Abbott's in Kensington because his grandparents and Angel's grandparents had both been married there. He chose the reception hotel and the music, the church was decorated in RAF colours, the cake had a sugar aeroplane on it, Angel's bouquet was to be in RAF colours using flowers sent from South Africa by Claude's Aunt Alice. He had smuggled the champagne in from Alderney on a flying boat. Cooper was to be Claude's best man, and one of his cousins was to be a bridesmaid. 150 guests were invited. Nothing was left to chance, and very little was left to the bride.

Then the wedding had to be postponed until 4th January 1922 because Angel got measles. Claude paid for his control, because in the middle of his latest RAF exams he had to contact the 150 guests and then organize a new wedding at short notice. The doctor said that Angel could be married four days after her spots disappeared, but she grew impatient and used scissors to cut off the scabs, which left her with at least two lasting pock marks on her face.

The wedding itself went off very well, apart from Cooper, the best man, being late. The only upset for Claude was that his beloved former guardian, Aunt Lotty, refused to attend because of the presence of Claude's Keith relatives – the Keith-Rogers feud, which had started 32 years before, smouldered on. A list of presents was kept by Claude – he commented that they received over 250 silver spoons, but no carvers or cruet! They were driven by hansom cab to his Aunt Nell Keith's house, where they had a meal before catching the boat train to France for their honeymoon.

Airman's Wedding.

Flight-Lieutenant C. H. Keith and Miss M. A. C. Montgomery, married at St. Mary Abbot's, Kensington, yesterday.

And so, a little after 2pm on 4th January, my days of batchelordom were ended. Perhaps it was as old Breeze had said, I had had a good run for my money.

So why did he marry Angel? Of course, we only have his account, written for his infant son after his marriage had got into difficulties. Angel would almost certainly have told it differently, and it's very difficult to see her motivation beyond wanting to get away from her mother [later accounts from her mother suggest that their antipathy was mutual]. She didn't marry for sex, she wasn't the sort to be carried away by a whim or by honeyed words, and she didn't want children. Claude, an obviously sensual and experienced man, married a woman whose very coldness and inexperience had attracted him. Her initial reluctance and his later attempts to have a long engagement suggest that they both had substantial reservations – later both of them independently admitted that they had considered pulling out of the wedding. However, the personal challenges and the social pressures and conventions, as well as the Ada Land breach of promise case, ensured that there was to be no way out [at least before the marriage] for either of them.

Chapter 11 'Pathetic and inevitable' – a blow by blow account of a marriage breakdown

It is rare to have such a detailed log of a marriage break-up as the one that Claude compiled. In addition to his account for his son, he kept all the letters [the sole communication between himself and Angel in the last years of their marriage] that passed between them.

As they set off on their honeymoon, the warning signs were already there: Claude had been attracted to Angel's froideur while Angel had seen Claude as a way of escaping her mother and siblings. These may be a good hook for an affair, but not good glue for a marriage. He had sniped at the 'plummy' way she and her family spoke. She was a firm believer in women's independence who must have known Claude's paternalist views before they married. Claude never recorded any affectionate action taken by Angel or anything affectionate any relative or friend said about her.

For the first two years things were quiet between the married couple. They agreed that they would put off having children because they were young and didn't have a lot of money. Claude was working hard at Eastchurch on the Isle of Sheppey, while Angel lived in the rather grand house that her uncle gave her – Pelling House in Old Windsor. Claude would visit Angel on his BSA motorbike whenever he had leave, but there was plenty of space between them, and not too much pressure. But the question of a child – a dear ambition for Claude – came to the fore:

During the spring of 1924 we both agreed that the time had arrived for us to start a family, but months went by and no family seemed possible. On the advice of Sir Lenthal Cheatle, the famous Harley Street specialist who had been treating your mother for some malady, I went and saw Dr. Martyn of Eton. He made light of what had become a sorrow to us and said that he could easily correct matters with a slight operation to your mother. She agreed to undergo this and in August of 1924 spent a week in a nursing home at Datchet and got over it. Dr. Martyn then said that his operation would be ineffective unless your mother more passionately desired a child.

Time went by and we grew to doubt whether his operation had achieved the desired result. Then, just before Christmas when we were staying in Paris on our way to Spain, at the Avenida Hotel, 41 Rue de Colises, off the Champs Elysees, one night your mother's wish must have been granted. We journeyed on and spent several weeks touring Spain, and then one day whilst we were basking in the early morning sun that flooded our room in the Hotel Biarritz at San Sebastian, your mother told me that a child was to come to us.

This extract suggests that Angel did not passionately want a child, and had been persuaded to undergo a gynaecological operation in order to conceive. The picture of her in

San Sebastian, taken on the morning when she discovered that she was pregnant, does not radiate happiness.

The birth of their son Colin did not bring Claude and Angel together. On 9th September 1926 there was a scare, but Claude wasn't due his leave, so he remained on the Isle of Sheppey until 18th September, leaving Angel in Old Windsor. In fact, he was home a week before the event. They had engaged Dr Andrew McAllister, a noted gynaecologist, who agreed to take the case for 30 guineas instead of the usual several hundred, because *"my practice is to ease up to serving officers but to sting profiteers and socialists."*

On the 25th September, Dr. McAllister gave Angel an anaesthetic and tried to induce a birth, but it wasn't until 8 o'clock on 27th September that Claude got a call in Windsor that the birth was underway. Claude raced into London on his motorbike, stayed until 3 pm watching his wife in acute labour pains, and then was sent home. He spent the evening worrying.

The phone call came through that night: Dr. McAllister had been called by the midwife, who said that Angel had become 'dangerously restive', and he had decided to give her anaesthetic, and induce the baby. The baby was a *'bonny boy, perfect in every detail'*. Cue Claude shouting, praying, and giving the dogs his own dinner. *'They were sick that night, but what did it matter? I had got a son!'* There's nothing about his concern for Angel's health.

Next day Claude was not allowed to visit his wife and son until the afternoon, so he spent the time writing to relatives, and to the Times, with an announcement of the birth:

KEITH. On 27th September 1925 at 33, Brixton Hill, SW2, to Angel [nee Montgomery] wife of Squadron Leader C.H. Keith R.A.F. of Pelling Cottage, Old Windsor – of a son. [Colin John Hilton].

The announcement of the name in the Times is interesting, and it was to spark of a battle between Angel and Claude. Claude explained:

I should tell you that we had already discussed your names. Your mother wanted your first name to be euphonious with our surname and we both agreed that Colin was good for this. I had suggested Clive …. John we both liked: I because it is an old Keith name, and your mother because it is her eldest brother's name. Hilton I insisted upon, as there have been but four Hiltons in the Keith family in all, and all have travelled and seen much of the world and life. You are Hilton V, and I hope the name may bring you all and more than it has brought the other four of us. I wanted you to be called Michael, but your mother said it was 'overdone' as a name, but I secretly intended that you be christened Michael, though I didn't press the point then. I knew it would mean loading you with four Christian names to carry through life, but it had to be, and to me you will always be 'Mickie'.

This dispute over Colin's name was to run and run. Claude continued to call him Mickie, and as the certificate below shows, Claude got his way at the christening. However, when his parents divorced, the Angel deleted the name Michael from Colin's identity, and he never used it again.

Baptism *solemnized in the Parish of* St Peter, Bayswater *in the Diocese of* London *and County of* London *in the Year* 1925

Alleged date of Birth.	When Baptized.	Child's Christian Name.	Parents' Names.		Abode.	Quality, Trade, or Profession.	By whom the Ceremony was performed.
			Christian.	Surname.			
Sept 27th 1925	Decr 1st 1925.	Colin John Michael Hilton	Claude Hilton + Mary Angel Constance	Keith	Welling Cottage Old Windsor Berkshire	R.A.F.	A. Hopkins Ass^t Priest St Andrews Catford S.E.6. (Kent)

I Certify, that the foregoing is a true Copy of the entry of the Baptism of Colin John Michael Hilton Keith in the Register of Baptisms for the said

Parish of S. Peter Bayswater

Dated this 30th day of June 1936.

Signed L.T. Maund.
(Vicar)

Claude visited his Aunt Nell Keith on the way to Brixton that first afternoon:

She was overjoyed that you had come into the world and were a boy. "Another Keith has been born" was her cry – a young life to carry into the future the names and traditions of her beloved family.

Claude found Angel with a *'pale face and gazing vacantly into space'*, *'unable to grasp the significance of it all'*. Was this the start of a prolonged post-natal depression? The portrait

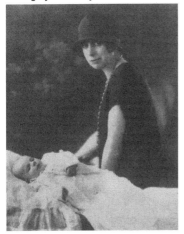

of Angel with Colin left] is not a picture of maternal love. On Saturday 3rd October, Angel gave Colin his first breast feed, but she found it so painful that it was permanently discontinued on the 7th October, being replaced with bottles of *'Humanized True-Feed, a desiccated milk food from Jersey cows kept on a special farm in Cheshire'*. On 17th October, nearly three weeks after the birth, Angel and Colin left the nursing home in Brixton and went home to Old Windsor. Ominously, Claude noted that Colin looked like a Keith, with little resemblance to Angel or her family, and that Colin was free from 'blemishes', contrasting this with the Montgomerys, whom he claimed were *'rich in warts and moles'*.

Colin was christened on 1st December 1926. Great Aunt Nell Keith hosted the event at her parish church and house, in Kensington, and the priest was Arthur Hopkins, Claude's cousin. It was a full family affair, with the Keiths out in numbers, with drinks beforehand and tea and cake afterwards. At the christening, the name Michael became an issue:

You were christened in the names Colin John Michael Hilton, your father whispering the names to your Godmother, who held you, when Arthur [the priest] turned to her and said, "Name this child." Your mother was furious at my including the name Michael, but she said nothing – then! She has said many unkind things about it since and forbidden anyone to use the name, so it'll have to remain your Daddy's own especial name for you.

The second potential flashpoint came at the end of the christening, when Claude secretly arranged for the lady who looked after Colin, Mrs. Deacon, to take Colin to be seen by his Great-Aunt Lotty Rogers. The Rogers family did not attend the christening because of the longstanding feud between them and the Keiths, but Lotty was distraught about missing the christening. According to Claude, Angel would have *'gone off the deep end'* if she had found out that Colin had been taken to Lotty. We know that Lotty had cautioned Claude against an early marriage to Angel, and they were to clash later as well. It certainly seems unusual that Angel did not hold Colin at the christening ceremony, and then sent him off with the nurse before the party had ended.

On 15th December, the nice Mrs Deacon was replaced as Colin's nurse by Miss Ada Peters [pictured below]. Claude infers that this decision was made by Angel against his wishes:

Everything that poor Mrs Deacon had done for you was condemned as wrong and Nurse couldn't understand how you had lived through such treatment. She was dressed all in white and moved about silently, like a ghost. I suppose she must be about 28 years old, and had a very thorough experience in the upbringing of babies. She soon grew to be very proud of you, and spared no pains to ensure that all was well with you.

One can only speculate as to why Angel decided in March 1926 to leave her five-month-old baby with the nurse and go to stay with her friend Mrs. MacMullen in St. Jean de Luz, near Biarritz. Claude rented rooms for Colin and Miss Peters in a house called Windermere, in Minster-on-Sea on the Isle of Sheppey, three miles from his work at Eastchurch. Claude used to visit *'every few days'*.

Already you became very intrigued by my uniform buttons, and used to hold them tightly in your baby fists. I flew over to see you one day, and from up among the clouds I looked down into the garden and saw your pram and knew that you would be peacefully sleeping there. My lovely babe, your father nearly burst with pride of you in those days.

On the 1st May, with Angel presumably returned from France, they moved into married quarters at Seacroft, Leysdown, on the Sheppey seafront. But soon Claude was posted to Iraq, a posting which did not allow accompanying wives, and he was not to see his son again for a long time. Months later he wrote:

I hate having left you, for I expect three years will elapse before I shall see you again, and I shall for ever miss three of your priceless baby years. I am thinking of getting a baby cinema and sending it to your mother to make a record of you. When I left you could only just stand by holding onto the rail of your crawl pen, you couldn't walk and you hadn't yet said one intelligible word. When I next see you, you will be a great boy of four. Your mother tells me that she has got a new nurse for you and that you are very well. Dear old fellow: I have only been away from you for less than two months, but it seems years. May God bless and keep you, and make you grow up fine and strong. My idea is to serve three years in this tropical hell and then get transferred home for another three. You will then be seven and ready for the junior school of St. Lawrence, where your Daddy went in the summer of 1902, and your mother and I will probably go out to India for five years. This is my idea, but much may have to be altered, but whatever may befall, I do not want to risk ill health to your young life by taking you abroad with us when you are young.

He was right – much did need to be altered to these fond plans.

Claude was posted to Iraq in October 1926. This was probably the month when his marriage became doomed to failure. While he could talk to Angel and could share some of her complaints, there was a slim chance that they could work out their differences. Once they were thousands of miles apart, living in totally different worlds which Angel could not comprehend [and made no effort to comprehend], communicating by a slow and erratic postal service, with no prospect of seeing each other, their differences and tensions were bound to be exacerbated to breaking point.

Claude kept a copy of almost all the letters he sent Angel from Iraq and later Egypt, and all the letters that she sent him. Later he bound them into a solid book marked 'Private' – it is one of the saddest and most complete records of a marital breakdown that can exist, because it contains every single communication between them during the last four years of their marriage – it's possible that they did not speak to each other face to face or by telephone ever again.

The very first letter that Angel sent Claude, dated 6th November 1926, clearly shows that things were not well before Claude left for Iraq. There is nothing positive in the whole [very long] letter.

Angel's strongest complaint in this first letter is about money, which she returns to time and time again over the ensuing years. She says that she has an overdraft, and has had several friends to stay, but she can't afford enough maids to look after them. She only has one maid '*plus a nurse for baby*', when she needs two maids. She needs a gardener, but can't afford one. She would like to have a live-in married couple '*to do car, garden, baby and house*', but she can't afford this. Her utility bills are high and the phone company are threatening to cut her off. She has had to turn down party invitations because she doesn't have a new frock. Her car needs repairs.

She complains about the house in Old Windsor, which was given to her [and owned by her exclusively] by an old uncle, Keith Hudson.

I felt that I simply could not go on being left alone in this place night after night and I could not expect visitors to come here and do all the dirty work and get no fun, even when that was finished on account of baby, so I had to have someone who could sleep in. I will try a little longer, but I am not very hopeful. It seems a waste to have a house this size and to see nobody and go nowhere at my age, just because I can't afford to have them here or to go to them, when by moving into a town or a smaller place, I could do both.

Pelling House, Old Windsor, 'before it was done up'.

She complains that he is having all the fun by being abroad, while her trip to Algiers is having to be cancelled [no reason given, but it wasn't lack of money]. She scoffs at Claude's descriptions of the smells of Baghdad – '*You don't seem to be able to get over the smells of the place, but Mrs Medhurst has had glowing accounts of Baghdad from her husband – so some people seem to like it*'. She rails at his concern for her welfare if she went to Algiers, and then gets into deeper waters:

You're very childish sometimes. I wish too that you would be more reasonable. You went abroad at my age, and it didn't kill you. Why should it hurt me? If you're thinking of the physical effects, look at Phyllis and Mrs McDonnell – they have been living in the tropics. Why, every other woman has been or is going nowadays. As for the rest, if you trust me so little, why bother to try to keep me? I'm blessed if I would lift a little finger to stop you if I thought that the moment my back was turned you were going to be unfaithful or wanted to be. You are simply driving me to it with your absurd attitude. One minute you tell me to go off and do my damnedest, and the next you are preventing me having a perfect normal decent time. As for going with Auntie Consie or Mrs. Wilkins, fond as I am of both, surely you don't think that all my society, till you return, is to be babies and old people. I don't grouse that marriage has not brought me freedom: I was perfectly free when I married you, or as you know, my people would not have allowed it, but I do object to being told where to go and who to go with, at my age. You may not want your wife to be a slave, but you don't want her to have any sort of life or individuality. It amuses me too when you talk of other women as 'vain creatures of pleasure', and say that you are glad that I am not like them. Have I hidden my love of these natural and very harmless pleasures so well that you haven't realized that I have missed them?

This is a serious cry of anguish, which would need lengthy face to face discussion, but such a thing was obviously impossible. She also answers his questions about Colin:

8th November 1926: No, Colin doesn't walk alone yet. He seems to have had quite a lull in the cutting of his teeth too, which is quite usual, I believe. No, I shouldn't call him funny, nor does he amuse me, but I give him full marks for good behaviour. He  *really is very little trouble and whatever you may say, I think it is because I have taken trouble over his physical well being, which, at this age is, in my opinion, very nearly everything. Those foul whining spoiled children that one meets would be greatly improved by sensible feeding and regular hours. I don't see any necessity for children to grizzle and howl, though the mothers of grizzling children will tell you it is unavoidable, simply because they have no method in their treatment of the poor little brats.*

PS. I can't find a picture of you holding Colin, so I suppose I must have sent it to you last week.

Angel ends her letter with a piece of gratuitous nastiness about the first of a series of circular letters that Claude was to send to his friends and relatives from Iraq, and which would eventually form the basis of his first published book, Flying Years:

You haven't changed much, have you? Your letter is very illiterate and full of jargon and affectations. I'm not saying this in an unkind way at all, but just in case you can change. It would make such better reading and I could show it to people – which I hesitate to do with this.

Your loving wife, M.A.C. Keith

This is all in Angel's first letter; it is very hard to see how these issues could be untangled by correspondence alone, and Claude repeatedly pointed out in his subsequent letters that he simply did not have any more money to give her. As it was, matters deteriorated from the first letters, with money, independence and the way that she treated Colin being the main issues, although they would snipe at each other about petty things, such as her omitting to date letters.

Angel's second letter comes from Kilmarth House in Cornwall, where Angel's Aunt Consie lived. [Consie later sold it to Daphne Du Maurier, who wrote about it extensively in her novels].

November 22nd 1926: Colin is very well and has another tooth. I have not succeeded in getting a nurse, though, so have had to leave him behind. It was a pity though, as Auntie Consie would have enjoyed him. He is not yet really interesting though, and to my mind won't be for another year. I don't think that you are missing the best part of his childhood at all. I think from 3 years upwards is their best, then they fall off again under the influence of a prep school.

Again, this suggests that maternal love and even maternal care for the infant Colin was in short supply. Colin's absence is seen as a pity for Consie, but not for either her or her son.

December 3rd 1926: I have decided not to go to Uncle Alick until the spring or early summer as the weather has been shocking and it is no time of year to take a teething baby about – also I still have no nurse so couldn't take him till I find one. At present Mrs. Deacon has him and I have no one – but it is better that he should have one atmosphere and that I should be free to go off and stay when I get the chance, as I cannot go on doing all this housework indefinitely. I mean to freeze on to Mrs Deacon. If I let her go someone else may take her and then I shall be in the soup – Mrs. Napier is always trying to get her and if it wasn't that Mrs. D is fond of baby and doesn't like Mrs. N, she probably would.

Angel later told Colin that she had loved her dogs more than she had loved him or any other human – and this next letter [which was two short paragraphs, rather than her usual thousand words] rather confirms it.

December ? 1926: This is just to let you know that Colin is well. Spy [one of her three dogs] has died and I don't feel like writing any more. He has brought more happiness into my childhood and later life than any human being, and never let me down in 17 years ..... I suppose that it is some consolation that the most dreaded day of one's life is in the past.

Christmas 1926 may not have been a jolly affair:

December? 1926: Mother sent Colin some presents, which I acknowledged for you. I imagine that they are the result of your renewed acquaintance with her as she didn't send any last year. Aunt Nell did not even write, so neither did I. In fact not one of your relatives or friends remembered me or your son, except Mrs. Baddeley [Claude's Grandmother] and Dockray, from both of whom I received a Christmas card. My Christmas dinner consisted of fried sausage meat which I fried myself on the one and only fire. I had a great many invitations but I didn't feel like going to them.... I can't stand this place any longer – everywhere I look I seem to see Spy and dream of him at night. I must get away and get something to do other than housework – it is making me ill ....Colin is well, except for more teeth.

It is possible that Angel was suffering from clinical depression, and her sense of isolation and alienation was certainly isolating her and Colin from friends and relatives.

January 18th 1927: Colin is still very well except for cutting more teeth. The cinema camera has come but I'm sure I shan't be able to work it – I can't take photos with any decent degree of success. Also I expect it will prove an expensive hobby and I have no money for such things at the moment. You are lucky to be busy on reasonably intelligent work – I get sick of spending all my time doing what should be done by the lower classes, while they are enabled by means of doles and pensions to pick and choose and live far better than I can – they know it too.

January 24th 1927: I think that you should know the way that I am living at present ...... if I don't tell, you will soon be hearing from others, who are already beginning to comment on the state of my health, and find fault because I don't see more of Colin.

Mrs. Deacon has Colin, and until recently used to bring him down to me during the day and take him back with her at tea time. This was a temporary measure until I found a Nurse General, but it has gone on so long now and I can't find anyone willing to stop here either as maid or nurse alone – they all say that it is too lonely. At the moment Mrs. Deacon has her father and child at home ill; she is not strong and the weather has been awful, with the result that she has given up coming down to me at all and says it is too much. She is however quite willing to keep baby, but if she does so I shall never see him for more than a few minutes at a time. I have tried to get a job but am looking so ill that people won't believe that I could stand it .... The people here are all very disapproving because I don't have Colin in the house, and I won't justify myself to them – they can mind their own business. But to you I will say quite honestly that at the moment this house is not fit to have him in – I could not look after him and do all the housework ..... as Mrs. Deacon can't be relied upon to bring him down [she hasn't been near me now for nearly a week], and I can't get one maid to stop here alone ....also this house is damp .... really Mrs. D in her cottage can give him more comfort than I can here. All the same this state of affairs has been going on too long and I should have him with me more now, I know, and also I can't keep up this hard word much longer, and know who is going to look after me if I knock up. It boils down to this .....

Angel goes on to write in great detail that the only solution is that she receives more money so that she can employ a nurse and servants. She has refused financial help from relatives. The postscript reads:

P.S. One thing I am quite determined about: I will have no outside interference in this matter. Anything you do, or don't do, must be on your own. You have made quite enough trouble between me and my family one way or another, and I refuse to have either my family or yours interfering, or dragged into this. I would rather starve – and may have to. You are gradually alienating all my family, but although I mind in a way, it does not alter me in the least – I can if necessary be independent of anyone and everyone. If the whole world gets up against me, there is always the next.

Claude's reply on 6th February was calm and conciliatory, and he enclosed a cheque for £5 to compensate for her complaints about him wasting money on a cine camera. But he writes that he simply cannot afford to pay for the servants she demands, and he warns that his pay is likely to be reduced later in the year.

You must realize that what you ask I cannot do .... I suggest that you shut up the house, and go away for a change, and do not worry if it does get damp. If you wish, by all means sell it ..... I have every confidence in Mrs. Deacon's looking after the baby with every care ...... I am afraid that you must try to cut your coat to your cloth: if you cannot live at Pelling, leave the baby with Mrs. Deacon, or I will arrange for him to be looked after, and go and live in some good rooms or at a boarding house – it is what hundreds of wives have to do. I know for a fact that you are far better off than most. It is no fault of mine that neither of our families offer you a home which you could, or would, accept.

Whether Claude thought that 'baby' would be better off with Mrs. Deacon, or whether he was just sacrificing 'baby's' best interests to pacify his wife is not clear, but certainly Colin's interests weren't foremost in the deal. Angel did indeed shut up Pelling, and went to live in London with friends, leaving Colin behind in Windsor with Mrs. Deacon. She justified it by writing:

I shall have to leave baby with Mrs. Deacon for the present, for which I shall probably be abused by all your relations. However, I have your last letter in which you suggest it yourself, and I shall keep this to show them if they get too noisy, though it probably won't make much difference – there is some satisfaction to be got from saying nasty things about me, but none where you are concerned as you are too far away for them to get any visible results.

Claude's family obviously hadn't completely ostracised Angel, because later in the letter she writes that Lotty has invited her to Cornwall with Nell Rogers [Claude's cousin], and she had visited the Baddeleys. She turned down the visit to Cornwall because she feared that she might have to share a room with Nell. Later in the letter she again accuses Claude of alienating her from her own family.

Angel's next letter, dated 15th February 1927, came from Hotel Riposo, Bexhill-on Sea, where she went to stay with a friend. This letter shows that 'possession' of Colin had started to be one of the battle issues in a rapidly deteriorating marriage:

Colin is well .... You write of him as "a baby ..... proud to possess". I wonder when you will realize that you don't 'possess' human beings – not until he teaches you, I suppose. Anyhow, you don't possess him or me, and the sooner you realize that we have lives of our own to live and for which we are responsible, the better for all of us. Is all this sententious jargon the real 'you' or do you affect it for some obscure purpose? If the latter, can't I be let into the secret – it would make it so much easier to live with you.

After returning from 'dull' Bexhill, Angel moved to London to stay with friends.

I have had to leave Colin with Mrs. Deacon, as for one thing I was afraid that if I didn't she would get another job and I would be left without anybody when I got back again. I went down to see him on Saturday with Violet and Wyndham, and found him full of beans. He tries to talk now, but is at his best when copying people, rather like a monkey! If I give him a piece of paper, he makes it into a spill and pushes it into the fire – very dangerous but quite intelligent. He also knows where wrist watches are kept because the first thing he did when I went to see him was to pull up my sleeve and look for mine.

Why isn't it surprising that the first thing Colin did when seeing his mother was look for a watch, rather than for a kiss and a hug? In her next letter from London, Angel again justified at length leaving Colin in Windsor, no doubt because Claude had asked why she could not employ a nurse in London. Her main justifications were that a nurse would have necessitated the sacking of her friend Vi's maid, as there wouldn't be room for both.

May 2nd 1927: I am glad that you are beginning to see reason about my going abroad. I never had any intention of taking Colin further than a possible few weeks in the S of France, during the worst of the winter. Certainly I should never be so foolish as to take a small boy sightseeing. Who would?

May 8th 1927: I must try to find a regular job, also a nurse for Colin, as I want to take him away for a holiday and Mrs. Deacon can't leave the village. Have you put Colin down for any Public School? I doubt if we shall ever be able to afford to send him to one, but still it should be done or he will never be able to get to one – most babies are put down at their birth, more or less.

The next letter is undated, but was sent from Pelling Cottage, which she had put with agents to let it. However, no one wanted to rent it because the garden was totally overgrown, and there were problems with the cesspit. The next letter is also undated, and was sent from London. There were still no tenants for Pelling Cottage, and still no nurse for Colin – the applicants were either too young or *'won't do anything except look after him, which is quite out of the question'*. The next undated letter was sent from Folkestone, but it shows that Angel had acquired a nurse for Colin:

I have come here with Nurse and Colin for a week, to give him a change and sea air before the awful summer prices. These are bad enough and the lodgings are so frousy and uncomfortable that I feel Nurse, who is new, may give notice any minute. She has a very sensitive nose and that is always trial in places like this.....

The next letter said that Colin was well and benefitted from the holiday, but that it had rained the whole time.

September 14th 1927: [Angel has gone to stay with a friend on Sheppey] *I left Colin very well, and Nurse quite contented. She is much more capable of taking care of Colin than I am so I have no fear of leaving him. She is a great success in every way except that she can't stand fog, so that I am even more anxious than ever to get away from Pelling for the winter, as I do not want to lose her. She is elderly and very reliable and also more educated than the average servant and speaks so nicely that she will do for Colin, as long as he needs a nurse.*

This shows that Angel's priorities for Colin's care include a nurse who speaks nicely. The next letter has no news of Colin, but in the following one Angel remarks that she does not give Colin toys – he prefers sticks and cardboard packets. She asks that Claude send money, not toys, for him.

Angel's letter of 1st October records that Nurse is thinking of leaving, and that Doc [Major Dockray] has visited because he wanted to see Colin – Claude has underlined this bit of the letter – Angel has written that she likes Doc. The next letter says that Nurse is a treasure but is very depressed at the thought of a winter at Pelling, but Angel has not been able to let it. On November 8th Nurse is again struggling with cold and fog, but Colin thrives on it, being fat.

Angel's next two letters are undated, but are from Felixstowe, where she was staying en route for Malta, where she was going to stay *'for a couple of months at the outside'*. Colin was staying in England with Nurse. The second letter gives a progress report on Colin:

Colin is very fit and flourishing and has grown a lot and is getting taller and not quite so fat, though he still has a round fattish face. He is not a bit like me. Some people, most I think, see him like you. I do sometimes, but more often like Roger [her brother] was at his age. I think he has your nature, though, if that is any consolation to you. However, from the very beginning I have tried to teach him self-control rather than to depend upon outside restraint, so I hope all may be well.

Colin remained a model of self control and even repression for the rest of his life.

Angel returned to England in February, after nearly four months in Malta, and wrote from her club, The New Century Club, in London. On 20th February 1928 she responded to an offer by Claude to arrange for her and Colin to fly out to visit him in Baghdad by writing that he shouldn't make the arrangements – she didn't intend to visit Claude.

The pictures that Angel sent may well have been the ones below, which are dated 1928.

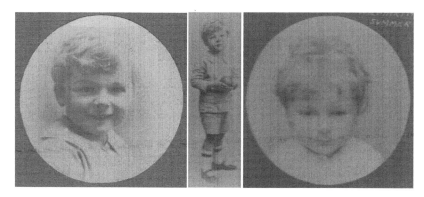

The next two [undated] letters from Angel must have been sent before she received Claude's because they are all about domestic and financial problems, with no mention of Colin, except that she prefers Marlborough to Lancing as a public school for him. Her third reply, dated 2nd May 1928, has been ripped from the book of letters. Instead, the row about the repairs to Pelling had moved centre stage in both of their letters. Having at last let Pelling, Angel, Colin and nurse moved to 46, Leinster Gardens, London W2, a *'sort of Bayswater boarding house hotel'*. There was Hyde Park nearby, and Angel suggests that Colin might meet other children there, whereas he never met children at Pelling.

Angel's letter, dated 13th June, 1928, from London, has little news, but does mention that Colin's rich godfather, Mr. Livingstone, has expressed an interest in seeing Colin, but because he will not communicate with Angel directly, she has rebuffed the approach.

Angel's letter of 26th June 1928 complained that Claude's Aunt Lotty, pictured below, who had met Colin and Nurse in the park, had criticized Colin's upbringing:

When nurse, hurt at being found fault with by a complete stranger, started to defend herself, Aunt L turned round and said, "Oh well, you haven't had him from the beginning, I expect it was Mrs. Deacon." Tactless, troublemaking and most unnecessary. Incidentally, no one has had him from the beginning except me, and once and for all I will not have your relatives criticizing me to my servants. It's bad manners, bad taste and calculated to make mischief and there is only one way to avoid it, by avoiding them. I shall not take any further steps to meet Aunt Lotty, or arrange for Colin to do so. .... Colin is very well and happy and most people volunteer the remark, quite unasked, that he has been excellently brought up. All children have their faults and Colin is no exception, but thank goodness he knows how to behave in public, and I think a mother and nurse may be trusted to know more about children than an elderly spinster with a kink, if not more..... Nurse and Colin have been away, spending a few days at some of her relations. They wanted to see him again. He remembered them all and seemed very pleased to go, and talked a lot about it beforehand.

Claude largely took Angel's side in the dispute, but Angel in her next letter is clear that the fences will not be mended between her and Lotty, and she also *'thanks goodness'* that she never sees Claude's Aunt Nell, either.

July 2nd 1928: Nurse, who shares our dislike of R.C. missionizing, came home chuckling the other day to tell me that a nun had come up in the park, and asked if she might speak to Colin. Having no reason to say no, she had to say yes, and so the nun asked Colin his name. Colin, who had had a lecture only that morning for not pronouncing it properly, hesitated, so the nun said, "Well, what does Mummy call you?" "Monkey face," replied Colin promptly. Nurse says the nun was terribly shocked ... I pointed out that no harm had been done, as she couldn't even pray for him as 'monkey face'!

Note that Colin, aged two, had received a lecture for not pronouncing his name properly.

Sometime in July 1928 the row started by Aunt Lotty erupted anew. It would seem that Lotty met Colin and nurse a second time, and that she wrote to Claude with her concerns a second time. Claude may have had reports from other people as well, because he also levelled anonymous accusations from 'people' about the conduct of nurse. In her letter, Angel expresses her 'disgust' at Claude's accusations, and threatens legal action against her husband if he cannot verify them:

Nature decided that a child should have a father as well as a mother, and I don't want to deprive Colin of either, as long as I can help it, but unless I get a satisfactory reply to this shameful letter of yours, I think seriously of consulting a solicitor, to find out what the terms of separation would be with regard to Colin. I fancy, when all the facts, including your treatment of me, before and after his birth, were made known, that you and your imbecile relations wouldn't see so very much of him, as you think.

This is the clearest indicator that Angel was prepared to use denial of access to Colin as a weapon against Claude and his relatives. Claude's reply, dated 29th July 1928, attempts to justify himself and Lotty:

Aunt Lotty considered Nurse unduly harsh and dictatorial with the child. It seemed improbable that Nurse would tell you of this, so I could only think your being upset would be due to Nurse's having led you to believe that Aunt Lotty had said something disapproving of yourself. If you did gain this impression from Nurse, then you are quite wrong. I wanted you to bear this possibility in mind. I cannot think that you would allow Nurse to deal harshly with the child when you were there, therefore it seemed probable that she did when she was alone what she would not have done in your presence.

Claude goes on to admit that it was 'unfortunate' that Lotty had seen Colin twice without Angel being present, and he admits that Lotty had no right to criticize what Nurse had said, and concludes by saying

Let me make it quite clear that, in writing to you what I did about nurse, I did so because what I heard from Aunt Lotty was enough to upset any man, abroad and away from his wife and child, as I am. I wished to put the other side of the case to you, and having done so am quite prepared to abide by your judgement in the matter. If, as your husband, I cannot write in confidence to you about a nurse whom you are hiring to look after your child, it seems that there is something radically wrong with the whole situation.

The 'in confidence' part of the correspondence was not honoured by Angel, who sent Lotty a copy of Claude's criticisms of Lotty's conduct, prompting Lotty to fire off a bitter letter to her beloved nephew. Claude, in turn, was more specific about Lotty's allegations in his next letter to Angel:

9th September 1928: In another letter she says, of Nurse, "I saw her lift her hand and strike him brutally. He did not cry – he is too brave for that, and possibly used to it, but he was deadly white when I went up to him some minutes later. She evidently guessed I had seen her though I made no mention of it. That was her idea of making trouble between her mistress and myself: she was afraid I should tell Angel." Now think for yourself what my feelings were when I read that? And all I did was to ask you whether you were sure that she always treated him as kindly behind your back as before your face? However, it seems as if we have flogged this to death. I have your assurance that you are satisfied with her, and that Colin is well and happy, and I am prepared to let it go at that. I put 'without prejudice' on my second letter because I gathered from yours that you had either told nurse or had shown her my former letter, and I am not fool enough to give any strange woman a chance, however slight, to run me for libel. What I wrote was for your information only.

Part of this correspondence took place while Angel was at Kilmarth [later the home of Daphne du Maurier] in Cornwall, with Angel's Aunt Consie. This time she had taken Nurse and Colin. Angel reports that Colin was very well and was enjoying the beach and croquet, and that she had taken some photos of him:

The picture of Angel and Colin at Kilmarth Manor is the last picture available of Angel – Colin kept no picture of his mother whatsoever, and if Angel ever sent another one to Claude, it has not survived.

Angel's letter from Kilmarth also outlined the differences between her and Claude over a choice of public school for Colin. Claude wanted Epsom College, being near Windsor and being a route into a medical profession, but Angel wanted Marlborough. She admitted that she didn't know very much about it, but she said that it was a place where the sons of 'poor gentlefolk' were sent, and she was anxious that Colin should have the opportunity to meet 'decent people'. She describes the people she has met as an RAF wife: '*I realize how small the proportion of gentle folk has been*'. Claude later agreed that there was a dearth of '*people of decent birth*' in the RAF.

Angel moved back to Pelling in September of 1928, together with Nurse and Colin, and also a maid. As usual, there were crises with the house [the drains], the garden [overgrown and overrun with rabbits and squirrels], and the weather [cold and wet].

October ? 1928: Many thanks for the cheque for Colin and my birthdays. I gave him as much or a party as I could, but I know so few children round here. With regards to the cheque, I got him one or two small inexpensive toys, but he really doesn't care for toys much, and breaks them all so soon and is much happier with chestnuts and sticks he can find in the garden, that seems 'real' – so I'll get some of his winter outfit with the money. He is growing fast that his clothes are becoming quite a consideration, and they aren't easy to let down, like a girls!

Angel's next letter, in November 1928, was from the Gower peninsula, where Angel had gone to stay for a couple of weeks with her newly divorced friend Lala Forrester. She reports that Colin was getting thinner again, after getting fat at Kilmarth, where she suspected that Aunt Consie's servants had been secretly feeding Colin.

There are no surviving letters from Claude and Angel over Christmas 1928, but by 25th January 1929, Angel, Nurse and Colin were living in rented rooms in Datchet, where they had obviously been for some time. Colin was becoming more expensive, and living in rented rooms caused Angel to complain that packing Colin's toys was a nuisance, because they took up too much room. She complained that Lotty had sent Colin sweets for Christmas, which she refused to give to him, and others, including Claude, had sent inappropriate toys:

It was so pathetic really when I think of the really sensible things I could have got him with the money. I wonder when you will realize that, for people like us at any rate, comfort should not be sacrificed for sentiment.

In her second letter from her club, dated 8th March, 1928, the simmering feud between Angel and Claude came to the surface, and Angel let rip. The issue started with the issue of Claude getting May Wadlow [see previous chapter] to buy Colin's Christmas presents, rather than trust Angel to do it, [presumably because he knew that Angel wouldn't buy presents – see earlier letters], but it went far deeper:

I realize that you don't trust me. It is mutual. Do you honestly think it is any good our going on? Even these letters seem inevitable. We don't trust or respect each other. We don't get on. We are not happy when we are together, but find fault with each other. All your feeling for me is desire, which I cannot satisfy and have learned to dread. We can't even stop quarrelling at this distance. Do you really think it is any good going on like this? You are the domineering type of man who wants to have everything his own way, with a cross between a mistress and a nurse-house keeper for a wife. I am a thoroughly undomesticated type of person, with strong likes and dislikes, who cannot be pressed into the mould you would make for me. One must give and take, I know, but to wear oneself out against a semi-self inflicted environment seems a great mistake....... Wouldn't you like to come to some other arrangement?

Claude suggested that Angel got herself a job to give her more income and independence. This appealed to Angel:

I am taking you at your word, and looking for a job, and feel years younger and less tired already. Why didn't you think of all these points before – it might have saved us so much unhappiness, if you had seen it all sooner. I don't mean about getting a job, but about giving more freedom and privacy, in fact, recognizing that one has a life to lead and can't merely be a shadow tacked on to someone else.

The job part is not essential on principle – it only becomes so where – as in our case – there is no money, it is necessary nowadays that a man should respect a woman's personality and individuality and not cramp her style in every direction, as you have tried to do mine. You have tried to alienate me from horses, dogs and people and outlook on life that I was used to and fitted for, and to make me like children and maps and talking about sex, and even to like the sexual practices of people foreign to me – by nature as well as race. I know I used to give in – I tried to like it, when I was new, and wanted to please you, or when you had got me drunk first, but no one will ever quite realize how I have suffered from it, and now I am no longer a bride, or even a girl, and can't keep it up any longer. I regret that the pendulum has swung so far the other way – for both our sakes – but it is the way pendulums have. Please realize this – that it is not, as you have expressed it so often, spite on my part.

I shall be only too glad to give you in the future, all I can, as you say, 'with sincerity', but I have learned in these last few years, from doctors and others, directly and indirectly, the folly of wearing oneself out, physically, mentally and spiritually, in what is not even a 'good cause'.

Claude in his reply could only agree that there was no use in going on as they had been doing. He lashed out as well, writing that she had persisted in rushing into marriage against his express wishes, and he calls her *'abnormal as a woman'*. He comes up with sentences like *'Women with brains should never marry'*. However, he also pointed out that he had suggested before a 'companionable marriage', an American idea, adding:

I thought it might make your life happier, and it certainly couldn't make mine more unhappy. It is no pleasure to me to realize that you are unhappy. It was the result of much deliberation that made me realize how disastrous it would be to attempt to live together again, as we lived when I last saw you.... again, let me assure you that I am not blaming you. I hope you will give me credit for having shown you every consideration I could since I came out here... It was no good upbraiding you for not doing what you obviously had no inclination to do, but it did not escape my notice nonetheless. It has become very clear to me that, whatever you felt in the past, you do not love me in the present. Again, let me assure you that I am not blaming you – love does not come to order or as a matter of duty, and it is mere hypocrisy to pretend what one does not feel. I am willing to admit that I do not love you today, and that I should never be able to love you unless you changed into what I once thought you were, and such change is, I am now convinced, not only impossible but distasteful to you. You say 'I don't like the sort of person you would make of me', so there seems no way out.

Then Claude gets down to details that show how deeply upset he was:

I am sorry that you rake up the sex question, but as you have mentioned it, I am going to refresh your memory in the matter. As an unmarried girl, when you came to see me in Paris with your friends, the Monktons, you may remember that you were overpoweringly anxious to see the seamy side of Paris. It was greatly against my inclination that you saw things there which were fouler than I had ever seen or have ever seen since – so much so that you may remember that I refused to look at them. After we were married it was you and not I who insisted in tearing away the last shreds of sex reserve. Do you remember insisting that I should strip before you? That we should bath together? Do you remember at Felixstowe denying me sex until I had, to amuse you, used unprintable words that I have never said to any other woman in my life, and do you remember tearing my hands away from my face as I tried to cover my blushes, and laughing at me? Do you remember at Felixstowe how you shocked me by saying you would like a whole regiment of naked men lined up in front of you, and for each to have connection with you? And, carried off my feet and satiated by it, I was taunted by you for not being able to satisfy your sexual demands.

And then, as I gradually became broken to these things, you cooled off and today you complain because you fear that I should treat you as you at first treated me. Having so aroused desire in me, you now wish to attach blame to me. Your present fears may be real, but at least be honest and admit that all your early conduct helped to arouse in me desires which you are now disinclined to fulfil.

You talk about pendulums – so will I. The pendulum of your sex desire has swung from one extreme to the other. Today you resent what your own Dr Martyn admitted to me were but normal happenings between man and wife. Martyn it was who suggested that alcohol might render you more normal to sex, yet you know that I have never encouraged or abetted your drinking inclinations, and you have never been drunk to my knowledge since we were married.

All of which is regrettable, and I only refer to it because I am not going to read false accusations in your letters. Now I have had my say, I will leave it.

Will you tell me if there is anyone you wish to marry or who wishes to marry you, if you can be free to do so? I will be the last to blame you if you have found someone to care for and who cares for you, whilst I have been away. I only ask you to be honest about it. You can't be happy with me, so you might as well tell if you can find happiness with someone else, and I will be sympathetic about it.

Claude, in his letter, moves on to the subject of his son:

What are your true feelings about the child? I know your attitude is that you have gone through more than I ever can for him, and therefore he is more yours than mine. Waive that. If we become divorced, do you wish to have Colin or for me to have him? Remember that you cannot have your cake and eat it. If you decide that you want him, you must have him absolutely, for I will not burden myself financially with a child which is virtually not mine. On the other hand, if you do not want him, I will bring him up myself and your disinclination for children will be spared. I respect your mother's right, and will abide by your choice. To me, he is only the memory of a tiny baby, and my own feelings would be purely sentimental, if I lose him.

After this exchange, Angel moved to London, and got a job in an accommodation agency called 'Useful Women'. Her letter is almost uniquely upbeat, especially as Claude had written about both of them being more independent.

The running battle over relations continued. Claude pointed out that Angel's refusal to allow any of his relations and almost all of her own relations [including her Great-Uncle Keith Hudson, who gave her Pelling House] to see Colin was against their rights as relatives, and that it would disadvantage Colin for the future [especially the rich relatives and godfather being excluded]. The other issue was Claude's upcoming leave – Angel was worried about having him around her for six months. The brief period of improved relations between the two in the spring soon gave way to the familiar wave of recriminations and accusations.

In an undated letter, Angel thanks Claude for books he sent to her and Colin:

I haven't read a book for some time, but will make another attempt shortly. Colin's I am keeping for him till a little later on. If he is given a book, he just tears it up, as he has a mania for turning things into something else. A book, for instance, is regularly reduced to tram tickets and shop receipts, and also the phraseology of this is at present beyond him, though he will appreciate the restrained wording on the first page: "To Colin from his father". I am not joking. I mean it. There is nothing he dislikes more than what he will later call 'gush'. Aunt Lotty sent him a book, 'For Tinies' or some such wording, and he was most indignant. "Why does she send me a book for <u>tinies</u>? I'm not tiny, I'm big." And if anyone calls him 'darling' or 'dear' he looks at them very gravely and says icily, "My name is Colin Keith", and puts them straight in their place. I suppose you'll think that this is my doing, but honestly it isn't.

In the same letter, Angel reports that she is planning to send Colin to live with her divorced friend Lala Forrester, who has a governess. She justifies it by saying:

I should have had to have a change soon, as I can't afford two nurseries [day care when she was at work] on the money you give me, and it was not good for Colin to go on living in one room. Not so much from the health point of view, as the mental. He was getting fidgety and bored and, I'm sorry to say, beginning to both pick and bite his nails. I'm doing my best to get him out of this habit before he goes to Lala's, but am not very hopeful ...

In an undated summer 1929 letter, Angel expressed her thoughts about Colin's future:

It is all I can do – think and worry above all - how to bring up a child to be a gentleman – in the only two alternative environments I can see ahead of him. I dread the influence you may have on a child of his nature, and equally dislike the thought of taking him away to a potty room [sic] and a boarding school education. Do you think all this is making life easy, or happy, for me? I don't reproach myself for having had him. I did it for the best, but I often wonder if it were not my second greatest mistake. However, we all make them and must face the consequences of our own acts. I realize this, but you still refuse to do so, and persist in your 'spite' theory.

In October 1929, Angel was again at war with Claude's relations. First she's cross that Claude's Aunt Nell [Keith] wants to *'restore relations'*, to which Angel says that she *'has no time for conceited and hypocritical old women like Aunt Nell, and her ignoring me for three years has been a relief and not a sorrow to me.'* Then Angel received a letter from Aunt Lotty [Rogers] inviting Colin and her to stay in a house she has bought in Cornwall near hers, and saying that she would like to send Angel some money. Angel reports that she has turned both offers down *'as politely as possible'*.

In the summer of 1929, Colin was sent to stay with Nurse and her family in the country. Angel spent time around the country, in Hull, Bicester, Godalming and at Kilmarth, and was planning trips to Norway, Canada and the South of France as well as a possible trip to see Claude in Egypt, so she had probably given up her job in London – she got a temporary job on a friend's stall at a pottery exhibition. In November, Nurse left Angel's employment, and Angel virtually abandoned Colin, who went to live with Lala, for which Claude paid £8 per month to Lala.

December 31st 1929: I went down to Lala's and spent Xmas there. Colin is thoroughly happy and wants to stay there 'forever'. He really is having a much better time – the flat was very small and he had to be quiet on occasions on account of all the people all round. There he has a garden, a large nursery and a crowd of toys. He has quite suddenly gone mad about toys – for a long time he didn't take much interest in them, and preferred cooking utensils, odd boxes and things, but now he can talk and think of nothing else. It is a phase no doubt, but quite a good one while it lasts ...Colin got a fair number of Christmas presents, mostly from my friends. Auntie Nan and Aunt Consie and Uncle Alick were the about only relations who remembered him. .... well, I'm glad Xmas is over.

In March, Angel and Claude discussed school for Colin. Georgie, Lala's son, was going, but Angel felt that Colin wasn't ready for it, being more 'babyish' on account of having been cooped up with two 'old women' – herself and Nurse. But Angel changed her mind about early school for Colin: Lala said that she didn't want to keep Colin beyond June, and Angel felt that she could not cope with both Colin *'and this business'* at the same time.

'This business' was the fact that Claude, going on some information from some unnamed source, had hired a detective who had produced evidence that Angel had committed adultery with Claude's friend Dockray back in 1926 and 1927. Dockray was the friend and colleague who had accompanied Claude through his adventures in Chile and other places, so this would be seen as a double betrayal by him. Angel admitted that they had slept under the same roof, but denied adultery. This is her account:

In 1926 I dined with him [Dockray] once in town, and he suggested getting up a party, and then I heard no more for some time [this was probably the time that I wrote to you, saying that I didn't know where he was]. The next thing I got was a letter from him saying that he was on his way to Siam. I cannot remember just when he returned, but your detective ſriend, I believe, said August 1927, and he is probably right. Anyway, I then dined with him once in town, and drove him to Victoria to catch his train and returned alone – and on that occasion he asked me to come up again one night to meet some people he thought I might like to know, and arranged a party. They couldn't come in the end, and the only person who dined with us was a man whose name I can't remember, but he was on leave from India and was going back shortly.

This was the night on which D saw me home, because I was very tired, having danced all the evening, and it was foggy, and we were not alone in the house, and even your witness admits that he slept in the 'green' room.

Next day he left, I imagine for town, and as far as I remember I only saw him once afterwards, and that was on a Sunday, when he came down to spend the day, and as I was going to town myself that evening, I drove him as far as Hounslow Station after tea.

Do talk over the question of letting me know the witnesses with your solicitors. Of course, I am assuming that you really want to find the truth, and are not merely trying to wangle to be rid of me. I have no objection to being divorced. I have suffered so much from you that I don't feel that a divorce would be any worse than some of the other experiences, but I am all against making an innocent person pay for my freedom, or yours.

It was revealed that Claude's principle witness was Angel's own brother, Jamie. He had written to Claude on 6th January 1927:

I heard from Angel for Christmas and she very kindly sent me some handkerchiefs. I wrote and thanked her and told her as briefly and kindly as I possibly could, that until she could explain what she thinks she is up to, I thought it better that we should not have anything to do with each other, so as to avoid quarrelling. I hated doing it, but I thought it best to have it out and finished. Best of luck to you.

Claude's divorce petition was filed against Angel, citing Mr. S.T. Dockray as co-respondent, on 10th June 1930. It was uncontested.

Both Claude and Angel may have claimed a sort of victory, but for both of them any victory was Pyrrhic. For Claude, he was able to portray himself as the injured party, and to get the freedom to re-marry, which he quickly did. But he was very hurt, and he lost contact with his beloved son, who was brought up by Angel to despise his father. It was only when Colin was at Prep School that he ever met his father, and even this was in the form of fleeting visits. Colin never read all the copious books that Claude wrote for him, and it was only after Claude's death that Colin became close to Claude's second wife, Gwen.

For Angel, she had her freedom, and she had prevented Claude from seeing his son, but her reputation in society was severely damaged; although Claude probably paid for Colin's education, her income [something that had obsessed her during her marriage] was drastically cut. She took Colin to live in a shabby house with a tin roof in the New Forest, where she became a recluse, living with her beloved dogs and never having another relationship with a man, as far as Colin recalled. She broke off all relations with both Claude's and her own family, and showed her son none of the love she lavished on her dogs. Angel never met her grandchildren, even though we lived only a few miles away. When Colin got news that his mother had died, he worried for a while that it was his stepmother, Gwen. When it became clear that it was Angel, he relaxed. He didn't attend her funeral, and she didn't mention him in her will.

It is easy to apportion blame for this catastrophic marriage. Angel is condemned through her own words, in her shocking treatment and lack of love for her child, in her constant demands for more money, her refusal to do anything she thought demeaning, her social and intellectual snobbery, her possible infidelity, and her outright cruelty, but she was also a victim. She was a young inexperienced woman whose husband was away, and who tended to be patronising to her his letters. She felt short of money, and lived in a miserable damp house that needed too much heating and upkeep. She suggested that she was in ill health for long periods, and felt that people and the world were against her – it is possible that she was suffering from depression or a prolonged mental illness [as her own mother suggested later]. It is also possible that the letters between Claude and Angel are not a fair reflection of what happened – they were typed up, collated and possibly edited by Claude at the time of their divorce, and in some letters it is clear that Angel is writing things to hurt or to reassure Claude, rather than to give an objective report.

Claude, too, was not a blameless father or husband. He expressed extravagant love for his son, but was prepared to give in very easily on custody and on issues of Angel's care for Colin. Angel regarded his love for Colin as shallow, sentimental and proprietorial, and she may have had a point. He was patronising, calling her 'dear old thing' for a long time after she asked him not to. He was always harking back to his good old days before he had met Angel, and writing to old flames. Angel says that he tried to mould her into something she could never be, and that he suffocated her with his control.

However, Claude was in a difficult position: serving abroad and with a large overdraft, it is hard to see what he could have done to have brought Angel round, especially from Iraq. The letters suggest that it was usually him who tried to compromise, and there is no evidence that he was malicious or cruel.

Ultimately, their temperaments were incompatible. He was sensual, she was intellectual. They both needed to be in control, as can be seen in their sexual history, and they had very different interests and background, despite both having a life rooted in the armed services. It's a sad story, and their child [my father] was the biggest victim.

Chapter 12 Flying Years 1: Iraq and the Persian Gulf

During the tumultuous years of his first marriage, Claude lived a very full life as an RAF officer, and it is for this life that he was known by most people. He was a very committed and enthusiastic serviceman, and a successful and popular leader of men. His early years seem dominated by relationships with women, but out in Iraq and Egypt he moved in a society where women were almost totally absent. Although there were some considerable discomforts, and some dangerous moments, this life was a happy and fulfilling one, notwithstanding his disintegrating marriage.

In 1920, Claude became Flight Commander of a Flying Boat Flight at Calshot on the Solent, and moved in 1922 to 230 Squadron as a Flight Lieutenant. In 1923 Claude was appointed as Chief Instructor at the RAF armament school at Eastchurch, on the Isle of Sheppey where he stayed over two years. These are the years of his marriage, of parenthood, and of establishing himself in the service, and Claude left no written record of his service life – only of his personal life.

In October 1926, Claude was assigned to 70 Squadron, based in Hinaidi, seven miles east of Baghdad in Iraq. During his four years in the Middle East, Claude wrote very detailed letters – over 100,000 words in total, which he typed and circulated to his friends and relatives in Britain and in America. Sometimes the letters read like a travelogue or adventure yarn. He kept copies himself, and had them leather bound when he returned. He was persuaded to edit and publish these letters into a single volume, which was published by J Hamilton under the title 'Flying Years' in 1937. The following four chapters are an outline of those years, 1926 to 1930, based on the original leather bound 'Letters From Iraq'. If the reader wishes to read more about this time, then 'Flying Years' can still be bought.

Iraq in 1926 was a colonial experiment: the idea of Lord Trenchard, Marshal of the RAF, was that it could be controlled very cheaply with only a small military presence by the use of air power – that local Iraqi forces be used to keep order, to be backed up by air squadrons who would be deployed to bomb any insurgents, rebels and bandits. It has a very 21st century ring to it, and its success in Iraq at this time led to it be used all over the world. The increasing significance of Iraq's oilfields and its proximity to the new communist state of Soviet Russia, as well as its strategic position on the new air route to India and Australia gave the mission a considerable importance. Iraq was unique at that time in that the RAF commanded the British Army deployment, rather than vice versa.

Claude landed in Basra in the troopship Assaye on October 13th 1926, together with a large contingent who had been shipped out from England. The troops jeered the Hydrabadi Indian band, who played 'Far from the old folks at home' as they disembarked! For the two day railway journey up to Baghdad, the airmen travelled packed in steel cattle trucks, while the officers had an old Madras Railway carriage. They stopped at Ur, city of Abraham, which Claude described as smelly and unimpressive.

Left: Ctesiphon on a 1923 stamp. Claude sent stamps home to Angel, who was less than enthusiastic about them. **Right**: A 70 Squadron Vickers Victoria over Alweyiah, Baghdad. Their huge size can be gauged by the cockpit just above the nose.

Hinaidi, on the Tigris floodplain very close to the ancient site of Ctesiphon, and prone to flooding, was a huge mud aerodrome, home to six RAF squadrons and two armoured car companies, together with an air depot and an RAF hospital. Claude remarked that they all ran independently 'as if none of the others existed'. 70 Squadron, which Claude joined as a Squadron Leader in charge of one of the two five plane 'flights', consisted of Vickers Vernon and Vickers Victoria bomber and transport planes, and one of the regular duties was to fly the mail to Egypt.

Claude's first impressions include the heat [up to 120 degrees in the day, but cold at night], dust, mosquitoes, and sand-flies that could penetrate mosquito nets, and the very real presence of the fatal disease bilharzias from the local water. They wore khaki, shorts, and a special solar tope [called a Baghdad bowler'], anti-actinic ray and dustproof goggles when flying. Claude 'inherited' an Indian manservant called Francis [pictured right], who had fought on the Western Front in World War I, spoke six languages, and wanted to do everything for Claude, even brush his hair!

Their day involved being up at dawn, working till lunch at noon, sleep in the afternoon with tea brought to them in bed, a bath at six, 'a yarn before dinner', and early bed. Mess food was better than he expected. There was an officer's club, a tennis court and a squash court, but Claude could not afford to keep a horse and play polo, or to belong to the Alwyia Club in Baghdad. However, he did have fun shooting 23 brace of sand grouse, black partridges and others from a car; they chased a great bustard at 35 mph, but it ran then flew quicker than them, and escaped.

Mortality is a constant theme in Claude's letters from Hinaidi. Scratches go septic immediately unless iodine is applied, graves are kept ready, and anyone who dies is buried on the day of their death because of the rapid putrefaction and disease risks. One of the first tasks for 70 Squadron after Claude's arrival was to collect the disinterred bodies of two British soldiers. The bodies had to be strapped to the lower wings of the planes!

This was also the first time that Claude mentioned freemasonry: his father was a known Mason, and later on in his life Claude rose quite high in the Masons' hierarchy. He attended the Baghdad lodge:

I met a very mixed crowd, which included some very good souls and many natives – as you know Masonry is no stickler over race or religion. Next Thursday I have been invited to attend 'Lodge Iraq'.

Claude was as advanced as anyone in the skills and knowledge of air navigation, having trained pilots in it back in England; 70 Squadron had to find their way over featureless deserts without any modern aids, knowing full well that if they got lost and had a forced landing, it might well be fatal.

Finding one's way in Iraq is difficult, to say the least. An airman can never hope for signposts, but usually he can hope for plenty of landmarks which he can identify with an accurate map. Out here the landmarks are few and far between, and their positions as shown on the very bad maps may be miles out. Often maps show a mountain range as 6,000 feet, and when he gets there the unfortunate pilot finds it is 6,500 feet. Out here the air is so thin that an aircraft won't go up as easily as at home. Rivers are, however, our best friends in showing the way, but even they have an ugly habit of altering their bends at short notice.

One of Claude's first long haul flights was to Kirkuk, to support the armoured car company that was clearing up tribal troubles amongst the Kurds. He mentions that Kurdistan is partly in Iraq, partly in Persia, *'and part of it doesn't belong to anyone, because no one knew about it until the other day, when they found that the maps were wrong!'* In Kirkuk Claude was educated on the use of bombing the awkward Kurdish tribes:

He showed me some photographs of villages before and after such action, and they were most educating. 'Air Control' is a marvellous means of bringing these wild mountain tribes to heel. It is swift, economic and humane, as we always drop warning messages some hours before we start to 'lay eggs' on their villages, so that they can clear out. The loss of life is usually nil, but by destroying their property and generally making life a burden to them, we usually get them to find it preferable to send in their headman to interview the government official with promises of good behaviour. Another important point is that the eastern mind forgets quickly, and if he is not punished for his misdeeds quickly, he has forgotten about them and feels that his punishment is not merited if it is delayed. They are a wild people. I had a look at the murderous weapons in the local gaol, and saw two gentlemen who are for the 'high jump' this week.

This is a fascinating variant of the tactic of bombing of civilians started by German World War I zeppelins, and then extended in the Spanish Civil War and then World War II, but it is closest to the drone bombings carried out today [except the warnings].

The trip to Egypt with the Christmas mail in December 1926 was exhilarating for Claude. Two planes undertook the flight, Claude in a Vernon and King and Stewart in a Victoria. The Air Mail route guide started with this warning:

In consequence of the great length of the track, the severity of the climatic conditions, the lack of water, the enormous extent and uniform appearance of the desert and the uncertainty of the weather in this area, a very detailed organization has been found necessary... the success of the route rests more in the hands of the pilots operating it than in the hands of those responsible for its inauguration and maintenance....

There had been heavy rain in Baghdad, so they had to take off on a runway of muddy patches, with only enough fuel to reach Ramadi. After taking on full tanks at Ramadi, they flew over the bitumen pools and eventually over the desolate outpost of Rutbah Wells, stopping at a fuel dump called L.G.I. In the teeth of gales, they had to set down unscheduled at an 'utterly desolate' fuel dump in the desert called L.G.D. Night was coming on, so they tied their planes down, dug wind shelters, fried sausages, brewed coffee, and slept in sleeping bags in the howling dust storm. In the morning there was low mist, and the radio contact with the next station, Ziza in Jordan, suggested that they couldn't land there. They spent the day in the desolate desert, while the sandstorm threatened to tip the planes over and smash their wings. The sand got in the engine of the Victoria, so that it wouldn't start.

They spent a second night hunkered down in their sleeping bags against the extreme cold, and in the morning one of the passengers nearly stood on a deadly venomous snake. Claude's managed to get his Vernon in the air despite the 35 mph winds, and got to Ziza, which was nothing but a railway station – the village having been destroyed in World War I. The Victoria limped there, where it had to be left for repairs. The trip from Ziza to the Red Sea was exceptionally turbulent, between the mountains at 4,500 feet and the clouds at 5,000 feet. They consoled themselves that they wouldn't sink if they ditched in the Dead Sea!

By the time they got over Egypt, they were in a sandstorm, but they got the mail down at 5.30 pm. They spent the evening in dress clothes in a club in an Ismailia French club, flew on to Heliopolis the next day, and hit the Cairo nightlife the next night, eating pork, watching a game of pelota, and having tea at the famous tea house, Groppi's. Next day they visited the pyramids at Gizeh, and in the evening went dancing with some English girls in *'some unspeakable haunt'* all the while armed with revolvers – AHQ orders. Next day they flew over the pyramids, taking photos, and in the evening had a party at Shepheard's and danced at Groppi's. The return trip was much easier – they had a stern wind and completed it in record time in a single day. They brought back 100 turkeys, of which 12 suffocated, and several cases of kippers – both unknown luxuries in Iraq.

Christmas 1926 was a round of jollity – a walking soccer match, donkey polo with hockey sticks and a soccer ball, officers serving their men at dinner, a lot of drinking, a visit to the sick in hospital with sticky sugary foods in matron's lair, more drinking, a pantomime [Babes in the Wood], and a visit from Sir Sefton Branker from the Air Ministry in the middle of it all.

Claude was constantly awed by the desert sunsets:

Sunset in the desert is still a joy to me. It is sometimes so vivid and unreal ... there was not wisp of cloud this evening, and as the sun sank, right down to the ground, it seemed, the whole sky became a lake of vivid colours – a peculiar burnt orange low down, fading through lemon and a great variety of greens to the cold indigo of night on the eastern side. The blending was perfect, and the ground is so flat that one gets an unobstructed view of 'the bowl of heaven'. No works of man cut the horizon except the two masts of our main wireless station, which links us with "heart of Empire' – London. On top of each burns a red warning lamp.

Claude was left as Acting CO while his CO had to accompany the Air Minister to Persia [where they were delayed by breakdowns and sandstorms], and then to Karachi; his first duty was an *'ugly Court of Inquiry. Some blighter put an 18 lb shell in an incinerator, and the outfit went sky-high, plus a coolie or two.'*

Claude flew to Anah, and also to Mosul [which boasted six European women in its population!], where they stayed with Jeffries, the political agent, who fed them royally, took them to an Arab drama and then got two of the cast to go back to his house to dance for the guests. Jeffries told them that many of his agents got imprisoned by the Turks, and that he himself had a large price on his head. Claude was impressed by Mosul:

In its narrow streets one sees travelling merchants on their donkeys or camels, who have journeyed from afar ... carpets, candlesticks, every sort of leather ware, daggers, Turkish delight, copper utensils – all were being made before our eyes in the curious low shops which fringe every street. The colour, the noise and the smell all create curious impressions ... storks abound, and being regarded as sacred birds, they build where they choose, and especially favour the domes of the mosques.

Opposite: coolies dance at Hinaidi.

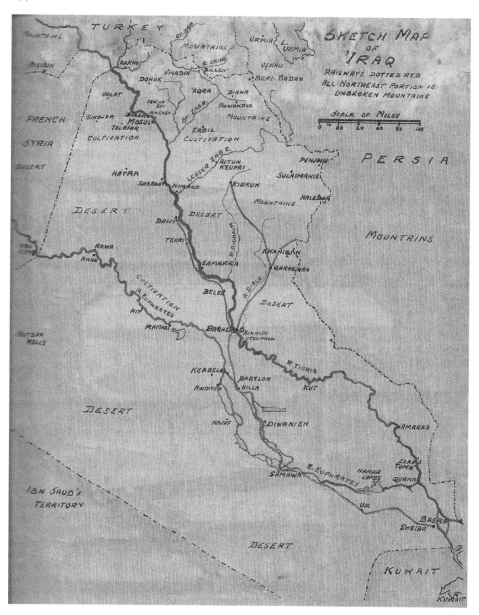

In March 1927 Claude's first leave was a fourteen day trip in a steamer down the Tigris to Basra, taking in the sights. He was able to dance with one of two nurses who were being transferred to Basra, and he saw Ezra's tomb, the tower of Sinbad the Sailor at Zobeir, the town of Kut-el-Amara where his cousin Garnet Richardson had been killed in World War I, and visited friends at Sheiba airbase and on the oilfields near Basra. Gliding down the smooth waters with a searchlight in the dead of night was a hypnotic experience.

Kut-el-Amara

Marsh Arab village

After returning from leave down the Tigris, Claude was off again, this time on a tour of the Persian Gulf with his CO and some of the political officers of the region. The Persian Gulf was administered by the British from India, but their military presence was light and a lot of the area was independent of them – Persia on the north shore, Ibn Saud ruling much of the south shore, and the independent sheiks of the Trucial States – Bahrain, Qatar, Raz-al-Khaimah, Dubai, and Oman along the rest of the south shore and into the ocean. The object of the trip was to explore a route for the increasingly vital British Empire air traffic to India and Australia. This was partly geographical – they would need level places for runways but more vitally ample water supplies, and partly political – these fuel and supply depots would need to be secure from both bandits and from any hostile local ruler. They needed sites for re-fuelling landing strips every 200 to 250 miles, and emergency landing sites every 20 to 30 miles. The arid nature of the Gulf area and the mountains of Oman, together with the volatile political nature of the states, presented very real problems.

Claude, accompanied by his manservant Francis and by his CO and Flight Lieutenant Switzer, flew to Basra, took a troopship to Bandar Jask on the Persian coast, where they met up with the Indian contingent, and sailed to Muscat, Oman, in the Triad, a converted pleasure yacht. Claude found Muscat a most picturesque place. They went swimming in the clear waters, having been assured that sharks did not enter the bay, and threw silver anna coins for the native boys to dive and collect.

 HMS Triad

Above: Muscat Bay, and boys diving for coins.

After the introductions to the English Wazir of the Sultan of Oman and a night at the British political resident's 'residency', Claude and Switzer took a trip inland. They got shaken up by camels, rubbed raw by horses, and suffered in the heat. Claude was interested in the open and widespread slavery: about £70 would buy an *'efficient buck Nubian'* and £30 a young girl. He also remarked on how all the men would be armed with a huge curved dagger and many with a carbine.

They rejoined the Triad and travelled north up the coast to Sib, where they were met by the Wali of Sib:

He came out in a native craft with some ten oarsmen, hefty slaves decked out in weird and wonderful colourful clothes, their strokes pulled to a monotonous chant, sung by the leader in the bows. The Wali, armed to the teeth and in his Sunday best and seated on a priceless carpet, is on a raised poop. The PR [political resident] didn't go ashore but we pushed off through the surf and shot off inland .... there is an old Portuguese fort , and an excellent site for a runway ... we called on the Wali and he gave us the usual Arab coffee, scented with rosewater and also produced a huge plate of hulwa – Turkish Delight. This is offered to you by a slave and you pluck out a handful with your right hand [the left is never used for eating, being devoted by the Arabs to nature's more basic needs].

They moved on to Sohar, where the Wali, who spoke no English, said that he would welcome planes. He had visited India, and was a Freemason! They travelled on to the northernmost tip of Oman, in the Straits of Hormuz. They called on the Wali of Khassab, and Claude went in the sea, where he observed the most intense phosphorescence – the shoals of fishes appeared to shine as they moved. The next day they landed at Lohi, where they were told that they were the first white people to ever visit, and they trekked inland, into the brutal jagged mountains. They visited two mountain villages, where the men were all away on fishing boats, and where there appeared to be no water and no greenery – 'nature had almost defeated them' – see below.

 Wa'abu Murbarraq

Next day the Triad sailed up the Elphinstone Inlet, reputed to be the hottest place on earth, and visited Telegraph Island [pictured below], where the cable relay station used to be, but it had been abandoned due to all the personnel there going mad or dying. *'Even the natives cannot remain at sea level, but only come down at dusk to fish'.*

Further exploration of the 'horn of Arabia' confirmed that it was too mountainous for landing grounds, so the Triad sailed west, down the Trucial coast, looking for further sites. What is fascinating about Claude's pictures and accounts are the picture of totally undeveloped places that are in the 21st century huge hubs of world commerce. Claude writes that

Few Europeans have ever landed on this coast, and never without good reason nor without guns from their ship being trained on the shore … Pearling is their livelihood, and the necessities of life are imported from India by Hindu merchants, and bartered against pearls. The Viceroy [of India] won't allow mechanical dredgers, and all the diving is done by slaves. They go out in big outriggers, and dive with a big rock in their hands, which helps them to the bottom. They scrabble up as many shells as they can into a pouch carried round their necks, and come up for a breather, usually staying down nearly two minutes. In time they get deaf and blind. They bump their stone on the bottom to scare away the sharks, and the sharks are only brave enough to sample a few divers a year... for a rupee they will let you pick one shell from any pile brought in by the divers – and you might find a 6,000 rupee pearl in it!

They called in at Ras-al-Khaimah, Umm-el-Quaim, and then at Sharjah where:

The British Agent came off with a Union Jack proudly flying astern. He is an Arab of extreme ugliness with a glass eye, which gives him great puissance with the tribes, and his name is Isa-bin-Latif [Son of the Beautiful!]. We went ashore and visited the sheik who put us through a cleaning ceremony before he gave us any coffee: we had scented water poured over our hands, and an earthenware cup with smouldering incense in it, was passed round for everyone to hold under their armpits.

Left: Ras-al-Khaimah and right, Dubai in 1927 – both totally undeveloped then.

They moved on to Dubai, anchoring in crystal clear water, and were entertained by the sheik as they had in Sharjah, by a feast with bareback riding displays, and a wedding [pictured below]. The sheik [pictured below] had a bad reputation:

He is a bad lad, and 'jumped' the sheikdom from his elder brother by shooting him in the back as he was going home after being invited for dinner! This is the first time a live murderer has been my host, and Saqar-bin-Zaid looked every inch the part. Abu Dhabi is inhabited mainly by the wild Bani-Yas tribe, who wear their hair in long curls over their shoulders.

The land was unsuitable for landing – sand dunes on the coast, and uneven surfaces inland. So they moved on to Yas Island, which had miles of suitable land, but no water – they trekked to the only well [pictured below] but it was bone dry.

They moved on to Dohar, where they were greeted by a hostile sheik [pictured above, second right], who was a Wahabi, renowned for asceticism and fanaticism. Switzer got into trouble for attempting to smoke a cigarette during the coffee party – a big sin.

At Dohar their comfort came to an abrupt end, because the Triad got called off to deal with the Sheik of Henjam, who had run amok, killing the customs officer and then the postmaster. This left Switzer and Claude to make their way back to Iraq via Bahrain on a tug with no electricity, charts, wireless, life buoys and a life boat that could hold only three, which was lashed so firmly that it couldn't be untied! They slept on deck as the tug weaved its way through the coral reefs to Bahrain, which Claude describes as a 'very go-ahead place' and where they found several excellent landing sites. The mail boat took them over to Bushire in Persia, from where Claude caught a steamer to Kuwait, and a car to Sheiba, from where he flew a night flight back to Baghdad.

Above: a street in Bahrain and a butcher's shop in Bushire.

What had become clear from their trip was that they needed to find another route through the mountains of Oman, and so Claude was soon off to Oman again, this time for an overland exploration.

Chapter 13 Flying Years 2: The trans-Oman expedition 1927

Claude and Switzer were joined for the expedition by O'Brien, a medical officer from the Aran Islands [off the west coast of Ireland] – *'a wild soul but a very good doctor'* – and a political agent called Thomas, who was in command. They travelled via Karachi, where they saw the enormous shed built for the new Britain-to-India air service, for which they were now engaged in finding the 'missing link'. They sailed from Karachi to Muscat in the sloop HMS Lupin, which was to be their support ship for the expedition. Their first task was to find a sheltered bay on the Oman coast for flying boats. They started in the north, finding nowhere suitable, went ashore at Khor Fakkan, where O'Brien treated natives, and which Claude described as *'a miserable poverty stricken place, backed by huge hills which might be the ash-heaps of hell.'* They stopped at Sohar, to talk to the tribes of the area through which they wanted to travel, but the head of the Na'im tribe had only sent a nephew, *'a wild specimen'*, which wasn't a good portent. They sailed down to Muscat, and saluted the Sultan with 11 guns and then fired another 21 for Empire Day.

In Muscat Claude had to draw out 10,000 silver rupees, collected in ten bags, each coin of which needed to be laboriously counted – they got a slave to do most of it. O'Brien went off to do a study on unsanitary conditions and mosquitoes, but all his collected mosquitoes got drowned in the outrigger that ferried them back to HMS Lupin. It was the start of extreme heat for the expedition:

Those nights at Muscat were a foretaste of hell. The rocks absorb heat during the day, and at night, with an offshore wind, the temperature rises. Standing on deck, scarcely able to open my smarting eyes against the fiery wind, and I was far from normal, and shouldn't have been surprised to have seen blue sulphurous flames flickering behind the mountains! Sleep was impossible and at all odd hours one heard people diving from the gangway, but the sea was hot and phosphorescent, and brought little relief.

They sailed north to Sohar again, taking Thomas, the Sultan's Wazir, and Murphy, the political officer. They identified a landing site on the way, but Claude got mild heat stroke sitting on a donkey, and was only revived with iced ginger beer and a shave – *'a beard is a horrible thing to me'*.

At Sohar they prepared to move inland, but the place was full of tribesmen, followers of rival sheiks, who offered their services as escorts. Each sheik demanded that they hire half his tribe. They finally managed to whittle their escort down to 77 tribesmen in three shifts of about 20 each, plus Suleiman-bin-Madhaffa, Wali of Khaburah [pictured left below, with his son] and his ten men for the whole journey. All the tribesmen were armed to the teeth [see picture below], but the British contingent was unarmed, as to be armed would have provoked trouble. The escort demanded daily payment, and landing the silver through the surf on small boats was a nervy business – it was tied to a buoy in case the boat sank or capsized. Before they left, the Wali of Sohar, apparently doing all he could to help the expedition, had treated them to a feast, but next morning Suleiman-bin-Madhaffa brought Claude a letter he'd 'captured' in the bazaar, showing that the Wali of Sohar was doing all he could to hinder them, calling on all good

Muslims to reject Christian silver, and threatening 'lightning will flash in every place'.

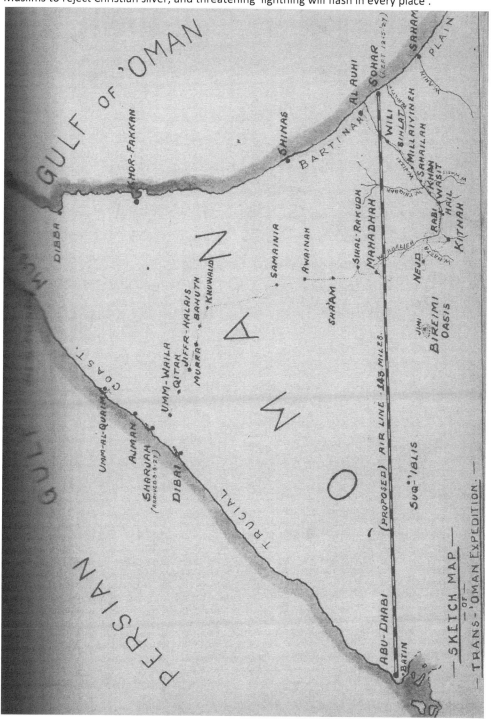

They set off inland on 12th May, leaving HMS Lupin to steam round to Abu Dhabi, to await them. Because of the intense heat, they agreed to travel at dusk and dawn, and to rest at midday. The first day covered only 7 miles because they were all adjusting to travel by camel. The ageing headman of the village where they stopped confessed that he had taken a young wife, and asked O'Brien if he had anything that would help him to perform with her. O'Brien gave him a *'good fat dose of cocaine'*.

That night the Bani-Kab tribesmen in their escort attempted to loot the village, which caused bullets to whistle around the night sky.

They followed the Wadi Jizzi, through blistering heat and a sandstorm, moving through date gardens. On the second day the cook got lost, and was found too late at night for any cooking. On the third day while Thomas, who was acting as interpreter, was away investigating some ancient Persian ruins, the rest of the party were fired upon, but Claude, Switzer and O'Brien had no idea what it was all about. When Thomas re-joined them it was clear that the Bani-Kab escorts had saved them from being shot.

When they reached Khan, where the natives spent the day in caves to keep out of the heat, they entered a new sheik's territory; he refused to let them proceed, except on his terms. Sheik Hamdan then said he'd been told to stop them, but he later relented and let them

through. This may have been because O'Brien did a roaring trade in doctoring and dentistry for his tribe [pictured below].

They proceeded towards Hail, but then they were ambushed by Sheik Hamdam's men in a narrow defile of Wadi Zumash. Both sides were ready for a shoot-out when Sheik Hamdam himself intervened and told his men to stand down. His men, who had waited through the heat of the day for this battle, were most disappointed. Claude and others climbed out of the wadi, up a saddle of high ground, to view what Claude described as an 'utter wilderness'. The picture below of Switzer, Sheik Hamdan [centre left] and two of his warriors was taken by Claude at this spot.

They halted at Hail because the sheik of the next area, who should have been there to meet them, had not turned up, so Suleiman-bin-Madhaffa was sent ahead, while they waited in the date gardens, where the picture below of Claude [left] and Switzer was taken. O'Brien did another full day of doctoring. His patients all refused anaesthetics on religious grounds.

On the second day at Hail they were attacked by a local tribe, apparently under orders from a powerful inland tribe, so they left in a hurry, in moonlight, and stopped at Najd, 'a *scorching hollow between two mountains, 1,600 feet above sea level, where the country to the west becomes sand hills'*. [Below left, Claude and camel at Najd]. At this place, the Bani-Kab escort refused to go further until Suleiman-bin-Madhaffa returned from Biriemi oasis with assurances of safe conduct.

Madhaffa met them at noon the next day to say that the country ahead had been declared by the Sheik Ma'im as belonging to Allah and Mohammedans, and that Christians should leave immediately if they wanted to live. Even Madahaffa was alarmed, saying there were 40 men ready to fight their advance, and he counselled retreat. Thomas refused. Eventually Sheik Hamdam took them all of to his village of Kitnah, from where they were going to negotiate with the Sheik of Biriemi. Although all the inhabitants of Kitnah came out to greet them, Claude was uneasy, as their route back to Sohar was now cut off. Claude reported that the place looked charming, but it felt like a Turkish bath with the atmosphere of Hades. They sent messengers off to the Sheik of Biriemi, who had moved south into the desert, and set up the wireless to try to contact HMS Lupin, but not all the equipment had not survived the

journey, so they could only transmit, not receive. The picture [above right] shows Switzer and Claude at Kitnah, fixing their position using a 'false horizon'. They were the first white people ever to visit Kitnah, and they attracted an audience at all times, and whilst they were fixing their position the natives believed they were praying to their God.

They dammed the stream to make a bathing pool, which they used each dawn, usually with a crowd of 'bints' watching from afar, fascinated by white bodies. O'Brien got excited when he got a collection of green leeches on him.

O'Brien became a hero in the place, treating even women [normally they were kept veiled and well away]; he was late back for lunch, saying that they were very charming.

He achieved great fame by removing a dead dung beetle from an old man's ear, thereby enabling him to hear more clearly. He lopped off a gangrenous toe, while we held the victim, and he brought relief to many with ugly eye infections. But even he gibbed when a mangey camel thrust its head into our tent at breakfast with its diseased eye hanging from its socket! Its owner was very offended because we wouldn't treat it, and immediately asked for baksheesh as an alternative – the logic of which we couldn't understand. Nearly all the cases he examined were suffering from enlarged spleens, a characteristic of malaria, but he found not one single case of venereal disease. Many of the women were suffering from the effects of childbirth at too young an age.

The Sheik of Biriemi was steadfast in his refusal to allow the expedition forward, and had himself arrived in Hail, searching for them, so they retreated north to Mahadhah, and decided that they would try to explore a more northerly route to Sharjah instead of Abu Dhabi. They left Kitnah on 24th May, the whole village seeing them off with good wishes, and after seven and half hours hard night riding, during which a camel died under Claude's servant Francis and threw him badly, they bivouacked outside Mahadhah.

At Mahadhah they had an elaborate welcome from the local Sheik [pictured below right] with camel riding stunts and then a mutton feast [pictured below left], even though they were exhausted. They camped in a pleasant date garden with a stream – the fishes in the stream nibbled their privates when they bathed.

They spent four days at Mahadhah, and found good sites for landing strips. They climbed the nearest mountain, and looked out over the sand sea to Biriemi. The heat was draining – 116 degrees and high humidity. They were attacked by giant poisonous spiders, and O'Brien achieved more fame when he excised a spider wound, so that the man could travel the next day despite what was often a fatal bite. Their tent was also attacked by some goats, who tried to eat it, and who left a sea of red ticks.

They moved to Khuwalid, where the water was black and foul, and then launched into the sand desert, entering a world where no white people had ever been before [Claude felt that they hadn't missed anything]. They had great excitement when they met a party of armed tribesmen, but it turned out to be the party sent out from Sharjah to meet them [pictured below]. They were going to stay at Murra, but the well had been hopelessly fouled by dead locusts, so they had to push on Jiffr-al-Halais, where they fell off their camels and slept dew drenched on the bare earth. In the miserable misty morning, Francis despaired of making a fire, but eventually did so and made their hot cocoa. Switzer appalled Claude and dismayed Francis by flinging his cocoa on the ground.

The party from Sharjah

Above: Claude drinks from a shoe, and right, the slave who made the coffee. Below: the well at Wadi Samaini. Claude's caption: *Some desert wells were 120 feet deep. Each of the 75 camels expected 5 gallons. All water is pulled up by hand in leather bags. It looks and tastes foul in most cases!*

They travelled across the sand, but at 7.30 am they had to stop at Qitah for the day, because of the heat and also a sandstorm. The sand covered everything, they couldn't eat anything, and they had to plug their ears with wool and tie muslin across their faces and mouths, so they could only drink through the muslin. Switzer had been sickening, and O'Brien was worried, and after they got drenched with dew the next night, O'Brien took Switzer off early, before the heat of the day.

On 3rd June [the King's birthday], they were very pleased to see the coast and the masts of HMS Lupin, but they could not get out to the ship because:

The sheik had a local war on. However, he had very kindly called it off to let Switzer through that morning, and now he had come to welcome us and give us the usual formality of an equestrian exhibition. It was a good show and I will say that they can ride, but all my thoughts were of Lupin and her wardroom and its ice supply! ... I learned that Switzer had got on board all right and was in his bunk ... Before we parted company, we took some of our escort aboard Lupin, and their wonder was profound: 'rock' that melted into water in your mouth was a great joy to them. Salem, having seen a Lewis gun fired, told us that he could defy all Arabia with one such mounted on Djebel Mahadhah.

They were also overjoyed to have cigarettes – they had run out at Kitnah, halfway through their expedition [O'Brien had been reduced to smoking random leaves rolled in toilet paper!], and to be able to drink something other than lime juice – their only drink on the expedition.

Claude's orders were now to return to Iraq. The journey went smoothly, but Switzer and O'Brien were hospitalized with heat stroke. Francis could not stop smiling on his return. Claude worked on his report for the Air Ministry.

The very detailed official report to the ministry was written by the political officer and Wazir to the Sultan of Oman, Thomas, who concluded that they had done well to confirm Mahdahah as a good alternative to the original route through Biriemi, since it was on a more direct route and was likely to be much more friendly to the air project. Thomas noted that there was a general hostility in the area toward the air project, in addition to the volatile tribal politics. The tension between Ibn Saud and the Trucial Coast sheikdoms had stirred up the tribes. Thomas compliments Squadron Leader Keith and his two officers for achieving 70% of what was needed to get the air route confirmed.

However, a sour postscript to the tour concerned honours. O'Brien had repeatedly said during the expedition that he deserved an OBE for it, and Claude, as his commanding officer, agreed, and, without informing O'Brien [which would have been against the rules], duly recommended him. Unfortunately, O'Brien talked about being recommended by Claude, and this got to the authorities' ears, resulting in no decoration for either of them, and black marks for Claude in higher circles. This was deeply upsetting to Claude.

Chapter 14 Flying Years 3: Iraq, and jaunts away

The summer of 1927 was no cooler in Baghdad than it had been in Oman. Claude writes back to England of all the candles melting before being lit, of his shaving razor being too hot to use, and all the rubber sponges having to be thrown away because they melted. His squadron spent a week of night bombing exercises, and found that the higher they went in the air, the hotter it was. He described how they had to land between petrol flares which lasted for two minutes.

Claude then took a planeload of VIPs on the run to Egypt, and once more had to battle with headwinds that caused them to have to stop for two unscheduled refuelling stops in the empty desert. The flight was complicated by the VIPs insisting on taking way over their allowed luggage/freight weights, making the plane dangerously heavy, and causing one of the tyres to blow out at one of the desert fuel dumps. They weren't able to change it, so they had to take off and land 'flat'. In the extreme turbulence, most of the passengers were very sick. They flew

across the Nile delta to Aboukir – a route not normally taken because there is nowhere for emergency landings.

The VIPs caught their boat, and Claude and his second pilot Potter ate *'the biggest meal that has ever been eaten in Alexandria'*. They then went and stayed a few nights at the San Stefano Casino Hotel, on the beach between Alexandria and Aboukir, where they enjoyed sea bathing – Potter and Ewens [from 70 Squadron] are pictured with some new friends. They spent a few nights in Cairo, which was even hotter and more humid than Alex, and where the best clubs were *'infested'* with a party of 400 American tourists.

On the return trip they only had two passengers, and it was much easier. They stopped in Jordan overnight, and enjoyed Amman, though Claude said that the roads and driving were terrifying. They spent the next day *'wrestling with death on a franticly hot day'* returning to Baghdad.

The next day Claude flew as navigator with Captain Wooly-Dodd on a new Imperial Airways 'special machine' – actually a prototype Hercules. They soon met a sandstorm, but this new aircraft was equipped with Reid Turn Indicators, which enabled it to fly through sand, fog or cloud, something that the RAF planes couldn't do. They spent the first night at Sheiba, and from there flew to Bahrain in just three hours. They landed in sand outside the town, and were surrounded by a vast crowd of people who hadn't seen such a plane before. They stayed just four hours, and then flew back at 10,000 feet, well above the sand storms and bumps, and far higher than the RAF planes went – Claude was very impressed by the view, and noted many dangerous coral reefs which were not on the British maps. They took five hours to return to Sheiba, making it a twelve hour round trip – a long day, even in such a modern aircraft.

Hercules aircraft at Bahrain

Switzer and O'Brien were on leave in England, and now, after Claude had flown three thousand miles in the last week, the CO offered him a fortnight of recreation in the 'summer camp' of Beribadan in the Kurdish mountains. Claude was down to just 10 stone one ounce, and his 'Masonic tummy', as Angel called it, had disappeared.

He flew up to Mosul in the north, had a second huge meal of the day, and then was flown on up to Diana, a landing strip in the mountains near to the Persian border, near to the enormous gorge and ancient Kurdish stronghold of Rawanduz. From there it was a two day mule trek up through the mountains, from Diana, at 2,000 feet, to Beribadan at 9,500 feet. Their escort, 'Kurdish and Assyrian levies', walked the whole way.

The mules were amazingly sure footed, but always walked on the outsides of the paths, so that the feet of their riders hung over the precipices, and there was evidence of mules and riders that had fallen to their deaths far below. As they climbed, the air got fresher and cooler, and the flowers and butterflies became more abundant. They picked wild figs, pears, dates and peaches. They took all precautions possible to be protected from sunburn and sunstroke.

At the overnight halt, tents had been erected, and each of the ten officers lucky enough to go on this holiday had a tent and a soldier to act as a servant. They had an icy swim in one of the many streams, and were served dinner before going to bed early. Next day the trek was ten hours to Beribadan. As they ascended there were abrupt changes as they got above the fly line, and then above the tree line.

Up at Beribadan, the altitude ensured that nothing too strenuous could be done, but the cool air was a blessed relief. Claude chose not to join the bear hunt, and instead set off with others on mules to conquer Mount Siah Kuh. They took in a magnificent view, took photos [Claude pictured in the snow, right], and returned at tea time, feeling smug that the bear hunters had seen no bears. Later in the week Claude climbed Beribadan peak without mules, and felt pleased that his lungs were fine, since he notes that he is accused of smoking too much and risking a weak heart – interesting that this is three decades before it supposedly became established that smoking damaged lungs. Later in the week they climbed Algor Dagh at 13,000 feet, where they actually crossed the Persian border.

Claude found the camp a bit monotonous quite quickly, and opted to return early, but taking in a trip down the Rawanduz gorge and stronghold, which Claude describes as one of the most amazing places he has ever been to. His pictures do not do it justice, so included below are some modern pictures: the town, the waterfall where they took tea, and the gorge from the ancient town. The precarious bridge Claude described has obviously not survived today, so his picture is included.

Alexander Bridge — Zakho.

They trekked to Erbil, where they stayed with the 'Admintor'. Claude found Erbil fascinating: a narrow maze of streets too narrow for vehicles, light skinned blue eyed Turkomans mixing with Kurds, unveiled women. They were picked up by Bristol Fighters and flown to Mosul, and the next day they flew to have a look at the frontier town of Zakho, where they landed and walked into town to see the bridge said to have been built by

Alexander the Great. The trip to Zakho meant that they didn't have time to fly up the legendary city of Amadia, which disappointed Claude; it is amazing that they could fly RAF planes through dangerous mountains and land in fields, just for a spot of tourism.

When Claude returned to Hinaidi, Baghdad, one of the Bristol Fighters stationed there crashed from a spin at 800 feet, and the pilot and passenger were killed. Claude described the crash and funeral in detail. Although the victims weren't close friends of Claude's, all the officers knew each other well, and it was a salutary reminder of the dangers of flying in these primitive planes.

In September Claude got a horrible shock: he was being transferred to an administrative post at the Depot at Hinaidi. This was because another officer doing the job had fallen out with colleagues, and needed to be transferred out of the Depot. Claude had a heartfelt rant:

Once again I am to be sacrificed to the service. 'I must consider the service before the individual', said the AOC. The whole affair disgusts me, because for years I have been kept in technical jobs which enabled the service to use my knowledge to their advantage, and after a hard struggle I managed to get back to a flying job, and to fly when one is not in a flying job is not easy. In three years I should be thinking of my next promotion, but I can have no hope of it unless I have held an independent command of a flying unit. I sacrificed part of my embarkation leave before I sailed last year in order to go to Manston and fly those heavy bombers, and the Air Ministry promised me that I should stay two years in this squadron. Now, because someone has to go to the Depot who is reliable, and Maxwell is sent to a job for which he is wholly unsuited ... not three weeks ago I turned down an offer to go home to take the super armament course at Woolwich because I didn't want to quit my flying job. Now the AOC won't even let me put in for that.

Before his transfer to the Depot, Claude's next jaunt was what he described as 'The Gulf Tour Deluxe'. The purpose was to finish arrangements for the air routes. He flew down to Basra, met the incoming troop ship, sailed over to Bushire in Persia, via Kuwait, and then off in HMS Lupin to Sharjah, rather over-celebrating his birthday with old mates en route. They then went to Henjam Island on the Persian side of the gulf, where Claude got marooned, because Lupin was called to Colombo. Henjam was [and is] an arid small island where there is nothing to do. There was only one other white person on the island. Claude got a black eye from a hockey game, shaved his moustache off, tried to avoid the ubiquitous red ticks, ate the marvellous small oysters, and worried about the cholera outbreak nearby.

On 28th October he sailed in the SS Bankura to Bahrain, very relieved to be able to have a bath again. In Bahrain he stayed with the local shipping agent in a beautiful house on the waterfront. At dinner he met an American who told a story about some Arabs at Hoffuf who, observing that he had a gold tooth, forced him to strip to see if he was growing gold anywhere else on his body!

The Foreign Secretary of India, Sir Denis Bray, C.I.E., C.S.I., K.B.E., arrived in Bahrain to a 13 gun salute, addresses of welcome, school children singing songs of welcome, incense, rose water, then a 150 person state banquet at the Sheik's palace [which included only two women]. There were 20 whole sheep, with five mountains of rice, all to be eaten with the right hand. Claude amused himself handing greasy innards to his neighbour, the signals officer from HMS Triad, because it is bad manners to refuse anything offered to you at a feast. *'The women had an ugly time, and were running in fat to their elbows before long.'* Claude reported that the Arabs are fast eaters, but they all felt that they had eaten themselves to a standstill.

Next stop was Bushire, Persia. After a few miserable days there, where they had to chlorinate the water so heavily that it tasted disgusting, Francis, Claude's servant, went down with malaria, and was taken to the local hospital. Claude visited him:

The place was cluttered up with hordes of miserable filthy Persian women, clutching diseased babies, and myriads of flies buzzed hopefully from room to room, working hard to spread every possible disease. In desperation I persuaded an Indian Medical Service colonel to take Francis in hand, and he was saved.

Claude was withering about *'rag time'* Persia:

Can you imagine a country which auctions all its public offices to the highest bidder each New Year's Day! They can't even run their perishing country; the Belgians run the customs, the French run the postal service, the Italians the railways, Swiss the police, and the Americans the finances! Recently the excise on imported tea and sugar was bounced up 156%, and that has made smuggling of these articles as profitable as gun running. The customs people had a good shoot up one night whilst I was sleeping on Prior's roof, and I awoke to the sound of bullets flattening themselves on the buttress above my head. There was a lot of shouting, and the customs snaffled five donkeys laden with sugar, but about fifty got through!

To make things even more miserable in Bushire, Claude received news that he didn't have to do the Depot job, but that Maxwell had still taken his job in 70 Squadron, so he was now without a job at all in Iraq.

The party set off in SS Chakdara for Oman. The political staff were always senior to the RAF or military staff, and the political officer, Haworth, had decided to travel with his family – wife, small child, son and son's friend, private secretary and private secretary's wife. This party took up all the first class accommodation, bumping Claude into second class.

They went on a leisurely tour of the Persian Gulf: Bahrain, Dohar, and then Dubai, where Haworth's wife and the private secretary's wife went ashore, thereby having *'the distinction of being the first European women to land there, but their uncovered faces called forth remarks from the Arabs which would have made a Leicester Square barmaid blush'*; Claude was unhappy at the political officer having so little tact. Claude obviously did not appreciate the political officer and his entourage: usually he was very cordial, but these people do not even get mentioned by name. In the picture below, Claude is sitting left, next to the rest of the Haworth party.

From Dubai they sailed up the coast, calling in at Ajman, Umm-al-Kuwain, and Ras-al-Khaimah. Claude surveyed the lagoons for flying boat anchorages, and took some good cine camera footage: *'Whilst we were waiting for a political pow-wow, a comic old Arab entertained the crowd by standing on his head. As I was taking a cinema of him, all his clothes fell off – so I think I have got a unique picture!'* Unfortunately [or fortunately], we don't have any of Claude's cine reels.

They then called in at Henjam again, Bahrain again, Bunder-Abbas in Persia, and Hormuz Island, where Claude was secretly rather gleeful about the bad behaviour of Haworth's eight dogs, which were also part of his entourage:

The ruins of the old fort at Hormuz had stood well until 1902, when an earthquake shook them badly. Two of the great underground water cisterns remain, and into these we went to photograph them. The whole island is very colourful, being mainly composed of red iron oxide, which was being shipped from shore. The natives were all dyed red with the fine powder, and the PR's eight dogs dyed themselves red with it, and made a frightful mess when they came aboard! One of them ate part of a dead eagle ashore, and then deposited it 'on master's mat' after he was back aboard. Another fell overboard, and two Arabs swam to rescue it.

Above: Claude's pictures of Hormuz cisterns and fort

Next they visited Khism Island, and explored the salt caverns, before sailing across to the south side of the Straits of Hormuz, to investigate a flat bottom valley that might be used if the British should want to control the straits. Of course the control of these straits, the entrance to the most important oil tanker route, is today one of the key strategic prizes in world geo-politics, but this was the start of it. They were met by the one ship of the Omani navy, carrying Thomas, the Sultan of Oman's Wazir, who had led Claude's Oman expedition, and three ships of the Indian naval force. The tribesmen of Khassab posed for Claude [below].

Although the local tribesmen would not help them, Claude later did some very bumpy aerial reconnaissance of the area, and then a very hot inland hike up and ravine and mountains, to get better photographs.

The Chakdara continued surveying the extraordinary inlets and cliffs of the horn of Arabia, and even encountered rain, but the coast proved very hostile to the chances of setting up air landing places. They called in at Sohar, where the Wali was having problems that Claude was very happy about: the Wali had secretly offered money to the Arabs at Biriemi to stop Claude's previous expedition, which they had done. Now the Biriemi Arabs had sent a thousand men, camped nearby to collect their money which Hammed, the Wali of Sohar [pictured left]

had failed to pay them. Claude comments *'I hope they loot this miserable place. It is no thanks to him that we crossed Oman with whole skins.'*

They called in at Muscat and rode camels up to Matrah, where they visited Stephens, who had completed the road between the two places, but was laid up with a crushed foot. It was people like Stephens, unsung and now forgotten, who changed the developing world, Claude claimed. They travelled a few miles down the coast to Yiti and Bander-Jissah, but the lagoon there was unsuitable for seaplanes. [Today it is the site of luxury hotel complexes]. Haworth's son and his friend came along, got tired and slowed them down, and ended up puking up their lunches, probably to Claude's silent glee – he certainly resented the extended holiday that Haworth's family were having.

They called into Sur, in southern Oman, where they were greeted by volleys of gunfire, which turned out to be the Sur way of friendly greeting, and then took off northwards, calling in at various places along the desolate parched shores of Baluchistan, still surveying for landing sites. They stopped at Bander-Jask, Charbah, Jiunri, Gwadder, Pasni and then finally Karachi on 14th December, where Haworth and his family put up at the Bristol Hotel and Claude avoided them, but the works depot accommodation was full.

As the PR [Haworth] talked of going to Hoffuf in Arabia to talk to Ibn Saud, I thought that it might be a good thing to seize the chance in Karachi of talking things over with Colonel T.E.

Lawrence, who was then serving at our depot as Aircraftsman Shaw, doing a tally clerk's job in the stores. A great fuss was made about the meeting and it was arranged to take place in the CO's bungalow – he being on leave. As we neared the compound gate, we saw a small erect figure standing there in brown overalls and tope, and he held open the gate and saluted briskly as we entered. And this was the 'great little man', Lawrence of Arabia, whose exploits in the war have thrilled all the world. His pronounced straight nose and deep-set slow-moving blue eyes reminded me of my CO in Cranwell days, IWB Rees, the famous wartime VC. And then I remembered that both these men hailed from Wales. He spoke slowly, almost wearily, as though he was tired of giving obvious answers. His voice was low and quiet, but rather forceful in timbre. His manner was one of shy reserve. It was hard to think that this little airman was the great 'Colonel Lawrence'. I hear that his work and conduct are beyond reproach, but he will never try to get promotion. It is unusual to meet a man who has won, and

then turned his back upon most of the things that men usually spend their lives trying to acquire! The PR interviewed him alone, as a man will talk freely to one, but not to two.

On 17th December, Claude travelled by train to New Delhi to report in person on the expedition's findings to Sir Denis Bray, the Foreign Secretary of India. On the train Francis refused to leave any of Claude's things, as he said thieves were rife – the carriages had no corridors, as they would aid the movement of thieves. They travelled across the Sindh desert, which filled the carriage up with sand overnight, and had to change trains in Lahore. It was raining when they reached Delhi, but a car was waiting for Claude.

Claude was most impressed by the layout and architecture of New Delhi, and by the hospitality of the wing Commander Pattinson [whom he had known at Cranwell] and his wife, who put him up and drove him round to see things. He loved the greenery, after more than a year in arid places, and Francis was very happy to be 'home', although he came from Pune. Claude had long talks with Sir Denis Bray, and returned to Karachi. He was very pleased to get a copy of a letter sent by Captain Rowe of the SS Chakdara to his bosses, thanking him for all the help that he had given on the voyage.

To return to Iraq, he and Francis embarked on the SS Varsova on Christmas Day, where he was the only first class passenger before the others embarked, listening to a distant carol being played on a piano somewhere in the depths of the ship as he wrote his letter home, telling of his 'Gulf Tour Deluxe'.

Chapter 15 Flying Years 4: Kurdistan

When Claude returned to Baghdad from Karachi he was expecting to have no job, but he was in for a very pleasant surprise: he had previously written a *'moaning'* letter to the Chief of Staff of the whole RAF, Terrence Higgins, and on the last day of 1927, he was called for a talk with the Chief of Staff at Hinaidi, who told him that he was getting his first command, of No. 6 Squadron, based in Mosul, in the northern Kurdish part of Iraq. He was told that the Air Member for Personnel, Air Vice Marshall Sir Philip Game, who had commanded Claude during World War I, had moved things for him. 'You stand very well in his opinion, and I don't think that you need to worry about your future.'

After a very good fancy dress party to 'see in' 1928 and to celebrate his improved fortunes, Claude flew some naval personnel down to Basra, and on the way down stopped off at Ur of the Chaldees, Abraham's home city, where he was shown round by the famous archaeologist, Dr. Woolley.

Before they pack up for the summer heat, they divide the spoils into three piles of approximately equal value. The Iraqi museums have first pick, and then the British and Yanks toss up for the remainder. You have probably seen the pictures of the recent finds: I saw and handled the real things. Woolley was clearing up a cemetery when we were there and getting up really large quantities of gold, silver, lapis and pearls. The workmanship was really fine and the age was between 5,000 and 6,000 years old – work done before Tutankhamen was ever dreamed of. We wandered through all the excavation and Woolley with his ready tongue and gift of reconstruction told us of things as they were when Abraham was a boy there. I cadged a little pot and a few cornelian beads – beads worn by women who were not so far removed from Mother Eve!

Above: TE Lawrence 'of Arabia' [see last chapter] with Lawrence Woolley on his right.

Claude's parting with his previous squadron came abruptly, as 70 Squadron was called away to take part in a desert war on the edge of Ibn Saud's territory. Claude was left to leave for Mosul as soon as he could, having finished his Gulf tour report. The weather was foul: sandstorms and then torrential rain. Claude was to travel north by train – a lucky chance, since all roads were closed and a plane from his new squadron that took off from Hinaidi to return to Mosul that day crashed, killing both on board.

Even so, his trip was not without drama – they nearly missed the train in the mud, all his luggage was dropped in the mud and his camera – *'the friend of the last fourteen years and with me on all four continents'* – was stolen. He and Francis were freezing on the train carriage which leaked water all over his bed. When changing trains at Quaragan, they sank in slimy mud, and got to Kirkuk on the second evening of the journey. Oil had recently been discovered in Kirkuk, and the only hotel was heaving:

The saloon reminded me of a tough joint in the woolly west: the place was full of smoke, nearly everyone was drunk, muddy and disreputable looking, yet there was money to burn. Yank drillers, the scum of the earth, were there in plenty, and food contractors and all the usual collection one meets in a 'new town' when a find has been made. I got lured into a game of snooker, and we played three a side with some of the oil guys. A drunken Scotsman was thumping out old music hall tunes on the ghost of a piano, two unshaven toughs talking heads over a stove, a Russian blonde with an eye to business making love to a sleepy fat oaf in a corner, boys rushing to and fro with whiskey and yet more whiskey being kicked and cursed for not being quicker – glaring lights, foul atmosphere, stench of smoke and drink and a veritable pandemonium of sound.

Next day the transport contractor, fearing that the mud would defeat the truck and trailer ordered, turned up with no less than five 'tourers' for Francis, Claude and their luggage. The route was on unpaved roads, now mud torrents, through hilly country, but the trip took exactly the seven hours the drivers had estimated, despite a bridge that swayed [with no balustrades] over a roaring torrent, a dodgy ferry and many mud 'flounders'.

The RAF base was two miles south of Mosul, a city of 100,000 people. It was a large compound, fortified with barbed wire, and supposedly supplied for a siege. It was shared with an armoured car section, a small hospital, a wireless station and a supply depot. The buildings were a haphazard jumble of random and dilapidated buildings, with the mess building in a Turkish private house, with the dining room being the old swimming bath of the harem. A blockhouse was being used as a turkey pen, but was about to be converted to a camera-obscura hut.

Claude was aware how lucky he was to have his new job – probably the most independent Squadron Leader's job in the entire RAF. However, he was also aware that there was a semi-hidden agenda: the AOC in Hinaidi had said that he wasn't *'entirely satisfied'* with how things were in Mosul, and had told him that he expected a crackdown in discipline there. Claude found the financial records in a *'gruesome mess'*, and the armoured cars and depot command, which only came under Claude for discipline, more trouble than help. He also now had command over twenty officers and over 200 airmen, liaison with the 'Assyrian levies', Iraqi army, and the local police, as well as his AOC in Hinaidi, two days away.

The squadron of Bristol Fighters were responsible for helping police and army to keep order in this tribal, turbulent and topographically awkward mountainous area, and to patrol the borders with Turkey and Persia, defending the new oilfields from the new enemy, Russia. In his early days at Mosul Claude was involved in a plane's pump failing as they tried to clear some high mountains, checking a lorry convoy stuck in the mud, dropping a despatch on a mountain village that wasn't on the map, tea with the sisters running the hospital and with the local army and police, and giving a lift to the archaeologist excavating Nineveh.

There were also visits to and from His Beatitude Ignatius Elias III, Patriarch of the Syrian Church of Antioch [pictured right], who was a refugee in Iraq. Claude was invited to a 'cleaning' ceremony that lasted from dawn to eleven o'clock. The cathedral was packed, the incense and candles overwhelming, and tame sparrows flew around. The Patriarch was in splendid purple velvet robes, and after the service he entertained Claude to coffee, tea, biscuits and chocolate; they got on so well that Claude invited him for coffee at the base. The Patriarch turned up, dressed in crimson silk, with a large retinue, and was entertained by a pilot doing some daring stunts. He was well impressed, and kissed the pilot on the forehead and blessed him. He then invited all the officers to another five hour ceremony. Claude and three others went to the last stretch of the service, and was given wine by the Patriarch, who told

him, *"Even as Christ turned the water into wine, so I pray that God may care for all of you who fly and turn your material lives into spiritual ones."*

As spring came, they were expecting war: a young sheik was claiming to be a divinity, and was waiting for the snows to melt so that he could send the women and children to hide in the mountain caves before starting his attack. There were also ructions over the annual taxation of sheep. Claude had his squadron practicing gunnery, to start with using a camera instead of guns. He found front firing *'rather thrilling'*. They also resumed patrols of the northern frontier, which could be terrifying – they flew into snow clouds which would completely cover their windscreens, and weigh down their fragile small planes.

Claude was called to unearth the seamy side of Mosul, due to trouble in the brothel area. He visited Charles Littledale, made famous in the best seller 'Two Years in Kurdistan'. He was a crack shot, 'despotic' in his methods, and in charge of the police. He gave Claude a tour of the prison. The prisoners were made to crouch in a compact area, covered by police with rifles, so that they couldn't rush Littledale and Claude. Claude was shown the scaffold – they now held executions inside the prison, because public ones caused too much excitement and unrest, but they then hung the bodies outside the wall, with a label listing their crimes. The prisoners did paid work, woodwork, spinning and rug making so that they had money when released.

Then Claude went to the brothel:

It opens off a street which has big notices forbidding all British troops to enter it. The actual entrance is through a cemetery [appropriate, eh?] and as we turned the corner I found my two Service Police quietly sitting on a grave, sipping little glasses of coffee and smoking cigarettes. The area is a tiny town of its own, with cafes, shops, washerwomen, but it has one entrance and is under police control. I had to wander through its tortuous little alleyways, photographing all the possible places that foolish airmen could climb in ... the best native hotel in the town backs onto the area and I had to place it out of bounds to airmen as they used to drink beer on its roof garden and then fling down the empties into the area, which greatly upset those within!

Above left: Mosul, with a Bristol tail-fin, and below, Evans' crashed plane.

Flying was a dangerous business in the mountainous area, and a young flying officer called Evans wrote off a plane in the crash Claude photographed, but both he and his passenger emerged relatively unhurt. Claude missed the first races of the Mosul point-to-point as a result of having to sort it out. A few days later he himself was involved in a dangerous situation: he and another pilot had flown to Erbil, and were returning over mountains when they were caught in a violent lightning, rain and sand storm, which completely obscured all visibility. This is before the time of radar, so they were flying blind below the level of the mountain tops, being thrown around by the wind. They managed to land, but the two planes were stuck in mud. They found some soldiers, who after the storm had past, pulled their planes out, and they took off, only to get caught in another storm, which caused them to fly blind for another period of time, until they flew into the sunshine and safety.

140

The rest of spring 1928 was spent sorting out financial records, patrolling, inspecting new ferries for the armoured cars, visiting outposts, flying down to Baghdad, and monitoring the coming war with the hill tribes. Claude went with Charles Littledale to see the villages of the Yezidis, a sect who worship the devil and hold blue to be an evil colour. They were mostly very poor and illiterate, and their mosques had pointed conical minarets.

Flying at dawn in the spring, with the greenery and flowers below and the snow on the mountains was very beautiful:

The landscape looks just like the Almighty had spread out a patterned carpet over the ground, but it won't last long: the sun will burn and blister it all up in a few days and reduce it all to that cursed drab monotony which is an abomination to my eyes. ... Flying near dawn among the mountains is much more attractive than when the light falls almost vertically, as in a slanting light the shadows show up in a wonderful way and you can distinguish the various ranges and peaks.

Claude commissioned the painting below, used it as the frontispiece of his book Flying Years, and presented it to the Officer's Mess of No.6 Squadron. The artist, C.E. Turner, was a well known war artist.

By courtesy of Wing-Commander C. H. Keith, R.A.F.   From the original painting by C. E. Turner, late R.A.F.

THE ROYAL AIR FORCE IN KURDISTAN, 1929
BRISTOL FIGHTERS OF No. 6 SQUADRON PATROLLING THE FRONTIER

As spring gave way to summer, there were more picnics, expeditions to Yezidi villages, one with an ancient phallus temple where infertile women went for a ceremony which Claude [normally not one to be over delicate] declines to describe in writing. He visited police stations with Charles Littledale, and met some interesting criminals, many of them awaiting execution. One was a holy man who had a magic cloak which entitled him to act as husband to any woman over whom he threw the cloak.

Above, left: Yezidi devil worshippers and right, Bizari Kurds at Ishkafta

There were plenty hair-raising episodes of planes taking off, nearly crashing, until there was a fatal crash in June. Claude was suffering from food poisoning when he was awakened with the news that a plane had gone down and two of his men were dead. Claude sent out three Bristols to collect the dead and to burn the plane. By noon the bodies were back, by 2pm the coffin lids were shut, and by 6 pm the funeral had started. Claude described the funeral, which was long, hot, moving, with flowers and representatives from the levies, the police and the townspeople.

The next day Claude set out on his long awaited trek with Charles Littledale. The medical officer was supposed to be going, but he had a fever, so a pilot, George Russell, went instead, together with *'a police escort, bearers, kit and grub'* and, of course, Francis. The trip was for Charles to visit and inspect some of the outlying police posts in the inaccessible northernmost mountains [see an inspection pictured right], but  also an opportunity for Claude to see some of the most remote places on earth. They travelled on mules, climbing 7,000 feet passes, camping, crossing perilous bridges with their mules, fishing [though Claude never fished, deeming it 'incomprehensible'], accepting the hospitality of an *'old foxy'* bishop and of tribesmen who had only recently killed detachments of British soldiers. The days were very hot and the nights cold, sometimes illuminated by lightning. The views were spectacular, and it was useful for Claude to see things from the ground, since they normally patrolled this area by air.

The highlight of the trek was the ancient [but dying] town of Amadia, set on a waterless crag. The women had to collect the water in leather skins every day from the river far below, and no animals were allowed in the town. Pictured below are the gates of the town, with the police lined up for inspection, and the police rest house, organized by Charles, where they stayed the night, listening to the waterfall cascading into the gorge below.

On the later days they visited a huge cave full of thousands of defecating bats [they hadn't brought an umbrella], which Claude noted as a perfect place for the locals to shelter from any RAF bombing raids. They visited the devil worshipping village of Shaikh Adi, whose mosque and priest are pictured below.

July in Mosul brought the hot south wind, which made everyone lose their tempers and find it impossible to get comfortable. A young officer flew low over the Tigris to wave to his wife, but flew into some wires, and ended up in the river. He appeared to be not too badly broken up, except for a smashed jaw and river water in his lungs, but then he suddenly died. His widow told Claude that he had a premonition of death, and that two young flyers had died waving to her in Cologne, Germany, years previously. Another officer was badly injured in a fall playing polo. And then, on Friday 13th of July, after the wind had turned to the north and everyone had cheered up, Claude thought that he was going to die.

He was flying with others up to the mountain airstrip of Diana. On the way out, over jagged mountains at 6,000 feet, near the upper limit for Bristols, the pressure in his engine built up to an unsafe level, and when Claude tried to release it, but petrol not air came spurting out, nearly gassing him. He managed to get his plane down at Diana, tested the engine, and found no fault, and so decided to try the return flight.

Ten minutes over the worst part [of the mountain], and then my engine suddenly petered out. I turned on to my rear tank and she picked up, much to my relief, but then she faded away again, and my rev counter fell from 1,900 to 1,200 and I was rapidly losing height. The thought of having to land there made me feel so sick that lethargy overcame me. Then I realized that seconds were precious and I set about trying to isolate the various branches of the pressure system, as I saw that my pressure had fallen to zero. Nothing seemed to cure things, and below me I could see those wicked crags rising up towards me. Franticly I pumped with my hand pump and my revs rose a little and I staggered on. My arm felt it would break, so I reached over and pumped with my left arm. Ahead I saw a rocky peak sticking up and I realized that I was too low to cross over it. Perspiring from every pore, I kicked over my rudder and skirted round it, pumping like mad. I knew by then that the fault was incurable and that it was a race: could I keep up enough pressure against some unknown leak to enable me to get over the first range?

Honestly, I have to admit to you, I was half choking with funk and my arms felt as though they were going to drop off, but I staggered on and got over lower ground where there were a few patches of ploughed ground. I was coming down rapidly and it didn't seem possible that I could reach a spot where I could safely land. It is curious what thoughts run through one's brain at these times. I was singing at the top of my voice that absurd little song, 'You may do as you wish – but not with me', and trying to picture what sort of creature my babe had grown into, and work out whether, in England at that time, he would have woken up for his breakfast. Then I chose my spot, and throttling back my useless engine, came down in rough plough, and my engine immediately petered out. I jumped out and felt drunk – my legs could scarcely hold me up. Just blue funk, and I don't mind admitting it.

A very hot August was enlivened by a liaison visit from the French air force in Syria. They crashed and lost two of their aircraft flying over, and then went wild in Mosul. When Claude took their colonel to meet the French consul, they found him sitting in just his shorts, eating his lunch.

He got up very excitedly. 'Attendez, mon colonel, I must put on a shirt,' he cried. 'On no account put yourself out,' said the colonel. 'If you persist in putting on a shirt, I shall remove my trousers,' and he proceeded to do so as he spoke! And so we dived down into a giant cave-like cellar below the consulate, and Maury, the consul, called for drinks. We all plumped for 'Vermouth melange' as being fairly safe. Just as well we did, as his clotted Arab servant had poured us full tumblers.

When they got back for tiffin at the squadron base they found the place in an uproar: the French pilots bringing the replacement planes had had arrived and had been drinking everything they could grab, and were singing round the piano. Claude then took them to meet Dominican monks and nuns, but the monks produced very good quality French wine, and finally back at the club things livened up even further!

Next day the French found it hard to rise, and when they finally got flying, one pilot tried to take off despite being warned that his wheel was squeaking. He shrugged it off – 'C'est la musique de l'air', and then slewed it round on take-off, nearly causing a major accident. His passenger, the colonel, was so alarmed that he decided to pilot it himself – which was brave since he was 52 and had a wooden leg! Claude reported that their planes were *'literally dropping to bits, rusted and filthy'*.

The French returned safely, but they had got lost en route, and a French colonel flew out to find them and his plane stalled and crashed, killing him. Claude comments that it had been an expensive liaison visit.

The weather turned exceptionally hot and nasty, and Claude worried about his medical officers. One was away at the summer camp at Beribadan due to ill health, and would probably have to be invalided home – it was suspected that he had the dreaded 'sprue' – an incurable and fatal tropical disease. His second medical officer was also sick, and had lost 8 pounds in a week. However, they both recovered after a spell in the mountains.

Charles Littledale and Claude motored south across the desert to meet the Sheik of the Bedouin tribe who controlled the desert, in order to keep him supportive. On their way they visited the massive ruins of the Parthian city of Hatra, which was then totally un-excavated. They were given a Bedouin feast, reclining on carpets in a tent, before driving back to Mosul. The desert air contrasted with the foul smells of Mosul; the cemeteries dotted around town, where bodies were only buried two feet down, were especially smelly.

Left: Claude's picture of Hatra. Right: Hatra [before being destroyed by ISIS in 2015].

Chapter 16 Flying Years 5: Lebanon, Syria, Iraq, Egpyt and Palestine

In October Charles Littledale invited Claude and some other officers to go on a jaunt to Beirut in Lebanon, driving across the Syrian Desert. They were going to two cars, Claude with Charles and his wife in one, and Oddie and Perry-Keane [the medical officer] in the other. However, Charles had to delay because their baby was not feeding properly without its mother, and so Claude set off with Oddie and Perry-Keane [PK] in an old dodge saloon that Oddie had bought for £17 in Mosul. Oddie was the mechanic, Claude the navigator, and PK the caterer and in charge of defence – the Syrian Desert was infested by bandits.

The journey was punctuated by the usual flat tyres and mechanical problems. They camped in the desert where it was so still and dark that they could hear dogs barking many miles away. They crossed the Euphrates into Syria, where the customs officials did their best to give them a hard time, delaying them long enough for them not to risk the desert run to Palmyra, so they had to stay in Der-es-sor. There they were bountifully entertained by the French military, one of whom they had entertained on the liaison trip to Mosul.

On the route across the desert they met some tribesmen:

A party of Arabs, each carrying a rifle, blocked our way, and as we hove in sight, they loaded. Oddie couldn't let the Dodge out as the road was too bad, so he slowed down and shot the bolt of his automatic. I did the same and PK got out the .303. They waved for us to stop, and we got a bead on them. Things looked ugly, and we knew that we'd have to shoot in a second or two, for it is the first to shoot who wins. Then they must have seen our uniform, for they reversed their rifles and waved us on. Keeping them covered we passed them and went right on and clear. What would have happened if we had not been in uniform I dread to think.

They passed an empty lorry with a man lying by the back wheel, apparently mending it, and another sitting in the cab. They passed with guns loaded, but didn't stop. They fell in with a couple of French armoured cars for the last part of the desert, and reached Palmyra safely. Here they stayed at the Zenobia Hotel [where 46 years later his son Colin and his family stayed], and marvelled at the wonderful ruins in this spectacular oasis.

The French hotelier was charming, and took them round the ruins himself, and his wife, who pretended that she had a good cook to cover their lack of staff, was the excellent cook herself. Claude was depressed about how the culture of the area had declined – the present day Arabs were living in miserable shacks surrounded by the stupendous architecture from two thousand years before.

They reached the Damascus to Homs road, where they had to stop for a night to get a new wheel, and while they were there they visited the tomb and museum of Saladin. Then who should roll up but Charles Littledale and his wife, who had travelled the same route as them, a day behind. They hadn't been held up, but reported that the lorry that Claude, Oddie and PK had passed the previous day had obviously been attacked and looted just before they had arrived, because both the men that they had seen were in fact dead!

Claude said it was 'comic' seeing Charles' wife not wearing a veil, as she was a 'pure bred Arab', who only went out veiled in Mosul. Claude obviously liked her – a he called her a 'wonderful woman' and he marvelled that she was only 24, with an eight year old son, but his attitude was an odd mix: on the one hand he remarked on her skin being whiter than most Europeans, but then he expressed disapproval of the Europeans who looked down on her because of her race, and says that Charles and her loved each other, *'and that is all that matters'*. From the picture of Charles and his wife [left] it looks as if Charles himself may have been of mixed race himself.

They stayed a night and day in Damascus, and then crossed the mountains of Lebanon, encountering several mechanical failures in Oddie's car, and then several crashes [not of their car] on the way down into Beirut. Beirut was very pleasant, but without a single 'decent hotel'. PK went off to visit friends in Haifa, and Oddie met his wife who had journeyed from England, and was not prepared to drive through Syria with his wife. Claude stayed in Beirut, enjoying the climate and sea bathing. He enjoyed dancing with a young German, went up into the hill villages, ate kippers, and went out to the hot spots with Maton, one the French flyers he'd made friends with in Dor-es-sor.

Claude joined up with Charles and his wife for the run home. They travelled north up the coast to Latakia, where they hired a ketch to sail round the bay, then inland to Aleppo, where they heard that 23 cars had recently been held up and looted on the road they had just used. They then motored on a very bad road across the north of Syria to Dor-es-sor, where the three of them had to share a hotel room, much to Claude's horror. They had a picnic in their room, then Charles, exhausted from the driving, went to bed, and Claude rushed out of the room to give 'Mrs Littledale' time to get ready for bed. They were both kept awake by Charles snoring. They returned to Mosul with no further mishap.

In November the Under Secretary for Air, Sir Philip Sassoon [pictured], visited Mosul with the Iraq AOC, and stayed for a night, having to take Claude's quarters and the care of Francis. The VIPs decided to change their itineries, wrecking all Claude's careful plans, and Sassoon was obsessed with finding pistachio nuts, which didn't seem to be available. Eventually Claude got someone to find some, and a whole branch was brought in, at which the Under Secretary brightened up, and wrote a very charming appreciative thank-you letter from his next stop, Baghdad. Claude was impressed that his politician knew all about him and his career, and he used the visit to 'pump' the minister on matters he wanted changing, such as cheaper beer for airmen serving abroad – this habit of trying to right perceived wrongs with politicians was to get him into trouble in World War II, but went down fine with Sassoon, who had apparently given hell to other places he'd visited. Sassoon later sent Claude a generous Christmas present; an inscribed gold cigarette box inlaid with platinum. [Apparently, Sassoon's family had been merchants in Madras, and had made their fortunes selling silver and opium].

No6 Squadron was also visited by Dr. McCurdy, a Cambridge don researching mental health. He was trying out a balancing test that tested mental stability while flying. Claude called it a 'great game', and came top of those tested! The summer camp at Beribadan had been used well to help personnel, but it was clear that the pressures of Iraq had got to a significant number. Claude's deputy while he was on holiday in Beirut had to be hospitalized after there were a number of complaints about his behaviour while Claude was away, and McCurdy said that his invaliding him to England had probably prevented *'a homicidal incident'*. Two of Claude's predecessors at Mosul had a apparently gone *'bats'* after leaving their command in Mosul. Claude reported that he himself felt *'jake'* [perfect], but it reminded him that mental breakdown was never far away.

They were visited by the Turkish Commission, which involved more speeches and drink and friendship pledges – Claude seemed to be very good at this, as he always ended up with invitations for reciprocal visits, and the Turks obviously had a good time. There were the usual winter rains and mud clogging up communications, and small-pox raging in Mosul town.

In the New Year they were visited by the new AOC, Air Vice Marshall Sir Robert Brooke-Popham, KCB, CMG, DSO, AFC, who looked old and tired, but who was very impressed when Oddie produced 100% gunnery target score. This had never been done anywhere in the RAF outside of No6 Squadron, and others in the squadron went on to emulate Oddie. The fame of the squadron, and of Claude's insistence on high standards of training, spread throughout the service, and Claude and the Squadron received a letter of congratulations from Lord Trenchard, the Air Minister, calling their achievement *'really wonderful and extraordinarily good'*. This achievement was one mentioned in Claude's obituary eighteen years later. Brookham was also frozen stiff when taken on a routine patrol, got to meet all the local notables, including the six local patriarchs and their bishops.

Just before Christmas, Claude got a wire that his old friend Major Dockray was going to be passing through Bagdad on his way from India back to Britain, and asking if Claude could meet him. Claude applied for a special leave, flew down to Baghdad, where the train was late, and there was no sign of Dockray. In the hotel he found out that Dockray was never going to travel, and that the telegram had neglected to say that it was Dockray's friend who was travelling, and that Dockray had thought it would be nice for her if Claude entertained her! Claude, who had had to pull in favours to get all the way down to Baghdad, was not impressed. Luckily, Claude's boss thought the whole thing very amusing. Of course, Claude was to be even less impressed with Dockray later in the year when Dockray was named as the co-respondent in his divorce case with Angel. Dockray's friend turned out to be an American war widow who talked non-stop but Claude admired for her spirit.

Christmas and New Year were strenuous times for Claude, keeping the cheer and discipline going simultaneously during a round of eating, drinking, donkey polo, an in-house pantomime, fancy dress parties, cross-dressed hockey and then getting back to normal.

In late March Claude took a trip to see the huge new oilfields in Persia. He took his excellent medical officer, whose short contract with the RAF was ending because the RAF was economising – Claude wanted to get his MO a job in the oilfields. He managed to include a series of lectures in Basra and Sheiba on his Gulf exploits, so he was able to fly down, taking in the annual RAF ball in Baghdad – both he and the MO were worse for wear in the air flying to Basra, and it wasn't helped by flying through a cloud of locusts, their green blood sticking to everything.

When they arrived at the 35 square miles of oilfields, they were most impressed by the scale of money being made, the 30,000 employees, the luxurious conditions for the Europeans, the well equipped hospital – all in sharp contrast to RAF conditions. Claude met his cousin, civil engineer Bertram Hopkins, who had been working for the company for seventeen years, and stayed a night in his tent. They were awed by the size, heat and noise of Abadan oil port. They went to a dance where there were actually plenty of women – a first for Claude in that part of the world. On the way home, Claude stopped at Hinaidi for the RAF boxing championships, and since two titles were won by men of his squadron, he received the trophy from King Faisal, who attended, and with whom Claude got 'matey' afterwards.

Spring 1929 was quite similar to spring 1928 for Claude: muddy car journeys, some extraordinary feasts put on by natives [the Christians in the area were great wine drinkers], and several near escapes including one quite severe crash landing that 'bent my kite'. One difference was that in 1928 there had been a plague of little red flies, but in 1929 it was a plague of caterpillars that completely covered the ground, and made walking a very squelchy affair.

April and May saw twin irritations arrive: the extreme heat and the auditors' visit – Claude hated auditors, whom he said thrived on other people's mistakes. The flooding Tigris had carried away the pontoon bridge at Mosul, and a bag of supposedly spontaneously combusting sugar had caused a fire which destroyed a consignment of two planes, 80,000 gallons of petrol and two tons of supplies on their way to No6 Squadron. There were various visitors, including a Hercules plane chartered by a rich American woman doing a world tour, a major from the Sudanese Camel Corps doing a study of Iraq [though Claude suspected that he was on some sort of extended sick leave]. Claude went down to the oil town of Kirkuk to stay with the Littledales, who had moved there. On the way back, his plane was thrown around like a rag doll in a huge storm, and he completed the 70 minute journey in 38 minutes.

Left: A Kurd at Shaklawa. Right: A Yezidi at Shaik-Adi

In June the pressure of one his men crashing and what he called 'the realms of higher mathematics' got to Claude, and he asked permission to go to the northern mountains to observe the Iraqi army training, as a break. There were 800 men practicing with machine guns, artillery, and an exercise of burning a village [not fully carried out, but enough to alarm the villagers!]. The Iraqi commander was very anti-British, having been 'punished' [tortured] by the British when fighting for Turkey in World War I. The British commander, Redding, was disappointed that they had forgotten to bring the white bread he'd requested, so Claude got Oddie to fly up and drop it by parachute! Redding then pulled out the smelliest Stilton cheese that ever existed, and insisted that they partake of it! There were also several visits to the local sultans or sheiks, with goodwill sessions of coffee, honey and cigarettes.

By July the heat was getting impossible, and war was brewing on the Syrian border, due to the French coming over the border into Iraq and seizing the goods of Bedouins, saying they were taxing them for being Syrian. This turned into a full blown border dispute between British Iraq and French Syria, with the local sheiks using the conflict to take sides and to settle old scores.

Claude took the High Commissioner of Iraq out to a desert camp for negotiations, taking Francis along to minister to the big man's needs. Claude and his men went for an evening feast with the Bedouin sheik Darwish in his encampment – it was totally medieval except the sheik had sent for them in two very modern motor cars! Claude had to fly the High Commissioner along the length of the border, knowing that one error of navigation would mean straying into French Syrian airspace, and an 'incident' involving the High Commissioner. Luckily the visibility was good, he didn't stray, and he got his passenger safely back to Mosul. The High Commissioner later wrote a very nice thank you letter. That afternoon Claude was having his afternoon nap, completely naked, when Sheik Darwish arrived to call on him. He dressed hastily, and over coffee and biscuits, continued the diplomatic campaign to settle the dispute. By the end of the month the war was over, and Claude was turning his attention to brothel raids to dissuade the airmen from going there.

Above: the High Commissioner arrives [left] and Darwish's Bedouin camp [right]

In August Claude was very pleased to join the 100% Club himself for a maximum score in the air gunnery test, and eventually all but one of the squadron achieved this, which caused them to be legends in the force.

Of more immediate importance was the order to move No6 Squadron from Mosul to Egypt. This was a complex business, moving all the stores, back-up technicians and their personal effects [and some families] across uncharted desert or through bandit country in Syria, or the long way round the Arabian Peninsula, with just one month's notice. To make things worse, their annual inspection was due on 27th August; then to cap it off, another 'war' reared its head.

A bandit Kurdish leader called Simko, who had murdered the Assyrian Patriarch and who had committed outrages in Turkey and Persia, had now moved over the border, seeking sanctuary in Iraq. The Turks were demanding that Iraq capture him and hand him over [something they'd failed to do themselves], but Simko had powerful allies in the northern mountains.

A distraction was that Claude and Francis had been gifted a young wild boar by a local sheik, and the boar became a favourite, befriending a kitten, with which it would play, chasing away all the dogs of the area. But Claude was feeling the strain:

Thank the Lord I am feeling a bit more chirpy today, but I have been feeling pretty cheap of late. I'm afraid that I must be going down to the prolonged effects of Iraq without home leave. I look, and feel, very ancient. Feeling oneself growing old in such a country makes one begrudge the passage of time. Old age comes so soon.

They had visits from the Chief Engineer and Chief Auditor of the RAF. Predictably Claude didn't like the Chief Auditor, a *'fat Scotsman'*, and Claude predicts a Royal Commission that will throw out all civilian control of the RAF. They had to fly him round the tourist high spots like the Rawanduz Gorge and Hatra. They also took him to meet the first ever editor of a Kurdish newspaper [circulation 25] – a man who was committed to the creation of an independent Kurdish state. Ninety years later, the struggle goes on.

On the 9th September Claude had to deal with two deaths: an Arab girl was found in the Tigris – she had been stabbed, and a young lad who had only just joined the squadron that week died of pneumonia. Then the High Commissioner of Iraq, whom Claude had flown around, died of heart failure in Bagdad.

There was a hectic round of farewell parties as the squadron prepared to leave: every section had them, and so did many of the Mosul worthies, military and dignitaries, and Claude was dragged to them all. A lot of alcohol was consumed, many speeches given, and every night was a late night.

In the middle of this round of parties, Claude was invited by his local pay clerk to a Syrian Christian wedding, presided over by Patriarch Ignatius Elias III. The bride was very young, straight from a school in Beirut. The ceremony was suitably grand and incense fogged, and after Claude took a photo, with the scrum of guests trying to get into it. [See right, with the Patriarch getting in the picture on the left]. The bridal feast was done in

Old Testament style, cutting the throat of a lamb on the doorstep, so that all guests slithered through the slimy blood. All the men feasted in the courtyard, whilst all the women went upstairs and nattered. Poor little bride: I am sorry for her. She looked so young and sweet in her white robes and veil. What sort of life will this be after that of a happy school girl in Beirut?

The overland convoy left first for Egypt, carrying the heavy stuff, with fears that the rains might bog it down. It left Claude in an almost empty room, reflecting on his time in Iraq:

Shall I live to hanker after a return? I wonder. And yet I have had an amazingly good time, and, with care, have not been off duty through sickness for one single day, although I have been damn near it. It is a marvellous service experience, and it is going to be many a long year before I get as good a job as this Mosul command – and well I know it! Oh, I shall never regret my days in Iraq, to say the very least of it. … My room is stripped, and nearly everything is packed – and I feel sad at leaving, just because it is the closing of a chapter of my life. Never may I re-live the happy times I have known here.

Left: the Squadron crest carved into a rock near Mosul. Claude is top left.

There were still more dinners, drinking and speeches to be made, but this time in Baghdad. Claude took Francis down with him, because getting Francis a visa to get into Egypt was ridiculously hard. He also had to fix up passports for two other local servants who had begged to go with them and who had been given permission.

Old Abdul Aziz Khan said he regarded himself as a part of the squadron, and he would go with it at his own expense if the service wouldn't send him. He is an Indian, and a masterly tailor, so we were glad of the decision. This leaving Mosul has shown so much loyalty amongst the natives that I could weep from having to leave them behind.

The most prestigious of all the leaving parties was an invitation of from King Faisal of Iraq, whom Claude had met at a boxing tournament the previous spring. This was not something the King did for all leaving squadrons, so the RAF high command was very impressed. Claude and his remaining officers were invited to a reception at the royal palace on 13th October.

We were warned that we shouldn't get any alcohol at the Palace, so I had several quick ones before setting out to collect Georgie. I found him doing the same, and helped him. We called at AHQ to join up with the AOC and the Air Commodore, and he said we had better have a cocktail before we left. Imagine my consternation when, as soon as we got into the palace, a much gilded lackey came up with the biggest tray of the largest and strongest cocktails I had met for many moons! However, it probably toned us up for a ripe appreciation of things in general. We were presented to the King. He and his Lord Chamberlain and his Aide-de-Camp were dressed quietly enough in black dinner jackets. The palace is not gaudy, but in very good taste and has an expensive 'kingly' atmosphere about it. A delightful string orchestra was playing soft music on the verandah, where a tiny fountain was peacefully plashing away. We were received in the audience chamber, which is big and has a polished wooden floor with a surface like glass. The King looked ill and seemed horribly nervous. He talked in French and apologized for not speaking in English. It was hard to think that this was the hard riding Arab who had been with Lawrence in the war.

The eats were distinctly good, probably the best dinner I have had in Iraq – which is just as it ought to be. We fed around a table in the middle of a vast room, about which soft-footed servants hurried, plying us with food and drink. The menu was normal European dinner and there was a flood of appropriate drink with each course. We certainly did well. The more champagne I drank, the farther the walls seemed to recede!

After dinner we went back onto the glassy floor, and the King had me over for a private natter. I hope he meant all he said! He was very pleased at the co-operation we had done with his army at Mosul, and then he produced a gilt-framed photograph of himself for me to take over to our new mess at Ismailia, as a souvenir of our service in his kingdom, suitably inscribed in much Arabic script. It was a bit trying to tell the tale to an Eastern King in a language that was neither his nor mine, in front of the AOC. We left soon after, as the AOC said the King was seedy and wanted to retire early.

Georgie and I put a finishing touch to the evening by racing back, changing into plain clothes and doing a last round of the cabarets of the 'City of Caliphs'. Next day we were given a slap up lunch at the Waverly Hotel – and so I saw my last of Baghdad.

Claude returned to Mosul that day, for a last round of parties. He went for a party with his friend Josef Hakkim at Tell Kaif, and they had a wonderful time – the family were Christian, and fond of alcoholic drink. The picture is from Tell Kaif, with Claude at the back. In a flood of final compliments from the Iraqi army, there was time for more farewell parties, including a party thrown on Claude's birthday by the motor-boat entrepreneur which featured Claude's first experience of what he calls 'eastern dancing by women', which impressed him enough to write a long description of belly dancing. They were blessed by Patriarch Ignatius Elias III, who also gave him a pen, so that Claude could write to him.

Finally the Bristol Fighters set off together on the three day flight to Ismailia in Egypt. They stopped overnight in Rutbah Wells, the oasis in the middle of nowhere, and stopped for re-fuelling at dumps in the featureless desert. Claude was in his element, because he was the only one in the squadron who had flown this perilous route before. They flew in strong headwinds over the Dead Sea and landed in Ramleh in Palestine where one of the Bristols crashing on take-off for the next leg. The crashed Bristol wasn't badly damaged, and flew on later. They landed on the sand runway at Ismailia – like landing on velvet – and a new chapter began.

In Ismailia they were part of a much larger base, guarding the Suez Canal, and Claude was no longer the independent head of the station, but having to defer to a senior officer on a daily basis again. He had been due to return immediately on leave to Britain, but his replacement was unable to leave Sudan, so he was only a stop gap in Egypt. With his marriage in its death throes back in England, it must have been an awkward few months.

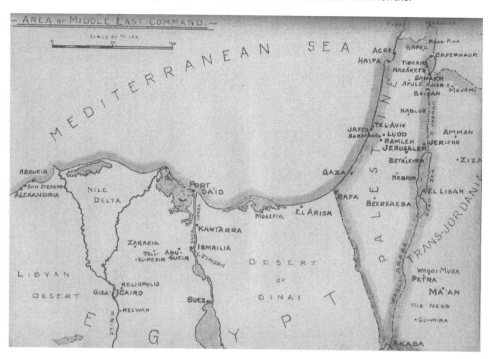

Almost immediately after arriving, things got more complicated, as Claude was informed that No6 Squadron was being moved to Ramleh in Palestine, immediately, to deal with the outbreak of riots between the Jews and Arabs. What made it worse was that Ismailia, unlike Mosul, was a station where families were allowed, and so many of the airmen's families [but not Angel and Colin] had just arrived in Egypt [pictured below, with Francis, right], and now their husbands were off away. Ramleh was the base for the Armoured Car section, and the army officer there was senior to Claude.

Despite all these irritants, Claude enjoyed Ramleh. He delighted in seeing the land of the Bible, marvelled at the excellent roads, and was delighted by the fertile greenery – their base was set in the orange orchards of the fertile Jaffa plain. The mess buildings were grand in comparison to Mosul, and Claude's quarters large and comfortable. Claude writes that *an instinctive feeling of reverence pervades me as I look out over the landscape.* Claude enjoyed walking in the footsteps of Jesus, and visited Crusader towers, too. The weather was bright and not too hot.

Claude found that there was no scheme for co-operation between the RAF, police and army, so he set about getting one straight away. He also set up signs on the roofs of the police stations and Jewish refuges so that the RAF knew where to drop supplies or messages. He set up a series of emergency schemes for the possibility that big trouble would flare up. He invited local police to dinner in the RAF mess and found them very friendly. He set up a debating society in the mess – the first motion was 'That State ownership of national commercial services is undesirable.'

On Christmas Eve a large party from Ramleh went over to Bethlehem.

The road was crowded with snorting, hooting cars. We queued up and fought our way into the waiting room of the Casa Nova at 11.30 pm, and there we found the station sergeant –major, who, being a RC, took it upon himself to look after us all, and brought us white wine. He had evidently been looking after himself in the same way! Then we squeezed into places in the north aisle of the great church of the Holy Nativity. Under the church, in a sort of cave is said to be the manger in which Christ was laid, just 1929 years ago. The service was a long jargon in Latin, with streams of richly robed priests moving to and fro, taking off their little pot-hats, crossing themselves and changing their robes. Incense was swung around the high altar, until it looked like a fog had crept in, and we were all inclined to cough. The church is used by all the various Christian sects, and at the top of another aisle some other denomination was running an opposition service in some unknown language. To and fro, along the dividing aisles walked Mohammedan guards, robed in rich oriental uniforms, tarbushes firmly jammed on their heads and with great curved swords in their hands, ready to slice up anyone starting a rough house! Soon after midnight we had our fill, and went off back to Ramleh.

Claude visited Haifa, where the British military commander lived in a nunnery, and complained that the nuns all tried to mother him. He spent New Year's Eve at a fancy dress party in Jerusalem, and on the first day of the new decade he walked around the historic and biblical sites of the old city. He described it in detail, but the striking feature to him was that Jerusalem did not live up to its translated name of 'City of Peace': the different ethnic and religious groups were hostile to each other and lived separately, and the British sentries were everywhere. He came away from the Church of the Holy Sepulchre *'sad and feeling that Christ wasn't buried there.'* His favourite spot was the tomb at Golgotha, because its simplicity contrasted with all the *'murky pomp'* of the Holy Sepulchre.

Next day they motored to a conference in Haifa, and visited Acre [*'delightful'*]. Georgie and he then motored up to Nazareth and Tiberias to investigate troubles caused by a band of forty murderers. They found the Sea of Galilee very beautiful, but the supposed landing strip by the river Jordan had been ploughed up. They returned to Haifa for a *'riotous'* party aboard HMS Royal Sovereign, which degenerated into a game of 'brown ball' – mixture of billiards and rugby played on a billiard table!

The day after returning to Ramleh, Evans [one of the young pilots whose crashed plane is pictured earlier in this chapter], had an accident with a shotgun, and blew his brains out. Claude describes him as one of the best looking men he'd seen – like a Greek God. Claude leaves unsaid any suspicion that it could have been suicide – it was always an accident in these situations.

Claude took a flight down to Ma'an in the Negev desert, where there was a very poor landing strip and a British Camel Corps station. They stood to while some tribal raiders were captured with their loot. Whilst there, Claude decided to explore nearby Petra. Their car got bogged down in the mud, so they never got there, but next day Claude flew over it. At first they couldn't see it, because it is so well hidden, but then they got some thrilling views. In 1930, there was no sign of life anywhere near the site that would one day become a huge tourist magnet. He then flew north to the Dead Sea, and enjoyed it when his altimeter showed that he was flying below sea level.

Sometime in February Claude transferred back to Ismailia, just at a time when war was brewing in Trans-Jordania. This was because Claude's replacement, Cox, arrived in Ismailia on 24th February, and Claude began the handover of his beloved squadron to him. One of his squadron had a non-fatal crash – the third such at Ramleh, and there was a double fatality from another squadron's crash, and with losing his squadron and facing Angel to add to the gloom, Claude gave way to an uncharacteristic wave of depression:

I feel it's time I got on leave. On service, death is brought so uncomfortably near that at times it seems an insignificant event, much like resigning oneself to chloroform for an operation that one hopes will soon be over. After all, is Death much more? One is taught that God is good, and that all will be well. Some days, when the wind blows sadly in the pine trees, I seem to lose the will to live. What sadness may the future not hold?

In March Claude travelled up to Ramleh, and handed the base over to Cox, before going on a tour of the area around Galilee, which was ablaze with flowers, to show Cox the landing grounds.

Back in Ismailia for his last day, he attended a christening of the child of his stores officer, and was made a godfather, and in the evening attended his Masonic Lodge – the Flying Six Lodge of the Antediluvian Order of Buffaloes. His farewell in the mess was a subdued affair, and he found it difficult to speak. The wives had all signed a letter of thanks and farewell. After the mess farewell he went over to the airmen's fancy dress carnival, judged the 'best ankles' competition, before being presented with a travelling clock. When he started his speech by saying that men are not allowed to present their CO with a present, they reminded him that he was no longer their CO, and a group dressed as convicts picked him up and carried him on their shoulders to the bar. Many drinks later, he was carried on the convicts' shoulders to his quarters.

Next morning his car had streamers, he was pelted with confetti, the car was chased through the town, and the airmen's jazz band played furiously. The airmen, still dressed as convicts, took over the train station, and pitched Claude through the window of the train so that he landed on Major-General the Honourable Stuart Worsley! In the carriage they had left every possible thing a man could want on a journey: fruit, cigarettes, whiskey, soda, a glass and much more.

And thus I left my squadron, feeling I should have liked to put my head over my knees and wept, and go on weeping ...

Chapter 17 A Passionate Wooing

Claude probably felt like weeping on many occasions after he returned to England in 1930, but the work that he was to achieve in the next decade turned out to be of global importance. Meanwhile, he had to forge a new personal life.

Apart from missing his beloved squadron and all the adventure and flying, he had to prosecute his messy divorce with Angel, face the prospect of maybe never seeing his son Colin again [despite paying his school fees], and adapt to a desk job in London, denied even the pleasure of wearing his beloved RAF uniform at work.

In Iraq and Egypt he had been served by an Indian servant, Francis, who made his bed, cooked his breakfast, washed and ironed his clothes, and would have squeezed out his toothpaste if allowed. Claude had eaten and socialized in the officer's mess every lunch and every evening. His entire world had been institutionalized and provided on a plate. Now he was going to have to find somewhere to live on his own, and to either look after himself or pay someone to do it. He had a London club and the Freemasons, but he would still have to create a whole new life for himself.

He had been away from England for over four years, and so he might have found it hard to revive old relationships, especially as he recognised that he was now a changed person: he was no longer young, and his former comrades were married and settled down. With his fortieth birthday arriving a month after his return, he was deemed too old for active command in the RAF, and he could no longer play the dashing airman to young women.

It's to Claude's great credit that he pulled through this undoubted crisis in his life. The support of his Masonic Lodge no doubt helped, but Claude was not one to remain lonely, so he would have set out to make new friendships. However, the most important element to creating this new life was to find a new love.

Unlike all his other romantic liaisons, Claude did not include his wooing and then marriage with Gwen in any book. Maybe this was because the rest of his accounts of his sex life

for written for his son Colin, who was still with his mother Angel, and thus still estranged from Claude. Claude may have thought [rightly] that Colin would not be interested. Because of this, we have no clear account of how Claude and Gwen met, and how and when they married.

When Claude met Gwendolyn Zara Dunkerly, she was employed in the higher echelons of the Good Housekeeping magazine. She was one of four children of Herbert Dunkerly, who was described as Canon W.C. Dunkerly, formerly of Singapore, in the 1967 death notice of Gwen's sister Elfrida. Apart from Elfrida, Gwen had four brothers: Lionel, Ronald, Cecil and Evelyn. Cecil, like his father, was a Church of England priest.

159

From my own memories of Gwen, she was in many ways the polar opposite of Angel. Where Angel was pessimistic, depressed, fiercely intellectual and antagonistic, Gwen was optimistic, kind, sunny, scatty, humorous, and one of the least confrontational people I have met. Where Angel scorned domestic arts, Gwen, in keeping with her Good Housekeeping job, was a sensational cook, was a mainstay of creative crafts within the WI, and loved flowers and gardening [although not cleaning or tidying]. Where they were similar is that they came from the backbone of middle England, loved dogs and were both virgins when they met Claude.

Although it is far from clear, it appears that Claude met Gwen through her sister Elfrida, with whom he may have been lodging. The time was either December 1930 or January 1931, at the time of his divorce with Angel. Claude left a set of untitled typewritten pieces of prose, which were found in Gwen's attic when she died over forty years later. They sound strangely adolescent for a man who had just turned forty, but Claude felt as if he was being re-born. The opening words give a good idea of his boyish elation:

This isn't the true beginning, for thousands of words have gone before – gone, perhaps forever. And perhaps these words may just stoke some very ordinary fire: they never may reach your eyes. At present I cannot say. For days I have tried to think normally – tried and failed, and it has taken me all my time to appear to act normally, and get through the sordid routine of my daily life.

I wonder if you have any idea of the havoc you have wrought in me. I have fought so hard against you – fought to prevent your becoming what none the less you have become. How Fate must chuckle! That I, whom no woman has ever completely upset before, should now be hit so hard! But I somehow think you do understand, and do realize that I am not playing, that I cannot catalogue you with any other woman in all the world. You are something new to me. In a handful of days you have completely changed my whole outlook on life.

Elfrida lived in the London suburbs, while Gwen lived in central London. He records running into 'town' through the foul winter weather, and avoiding to tell Elfrida where he was bound. Claude is barely polite about Elfrida, even to Gwen. This was either because Elfrida was protective of her sister [after all, Claude was going through a divorce at this time] or perhaps because Elfrida wanted him for herself – she never married and was known to be a 'difficult' person.

Gwen wrote back in reply to Claude's ardent missives [typed, with him keeping a carbon copy], but at first she kept him politely at arm's length. However, in a letter of 14th February 1931 Claude exults that the fog prevented Elfrida joining him and Gwen in London and prevented him from leaving Gwen's flat. But with the conquest made, there was still a long way to go. He wrote:

How will all this 'illicit love' go on? I dread to ponder on the future, for God knows, there may be no future! It is so still, so cold, as I write, and I feel so miserably lonely.

It is hard to draw firm conclusions when reading this collection of feverish writings. His dismissal of Gwen's sister, Elfrida, can be forgiven on the grounds that during my lifetime

Elfrida was still known to be exceptionally difficult by all those who knew her! It's possible, even probable, that Elfrida, who never married, fancied him for herself.

We can presume that the *'ugly cloak'* of secrecy was needed because his divorce from Angel had not yet come through. It was obviously very important for Claude, both personally and professionally, to be seen as the injured party in his divorce with Angel, and so he couldn't be perceived as having an affair until the divorce was fully finalized. On the other hand, he seems to take a delight in the *'illicit love'* idea – maybe it reminded him of his pre-marital adventures recounted in his book 'My Rosery'. The fact that Claude wanted to keep it all *'hallowed, sacred and secret to us both'* didn't prevent him from writing it all down for Gwen, and keeping a copy for himself and for posterity!

There are frequent allusions to his mortality in these papers: this could either be an affectation to heighten the romantic tragic tensions, or could be a reflection that he knew that he had genuine life threatening ill health, on which he doesn't elaborate anywhere else. It may explain the fact that he never held an 'active command' after 1930. It could be that he was still scarred by all the deaths out in Iraq and in World War I. It may tie in with his comments that he can never give Gwen what other men might – was he rendered infertile by illness? We can assume from his writing of 14th February that he wasn't impotent.

Claude's account of his wooing of Gwen is in stark contrast with the tortuous difficult time he had wooing Angel. We don't know when they finally went public, or when or where they married, but the divorce from Angel wasn't final until the summer of 1931. The marriage to Gwen was by all accounts one of blissful happiness through to Claude's death. It sustained him through the difficult years when he was working feverishly to ready the RAF for a war with Hitler's Germany as his health waned, and then as he faced up to life without his beloved RAF.

Chapter 18 Putting the fire into the Spitfires: arming the RAF for World War II

Claude told the story of his part in winning the Battle of Britain in his book, 'I Hold My Aim'. The technical details are very full [and often dull to the non-specialist]; the personal story is vibrant, full of cheery anecdotes, but maddeningly fractured and incomplete. What is clear is that Claude was one of the few people who made the vital decisions that staved off the German threat in World War II.

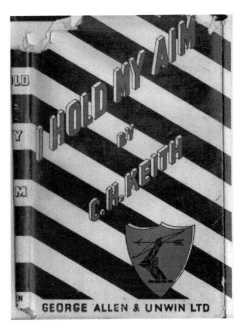

When it was announced in the Times of 19th September 1930, that Claude was appointed to the Woolwich Arsenal as Superintendant of Design, it heralded him as a double specialist: holding qualifications in both navigation and armaments. After World War I he had opted to become a navigation specialist to aid his work in seaplanes, but when he worked at HMS Vernon in Portsmouth on torpedo development, and then when he became an instructor at the armament school in Eastchurch, he gained the armaments specialism, although Claude remembers the gaining of it as being unmerited.

Once at Eastchurch, Claude had become fascinated by armaments; he recruited some men who later became famous in their field, and was responsible for setting up standardized bombing tests for the RAF, so that one squadron could be compared with another. Add Claude's unique experience as an electrical engineer for Marconi, and it's easy to see why he was chosen for Ministry job.

From 1930 to 1933, Claude supervised the design of all bombs used by the British armed forces. To the layman, this may seem a relatively easy task: just find the best shape for heavy things that drop, and then fill them with the best explosive. Of course, this hideous task was much more subtle. The bombs had to carry a wide variety of different lethal substances: high explosive [TNT], incendiary material, poison gas, anti-personnel shrapnel and many others, and each substance provided a different challenge. The bombs would have to detonate at different heights – some well above ground, others on impact with the ground, and others that needed to penetrate earth, armour or concrete before exploding. Thus a range of detonating devices was required. Claude and his team also worked on how geology made a difference – how bombing hard rock areas required different bombs from soft clay areas. When World War II started, Claude had the test results to be able to advise the War Ministry on exactly which London Underground Stations, under soft clay, weren't deep enough for safe civilian shelter.

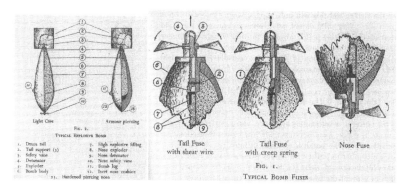

Light Case   Armour piercing

Fig. 2.

Typical Explosive Bomb

1. Drum tail
2. Tail support (3)
3. Safety vane
4. Exploder
5. Bomb body
6.
7. High explosive filling
8. Nose exploder
9. Nose detonator
10. Nose safety vane
11. Bomb lug
12. Inert nose cushion
13. Hardened piercing nose

Tail Fuse
with shear wire

Tail Fuse
with creep spring

Nose Fuse

Fig. 1.

Typical Bomb Fuses

Bombs also had to be delivered accurately from a variety of planes and vehicles, and had to be reliably safe when in the bombers' hands or vehicles, including abnormal situations of altitude, extreme cold or heat, and considerable buffeting. Thus the development of accurate bomb sights for planes became a priority. Much of the work of Claude's team was very boring and dangerous: repeated testing under great varieties of conditions, as well as trying to find solutions that satisfied the often irreconcilable demands of both the users [the armed services] and the government department that paid. One of Claude's personal innovations was to use slow motion photography to record exactly how bombs penetrated their targets, which greatly speeded up testing and gave much better evidence to sceptical paymasters and servicemen.

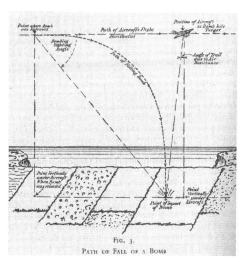

Fig. 3.

Path of Fall of a Bomb

In 1932, Claude was promoted from Squadron Leader to Wing Commander. We don't have his comments on this, but his intense pleasure would have been tempered with reflections that it should have happened several years earlier.

At Woolwich Arsenal, there was no great urgency about the work. They were able to evaluate experiences from the First World War, and to use their experiences from Iraq and other places. Although Mussolini had seized power in Italy and Hitler was a rising force in Germany, the nation's focus was on the financial crisis and the Great Depression. There was not a lot of money to spend on armaments. The politics changed in 1933, but in fact Britain was slow to invest strongly in re-arming their forces until 1937.

In September 1933, Claude was moved, and to his initial horror, he became a civilian. He joined the Air Ministry as an Assistant Director of Armament Research and Development with responsibility for armament; he worked in Room 707 at the Ministry on Kingsway, London. In place of his uniform he sported a natty bow tie; he was now moving in the world of politicians and the RAF high command.

My rank and my identity were at once sunk into the cipher which described my appointment. Plain clothes and a bowler hat were my uniform and I answered my telephone by 'A.D. [R.D. Arm:] speaking'.

Although he could claim much crucial success at this level, he was much better at schmoozing businessmen and inventors than he was with dealing with politicians and the top echelons of the services. An RAF website claims for Claude:

His role in the arming of the RAF over the next three years led to key decisions that were critical for the success of the RAF in the battle of Britain.

With Hitler's ascent to power in 1933, there were elements within the British government and services which saw the urgency of modernizing Britain's armed forces, still little changed from World War I. However, there were powerful forces against change from the traditionalists, who believed their present practices to be near perfect, from those who believed that Hitler was no threat and should be supported or appeased rather than opposed, and from those who argued that it was wrong to spend money on armaments in an economic depression. Claude himself wrote:

Spending government money is a very serious matter in England. In order to obtain money to do so, it was necessary to make out the most exhaustive case, and this receives minute criticism from a chain of experts whose job it is to stop anyone spending anything, if this may be possible. I have always believed that negative information is a valuable purchase, because a succession of failures is often a prelude to a startling success. But this is not the line of thought of the financial advisers – oh dear no! With the greatest of care I used to prepare the details of proposals for my annual budget. Then I had to go 'on the mat' and then justify each item before a cold blooded collection from the finance department.... My first two budgets were pitifully small, but I had been warned to keep them small. My last budget was for the year 1937-1938 and this indicated a complete reversal of policy. I was told that I could ask for more. I did, and my proposals were sent back with instructions to inflate them. The realization of the necessity of re-arming had broken on high places!

In July 1934, as a result of meetings with Air Commodore Sir Arthur Tedder, Claude held an informal conference to consider air gunnery which led to the formation of the 'Air Fighting Committee'. This was a subject close to Claude's heart – after all his Squadron in Iraq had become a legend for their 100% gunnery test scores. This group met to consider how to modernize the RAF. The planes and their armaments used in 1934 were a ragbag of different designs, often highly idiosyncratic and technologically backward. Many planes were still made of light wood and canvas, with guns that fired the same rifle bullets fired by infantrymen. They were slow, easy targets, with little capacity for defending themselves or of doing significant damage to the enemy.

Claude inherited one project from his predecessor at the ministry: gun turrets. In February 1933, two RAF Captains, Frazer-Nash and Thompson, had been awarded a contract for a mock-up of a gun turret, which would hopefully revolutionize the defensive firing of machine guns by the observers – until this point observers had only hand held guns, which were highly inaccurate, needed to shoot through open windows in a plane, and could only be very light [and therefore not powerful]. Frazer-Nash and Thompson invited Claude to Kingston to try their prototype electrically powered turret as soon as he took up his post. Claude was most impressed, and subsequently fought for this development.

It was a long hard battle for Claude to nurture this development from its very awkward first installation in a Demon bomber [see above left] to the ubiquitous turrets in the mass produced Lancaster and Wellington bombers. The RAF were sceptical, and Claude repeatedly sent doubters down for demonstrations; but the financial people ruled that as the Demon bomber was nearly obsolete, the gun turret would not be needed. At this point, Fraser-Nash and Thompson were running out of money, but Claude was able to get enough orders to keep the project running.

Claude helped the development with an innovation of his own: he proposed and developed a beam of light that shone down the length of the barrel of the guns, to show the gunner exactly what he was aiming at. This 'invention' became common practice in all gunnery schools, and Claude applied for the patent for it. However, he alleges that the Ministry 'lost' his patent application, and he was never paid for it.

Frazer-Nash and Thompson were world pioneers of gun turrets, and they rightly got a lot of credit. Above are pictures of them demonstrating their invention to King George VI. However, the real breakthrough on the practical problems came when Claude was on a visit to Paris. He had gone to see the Hotchkis gun works, but it was a holiday, so he couldn't see anything officially, but the manager, Herlanger, was friend, and invited him to lunch at the Cafe de la Paix. Herlanger said that he had a secret gun to show Claude, but Claude already knew about it, so Herlanger challenged him to visit his friend M. De Boysson, who might have something to impress Claude.

Fortified by that ample and excellent lunch, and having yarned pleasantly over coffee and Armagnac, we bundled into a rickety old taxi, and gave the driver the address which Herlanger had scribbled on a piece of the menu. It was a long and bumpy journey, and the driver had some difficulty in finding the address. Eventually he flung open the taxi door and pointing to a shabby double door, he exclaimed 'Voila!' We paid him and clanged a bell. Nothing happened and we were beginning to think that had come on a wild goose chase, when the door opened. A benevolent blonde-headed old man looked out, stroking a pointed beard and looking at us through his pince-nez with one normal and one sightless eye. 'So you are come', and beckoned us inside. I found myself inside a grubby garage annexe, looking at a turret mock-up!

De Boysson had been so disgusted by the indifference shown to his work by the French, that he was prepared to sell to the British. This turret proved the perfect design for the belly and for the tops of planes, the Frazer-Nash design being used for rear gunners. The design was taken up and licensed for manufacture by the British firm of Boulton Paul. Their chief designer, John North [below right], was trying to sell to the Ministry a revolutionary fighter plane, where the pilot was just a chauffeur, and the shooting was wholly done by a gunner in a turret [the Defiant]. The Boulton Paul turret [below left] proved remarkably effective for bombers [though not in the Defiant], and was immediately very popular within the service.

Claude does not feature in the pictures of Frazer-Nash, Thompson and King George V, but he must have met the King at this time, because there is an invitation from the King to Claude to dine at the Palace. Unfortunately, we have no account from Claude of how the dinner went, and there is no year on the invitation, although it almost certainly dates from this period [1936-7].

The Chamberlain *is instructed by* His Majesty The King *to request the honour of* Squadron Leader Keith's Company *at dinner on Sunday Oct 13th at 8.15.* White Mess Kit. The Palace.

One of the first presentations of Claude's new Air Fighting Committee showed that future aircraft should carry eight machine guns capable of firing at least 1,000 rounds per minute. Both the number of guns and the rate of fire was seen as revolutionary at a time when many officers thought four guns were adequate and Air Marshal Brooke-Popham is famously quoted as saying "I think eight guns is going a bit far." As things turned out in World War II, Claude and his team were more than vindicated. Claude noted with pride that in 1936 Britain led the way in gun turrets – that the Americans had not solved the problems, and during a visit to Berlin in 1936 he noted that the Germans had not yet come close.

Once they had agreed on the number of guns and while they were hunting gun turrets, Claude set to work scouring Europe and the world for the best machine guns to put in their planes. The existing guns were made by the British firms, Vickers and BSA, but, despite passionate wooing by Vickers, Claude and his team believed that their guns were too unreliable. They used BSA to manufacture, under license, the best guns of foreign origin that they could find. Whenever possible, they bought examples of all the guns that were available, but they were compelled to travel round Europe and the United States, seeking out the latest experimental prototypes, and getting in their contracts before the opposition. This where Claude was in his element - he was good at charming armament magnates, and good at testing prototypes under constraints of time and place. He also enjoyed it immensely.

Their tour of the machine guns of Europe started in *'dirty and grim'* St. Etienne, where they were booked into a hugely expensive hotel, and greeted like royalty by a crowd that was there to meet them. The owner and designer of the works, M Dharne, an alarming driver, wore a blue smock, looked like a butcher, and *'his big intelligent eyes shone with an alarming ferocity'*, a total hatred of 'les Bosches'. He plied Claude with coffee and brandy at the factory, and then a very good meal en famille. Claude got on well with 'Auntie' – Dharne's spinster sister: he explained the British significance of mistletoe and found it hard to extricate himself!

The second gun they investigated was from Finland – Claude struggled with the language, as the inventor did not speak any other language. Next they took off for the Danuvia company in Budapest, where Claude also found the language impenetrable. However they had fun touring the nightspots of the city: they started drinking tokay in a cafe, and then looked for music and dancing. The Prince of Wales Cafe was painfully correct and dull, and so they moved on to the Parisian Grill, which they entered 'coatless and hatless', which peeved the cloakroom lady.

Then we, three very obvious Britishers, had to get through a foyer in which 'unattended ladies' had to wait until they could acquire an escort to take them into the cafe, as unescorted ladies were not allowed in side. Of course, trying to get through that room was like going through a rugger scrum, and we did not get through in single blessedness. I found that I had collected a dreamy wench of startling dark beauty and a voice of dangerous appeal. I danced once or twice and then we cleared off, on the plea that the long train journey had made us weary. I promised to return the next night, but the bewitching Yska was lovely and I know how frail is human nature – I never did go back!

They met the British Minister [diplomat], who warned them that they would be tailed in Budapest by two different sets of spies [this turned out to be true], they visited the Hungarian Army Deputy Chief of Staff, marvelling at the tight crimson trousers worn by the guards, and then visited the Danuvia works. They were impressed by the most perfect and beautiful gun that was put through its paces for them, but it was too perfect for their use. The Danuvia company entertained them royally:

We visited the stately Houses of Parliament and sipped royal tokay in the lounge; we dined to gypsy music in the Kis-Royale Cafe in ancient Buda; we danced on the illuminated glass floor of the Cafe Capri; and for the whole of one gay night we kept alive on much champagne at the Arizona Night club. I had the idea that I knew a little about city night life, but Budapest made me realize how little. They do not believe in segregating the sexes in their leisure hours, and at the Arizona the thoughtful Bentinck had provided us with gay Hungarian dancing partners. It was the usual routine with foreign visitors, he told me, but he added that there had been some difficulty when the Japanese had come, as Hungarian girls did not like the smell of them!

This last sentence gives an insight to the game Claude was playing: all the powers were doing the same as the British, trawling the world for the best arms for the next war.

Next Claude and his team went to Switzerland. Here they had the best shots and the best machine guns in the world. Given a demonstration of the Furrer machine gun, Claude asked if he could buy some, but was turned down.

The old colonel raised his eyebrows. "Because they are secret," he exclaimed. I asked why we had been allowed to see them. "Because I wanted to give you the joy of seeing the finest machine gun in the world," was his laughing reply, "and I knew it would be quite impossible for you to copy it from what you have seen." He was right ... but it would not have suited our purposes...

Whilst in this part of Switzerland I welcomed the chance of looking over the Arms Factory at Solothurn. When we went there it was completely idle, having already served its purpose. During that time when the German nation had been prohibited from the manufacture of arms, the Solothurn Company had undoubtedly done much useful work for the Hun. The factory had been designed and then chopped and changed as experience was gained, until it represented the ideal layout for mass-production of machine guns. As soon as it had been perfected, it closed down and I doubt not that dozens exactly like it sprang into existence all over Germany.

This cat and mouse arms race with the Germans was not a straightforward tale of outright enmity. Later in 1936 Claude visited Berlin, having arrived via Prague to avoid letting the Germans know they had been to Budapest first. The Germans received them courteously, and their hosts, Lowenstein and Herring of the Borsiz Arms firm, were very friendly.

[In WWI] Herring had been 'ditched' when the Scharnhorst was sunk during the Falklands battle. He had been rescued and imprisoned in Donnington Hall. He was one of the crowd who broke loose during the autumn of 1917, through an amazing tunnel they had dug. I was serving at Cranwell at the time. All of us who had our own cars were given unlimited petrol to go out and scour the countryside for escaped Germans. We did not find any, but we all rendez-voused in Nottingham that evening and had a grand party. Herring told me that he had been at large for three days, and then walked slap into the arms of the Camp Adjutant in Piccadilly! He got six months hard labour for 'damaging His Majesty's foundations', but he did not seem to bear us any ill will. On my last night in Berlin we gave dinner to Lowenstein and Herring at the Adlon Hotel. As we said goodbye, Herring shook me warmly by the hand and said, "You know we were fools to fight each other in 1914. It must never happen again." Did he know then what was brewing for 1939?

They were given very impressive demonstrations of the German machine guns, which seemed very reliable and easy to manufacture, but they were unimpressed by the bigger 'cannon' developed by the Germans with the Solothurn company. They had a terrifying incident when Lowenstein's car broke down in the middle of one of the new autobahns, leaving them stranded as cars tore past on either side of them.

Above: Claude [centre] and his ministry team, with Thompson on Claude's left.

Despite all the European manoeuvrings, in the end Claude and his colleagues plumped for the American Browning machine guns for the RAF, made by Colt at Hartford. The other decision they made was that if they were going to have twice the number of guns as previously, they would have to be mounted in the wings of the plane, a revolutionary idea, which required a lot of work on how to get accurate sights for the pilot. They designed the 'Hendy Heck' – a flying laboratory for gunnery to try out all the new ideas. Thompson and Claude took off to America in a Cunard liner, the Aquitania, and visited the Colt factory and also various US military establishments such as West Point and Langley Field. Connecticut and West Virginia were 'dry' states, which presented challenges getting hold of their gin and whiskey. At the US air development base in Dayton, Ohio, they saw a lot of interesting work on bomb sights. They learned that the Americans were encountering a lot of similar problems with development work, and were finding similar solutions, but they were often kept at arms' length from seeing the details – they were allowed to see a P.41 fighter in Dayton, but only in the distance, but then they wangled a closer look in Detroit.

On visits such as these one has to develop a sort of photographic mind, for it is not done to take notes as you go along. Back in our hotel, of an evening, Thompson and I set to and wrote up our impressions, and compared notes. It is rather like one of those dreadful party games when you are given five seconds sight of a tray of various objects, and then they are covered up and you have to write down as many as you can remember.

Claude and Thompson were entertained, but found American women a mixed blessing:

They were certainly a joy to behold, but their voices were hard and insistent whilst their candour when discussing delicate matters was quite embarrassing.

After Detroit they visited mobster-era Chicago, where Claude was impressed that his hotel boasted that all its beds were made of steel and were bullet proof! They were impressed by one of their hosts who proceeded to eat his huge cigar and to spit jets of tobacco across his office, hitting the cuspidor every time. Thompson and Claude, now with a raging cold, next went to St. Louis and to Scott Field, Belleville, to discuss how to protect artillery observers from friendly fire. From St. Louis they flew back to New York and Hartford to firm up the contracts to manufacture Browning machine guns in Britain.

The introduction of a new weapon such as a machine gun into service is a big undertaking. Training must be organized so that all personnel may become fully conversant with the new weapon, and they have to be taught the proper names of hundreds of new and unfamiliar parts. Changes are not popular with users; to begin with, pilots looked askance at the Browning. Once drawings and specifications were ready, we lost no time in placing orders with firms in this country. It was this Browning which saved the BSA gun shop from taking on bicycle manufacture. Our choice of the new gun received it s baptismal trials when our fighters went into battle against the German bomber hordes. The sterling reliability of the Browning won it a place of great affection and reliance with fighter pilots. They were able to give the guns a more realistic testing than we could ever devised in peace time conditions. Thank God the guns did not fail!

Apart from machine guns, the RAF also needed more powerful guns – cannons – in order to enable their planes to shoot at armoured vehicles, tanks and installations on the ground. The two candidates for this were from the Oerlikon Company of Zurich, Switzerland, and the Hispano Company of Paris. The pictures below show Claude, Thompson [in the bowler hat], and others trying out an Oerlikon cannon in a Swiss valley, examining the damage, and then sitting down to a picnic.

Hispano were a company that made automobiles and aero engines, but because they were having a dispute with Oerlikon over supplies of guns for their aeroplanes, one of their designers, who had originally been a Swiss clockmaker, decided to design a gun. The French government gave Claude and his team permission to see the gun, and later permission to buy six guns, but it took a lot of bargaining and 'quid pro quos' with the French government before Hispano were allowed to set up a factory in Britain to make guns for the British. The factory had to be built secretly under the name 'British Manufacture and Research Company'. It finally opened near Grantham in January 1939; the King and Queen and the Duke and Duchess of Gloucester were among the guests with Claude and Thompson, who, as the only person with an umbrella on a rainy day, was very popular.

The gun only fired 60 rounds before it needed re-loading, which was unpopular with pilots, but once they saw how destructive the 60 shells could be, blasting holes where many machine bullets had made little impression, they were quickly converted. The Hispano cannon was also harder to make, and difficult to mount in the planes, but its ability to destroy large targets, including whole trains, made it indispensible as the war progressed, and Claude, as well as praising many others who played their part, was personally immensely proud of the success.

Below left: Hispano cannon being used as light Anti-Aircraft gun, with [inset] Dennis Kendall, who set up the factory in England. Right: Hispano cannon being mounted in fighter planes.

In the course of the re-arming of Britain, Claude had to deal with people he called 'the merchants of death' – the independent arms dealers and gun runners, many of whom were

171

very colourful characters. Captain John Ball lived in a secret house in London, scruffy from the outside but stuffed with priceless art treasures inside – he often sold arms for art or for gold. He entertained Claude and Gwen with a tour of his treasures: Etruscan gold, Japanese swords, Louis Quinze furniture, Buddha shrines.

Ball was amusing, direct and honest, which made him a rarity in his business. Other dealers tried to sell the British government bogus new inventions for various things such as cutting enemy telephone/telegraph lines from planes. Many German and Austrian Jews and anti-Nazis were defecting with weapons or devices from Hitler's war effort. One such man, called Mohaupt, gave a demonstration of his armour piercing explosive which could be used on gun propelled grenades. The demonstration took place in a quarry in Switzerland, near the German border. It got very dark in the evening so they adjourned for the night, only to find that the Germans had crossed the border in the night and stolen back all the armour plates that had been blasted the previous afternoon. However, Claude had seen enough, and taken enough photographs to be able to replicate it back in England.

They also had to deal with a Norwegian who had patented some torpedo dropping gear, but they were sure that he was simultaneously selling it to the Germans, despite assurances to the contrary. But the Norwegian fell out with the Germans, and revealed that the Germans had been spying on British tests being carried out in the Solent, by filming from the Lloyds mail steamers that berthed at Southampton. After that the Royal Navy put on specially misleading shows whenever a Lloyds ship passed.

They had several dealings with men trying to sell them 'super-explosives'. One smuggled it into Britain in a tube of toothpaste. Another left a consignment of 'super-explosive' in the cloakroom of Charing Cross station for 'safety'! A third, who called his explosive 'Totalite', demonstrated his product at Zurich University. He had wild long yellow hair, a frantic way of declaiming the virtues of his explosive, and he assured them that it was safe to strike it violently, terrifying Claude's assistant.

The salesman for Oerlikon, Antoine Gazda, was a racing driver, who loved to drive Claude and others at insane speeds around the Swiss alpine roads, and also flying a plane at dangerously slow speeds around the mountains and lakes. He also gave demonstrations of firing across agricultural fields, where men worked – *"They seldom get hurt."*

Another wild looking gun salesman, with a mass of grey hair that flowed in every direction, was an American named Accles, who had been a friend of William Cody in the Wild West, but who now made an astoundingly different machine gun in Birmingham. Unfortunately, the ammunition feed worked on gravity, so the gun would not work in a plane when flying upside down. Accles is thus best known for his other invention – the Accles Cattle Killer.

Claude enjoyed dealing with these people, and also with the boffins within the British military establishment:

There were, and are, many very interesting personalities on the staffs of our own technical establishments. Unfortunately, the best brains do not always go with the easiest natures, and 'private wars' between members of staff can greatly hamper the orderly progress of investigations. I have always found it worthwhile to make a careful study of the susceptibilities of 'spike' individuals, so that they may be handled with due care. It is possible to get a tiger to purr – but it has got to be done in the right way and it needs a lot of patience and bravery!

In November, 1937, Claude was appointed Station Commander of Worthy Down, an air base north of Winchester. At that time it was a large, busy base, with three squadrons based there. He remained as Station Commander there until August 1938. This is a curious interlude in his career: it isn't clear why he was suddenly sent there at a time when the arms procurement race was in such a critical stage. The only mention Claude makes of it is in I Hold My Aim:

I enjoyed my three strenuous years at the War Ministry, but I was glad to escape and go to Command my own station at Worthy Down – to be able to wear uniform again and to have my own service family of officers NCOs and airmen. I did not enjoy it for long. The following year I was promoted and appointed as RAF Member to the Ordnance Board!

In 1938 he was promoted to Group Captain, and elevated to the Ordnance Board. This body had existed since 1414, based at Woolwich Arsenal:

The Ordnance Board is a dignified body, and a place thereon is, to many, the ultimate goal of their ambitions ... the business is carried out in sub-committees and thrashed out at a full Board meeting twice a week ... the Board is law unto itself, in that its word is final and can never be upset ...... it caters for all the technical requirements of armaments for all three services throughout the Empire ... slow it may be, but it certainly is sound. It takes the newcomer some

time to get into its stride, but once he has been deemed worthy of appointment, he is at once made to feel one with them. At least in one sense he is 'arrive', and for centuries after he has departed his photograph will be preserved in the gallery of departed members, decorating the walls of the sombre corridors. The outside world knows little or nothing of this institution, and the Board recks little of the outside world. The stranger within its guarded gates is never invited to linger.

Claude was obviously thrilled to be a member of this arcane and powerful group. The Navy had five members, the Army four, and the RAF three members. In addition there were three secretaries, and a department of 'ballisticians'. Claude led a very comfortable life:

I was become a technical machine – or perhaps I should say, a little cog in a great machine. I was required to move smoothly and do my part, but whilst I must never lag, there was no possibility of hurrying unduly. When I left my office, my job stopped until I arrived the following morning – like myself, it slumbered during the dark hours and only awoke to life when I was at hand to rustle my way  *through the mass of complicated files which poured ceaselessly into our offices. I and my wife lived in an exceedingly comfortable flat in Dolphin Square [pictured], and I journeyed to and fro in my car over twelve miles through darkest London, mostly over tram lines. I led an ordered, unruffled life, during which everything possible was done that I might make the best use of what little brain and learning the good God had given me.*

When we think of the hideous bungles of recent military procurement, of delays and write-offs, it is remarkable how good a job was done before World War II, when any mistakes would have been fatal for the nation. Claude's own account obviously focuses on the successes, but the ultimate result was defeat for Hitler and Nazism.

Chapter 19 World War II: Station Commander, RAF Marham

Occasionally we Members of the Board of Ordnance went away to visit works, attend conferences or witness trials. The morning of Friday 1st September 1939 found me with a large number of officers out on the marshes at the Experimental Station at Shoeburyness, intent on some urgent and important Air Force trials. It was a glorious still morning of early autumn, and the fresh sea air had livened us all. Suddenly a gunner sergeant-major came running across to us. He halted, out of breath, and then stammered out, "News just received, sir, that the Germans have invaded Poland and there has been fighting since dawn." So it had come. The trend of the previous day had left little doubt in the minds of anyone, but now the thing had come about: another war was upon us. It was with very mixed thoughts that I sat on a grassy bank and watched the trials go through. How was it all going to develop?

In our little flat we listened to Chamberlain's speech on the following Sunday morning, and we knew that we were once more at war with Germany. Within a few minutes the air was filled with the wail of the air raid sirens. We had been schooled to know their meaning, and what we should do. I bundled my wife off to the shelter and dashed off to lock up my car, which was in the street. As I ran, a bewildered labourer asked me "What's this?" As I ran, I shouted to him, "It looks like Hitler's answer." But of course it wasn't, and some weeks later I met the charming French technical attaché who had caused the alarm by landing at Croydon in a plane which had not been identified.

Gradually the minor discomforts of war descended on us. For weeks we got used to the wail of 'L-I-G-H-T-S' as some delinquent was warned that a crack of light was showing from his flat windows. The hours of daylight dwindled and my office hours increased so I knew that it wouldn't be long before I was driving home under 'blackout' conditions. In something like a fit of hysteria, the great and staid Board of Ordnance uprooted itself from its traditional home and hopped off to a temporary country residence, where confusion and discomfort reigned for many days. My Gwen, my wife, was called up for her Red Cross work, and sent off to cope with an influx of volunteer nurses, cooks, dispensers, masseuses and clerks at the Royal Herbert Hospital at Woolwich, and had to live in a nearby billet. Left to my own resources, I summoned an aged spinster, Miss Frith, to 'do' for me, but my home was never the same when Gwen left it. I still ran to and fro in the car, but the going was more difficult, my hours were longer and my midday meal had to consist of sandwiches.

Claude and Gwen made arrangements to put their possessions in storage, and planned to move into digs together in Eltham. But their plans came to nothing: on the very day in November 1939 that Claude was going to apply to leave the Board of Ordnance and return to the RAF, he got a notification that he was leaving the Board. It took him several days to find that he was being given command of the air base at Marham, a large bomber station in Norfolk, between Norwich and King's Lynn. The serving commander there was surprised, because he himself had only taken over there six weeks previously, and was very much enjoying it.

Claude gave way to a wave of depression. He didn't want to be separated from Gwen, who was indispensible in her job in Woolwich, the weather and smog was foul, and his Great-Aunt, Nell Keith, had died the previous month:

She had died as she had always lived – as an autocratic patriot. Her end was undoubtedly accelerated by her breathing defiance at two errand boys who had jeered at the union jacks she had hung from the window of her house. The war had created a beastly atmosphere in London.

At Marham, which Claude saw as being a world away from his beloved London, he had two squadrons of Wellington bombers, 70 RAF personnel, a battery of anti-aircraft gunners, and about three dozen WAAFs on site. It was, at that time, the largest RAF air base. The RAF officers were drawn from all countries of the British Empire and as well as all corners of the British Isles. Claude was anxious about the WAAFs: at the first dance on the base, they seemed dangerously close to the men, and Claude quoted the case of his cousin Pauline Heath, who as a WAAF driver had been sent to the other end of the country due to her CO falling in love with her and proposing marriage. He could have quoted a few cases from twenty years previously where he himself had got involved with female personnel under his command. However, soon afterwards a very strict order was issued, forbidding WAAFs from having any off duty contact with the men on the base, although it made no provision for what happened off the base.

In some ways, life at Marham rapidly improved for Claude. He quickly got back into the routine of mess life, of Christmas parties and making himself obeyed but popular with his charges. It appears that Gwen was allowed to leave London and join him, and he was also looked after by Flint, the *'unique'* manservant who had worked for them at Worthy Down. Cook, his service driver, and Chou-Chou, their Japanese spaniel, completed the household.

However, he was confined to his quarters for a week because of 'a cough of long standing'. Claude had been of delicate health ever since he caught the chest infection in Tierra del Fuego in 1914, and had been obliged to recuperate at the Linford Sanatorium, having been warned that his illness was life threatening. Claude seldom referred to his health in his writings, but it is clear that the RAF took the view that he wasn't in good health, and some of the moves that transferred Claude during World War II were most probably due to legitimate concerns about his health. In March 1940 he wrote:

Marham is 'strong air' and I don't seem to have the energy I had in London town – or perhaps old age is suddenly falling on me. At the end of this year I shall have scored my half century. This war depresses me, compared with the last. Why, I wonder? Is it because I am so much older? Is it because I miss the gaiety of France? Is it the grim methodical beastliness of these days? I think that the blackout is a curse that weighs heavily on everyone. The last was 'my' war, but this is not: I am merely become a peg upon which hangs heavily much responsibility and anxiety.

Whilst he was recuperating at Christmas 1939, he listened to the wireless a lot. He reminded people that back when he worked for Marconi, before World War I, he had suggested to his bosses that they should consider broadcasting dance music to the masses, an idea which was not taken up at that time, but which clearly became an enormous phenomenon since then.

The winter of 1939-1940 saw some extraordinarily cold weather. Claude ensured that Marham was one of the few bases which remained operational throughout the heavy snowfalls [pictured left]. It was reported that the German navy became stuck in sea ice off the Heligoland Bight, and thus uniquely vulnerable to being bombed; Claude's squadrons were raring to go, but the order from the ministry did not come until the sea ice had melted, and the German navy had escaped.

Claude found his role as a Station Commander challenging – the weight of responsibility for a soft-hearted man could be crushing:

There seem to be three stages in the life's work of a man: firstly he is hired for what he can do, then for the experience he has gained during the first stage, and finally he is merely required to accept responsibility. When one is in the first or second stage, how easy does the third stage seem! The 'heads' never seem to do much or put themselves out, for when there comes something to be done, they always seem to be able to off-load it upon someone else. But responsibility may bring more anxiety and be more wearying than either of the subordinate stages. In letters from my 'higher command' the phrase 'the personal responsibility of the Station Commander' occurs ad nauseam. In the last war, for a while, I myself was doing much the same sort of work that is undertaken by my squadrons now ... yet one got along quite easily. I was in the first stage then. Today I am in the last stage, and often I feel quite effete and impotent, when I dish out orders for others to go out and risk their all. 'The decision is left to Station Commanders' – what if they make the wrong decisions?

I prowl around my office like a caged beast, sometimes. It is the nerve centre of all activities, the buffer between those who do and those of the higher command, who require to be done. No one ever comes to see me but to report some trouble or irregularity which I must sort out. When 'the Station Master has decided', and I hear a mighty roar above my head, and I see the grim forms of bombers passing overhead, off on some perilous quest, I go to my window and gaze at them as they tail away into the distance. I find myself standing there, looking vacantly into the immutable inverted bowl of heaven, my hands clenched and my lips murmuring "God go with you." What else can I do? For hours their safety must lie heavily on me. I pick up the telephone and demand to be told when the first word comes in of their return, and then I try to put them out of my mind, and take up the banal threads of the administration of this great complex 'family' which is under my charge.

But it isn't so easy. I find myself looking at the desk clock, and wondering if they have yet reached the extremity of their allotted patrol. What has happened on the way? I gaze at the sky, and wonder whether their weather favours or endangers their flight. Time lags intolerably, and it seems an infinite time before their estimated return arrives. Just as I am about to ring up 'Operations', they call me, with the heartening news that the 'return call' has come in. I order my car, and am soon whirling down to the watch office. The Medical Officer is stepping out of the ambulance and the Intelligence Officer soon arrives, holding a sheath of forms in his arms. His duty is to interrogate the captains of the aircraft directly they land, and to flash off a signal to higher command, which will whet their appetite for the fuller details which will follow later on. The Fire Tender driver starts up his engine: one can never be sure, and an engine that won't start in an emergency may spell disaster.

Claude follows these paragraphs by recounting a case of a patrol of fifteen Wellingtons that went out in deteriorating weather. Twelve planes got back safely, but the remaining three were missing. Two of those planes then landed at other bases away from Marham, reporting that the last plane had a problem with its undercarriage. Claude worried about the pilot's pregnant wife, and about 'his boys'. Eventually, they learned that the plane had successfully landed under difficult circumstances. Everything seemed okay, and Claude went for a cheery dinner. But during the dinner he was phoned by high command, and ordered to arrest one of the pilots involved for allegedly bombing a forbidden target!

I went over to wake up the unfortunate Glencross, and put him under arrest. He had been up since dawn, had flown over the North Sea for some six hours, and had then had a sticky landing away from his station – and then to be placed under arrest! However 'orders is orders'. And the next day was Christmas Day!' The following noon, I got permission to release him 'without prejudice', and finally it was upheld that he had bombed a permissible target, and the whole affair fizzled out.

However, later that Christmas Day it was revealed that the other plane that had come down did not have faulty radio gear or a faulty undercarriage, so the radio operator and pilot were in line to be arrested for faking the problems. Luckily they then found a broken filament that created an intermittent fault, so that charge was also rescinded. These incidents show clearly that Claude was on the side of his airmen, and not being the most diplomatic of men, he may have already upset some in high command, even before 1939 was out.

Glencross, a daredevil pilot whom Claude obviously saw as a bit like him in his younger days, was later arrested for an emergency landing in Guernsey – he alleged that he had run out of petrol. However, Claude recalled that Glencross had a girlfriend in Guernsey, and it then emerged that Glencross had two WAAFs in his plane when he had come down in Guernsey! Although he escaped a court martial, he was transferred away from Marham.

Claude also instituted a reform across all bombers in January 1940, laying down what survival supplies would be put in the life rafts for bombers that came down over water. His list was taken up by the whole force.

At first, the patrols and missions from Marham were not too dangerous, being mainly out over the North Sea. In February they started night missions over Germany, but they were dropping propaganda leaflets, and Claude speculated that the Germans might put up more defence against bombs.

On 20th February 'the luck of Marham' finally ran out, and they had their first fatality; a bomber flying into a Thames estuary barrage balloon, crashing and sinking. Claude dreaded writing to the pilot's mother. In March there were more fatalities: a Sergeant Evans 'fell out of the sky' when towing a target for gunnery practice over Sutton Bridge. Then Claude returned from a couple of days leave to find that three had died in a crash, and three others had survived but were terribly burned. One of the dead, a young lad called Fanshaw had, before his death, invited his mother to a stand-up supper at Marham, and Claude had talked at length to her.

She seemed very apprehensive at her only son flying ... but what could I say?

On the Saturday after Good Friday, we held a funeral service for poor young Fanshaw in the dear little village church at Marham. Then they took his body away to Winchester, for interment in the family tomb. I had all the mourners to my house, before, to meet the padre, and afterwards, to tea, before they went back. They sorrowed deeply but they bore up nobly, and I coined a new epigram: 'The better the breed, the stiffer the lip.'

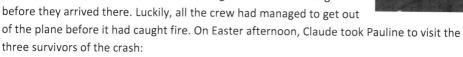

Over that weekend, Claude had 'Pingo' to stay. Pingo was Wing Commander Lester, the CO who was madly in love with Claude's cousin Pauline Heath [right]; she was staying with Claude due to her having an in-growing toenail taken out by Claude's Medical Officer. On Easter Saturday, there was a report of another crash, and they jumped into Claude's car, and could see the flames rising from the wreck long before they arrived there. Luckily, all the crew had managed to get out of the plane before it had caught fire. On Easter afternoon, Claude took Pauline to visit the three survivors of the crash:

Stathan looked a bit knocked about and his eyes were two pools of blood, but he will be all right. The sergeant was pale, had a broken arm and a few burns, but he will be all right. But Curler! It was my duty to go and see him – yet I dreaded it. I had to keep a brave face, or he might have guessed – for he hadn't seen himself in a mirror. Oh God: I came home and dreamed of him. They had treated his horribly burned face with tannic acid, and that had sent all his head black. It was swollen to such a grotesque size, and his eyes showed up as two blood red slits. His nose seemed eaten away, his lips were swollen to those of a nigger and an unearthly red. And he, gallant fellow, even tried to smile at me – I could have wept. Oh God: why did this have to happen? As I went away, the Matron said to me, "He may live to curse us all for keeping him alive."

The fatalities kept coming: in early April, on a lovely day when Claude played hockey while his planes were out, news came in of the squadron being attacked by Messerschmidt 110s, and two planes were lost with their entire crews. Claude arranged for the widows and mothers to be told, or told them himself. Of course, there was lots of talk about 'giving it back to the Hun', and the ship they had been attacking was reported sunk, but as the war spread and deepened, there was little good news.

Marham was obviously a showpiece airfield, because Claude received a stream of important visitors there, including the Marshal of the RAF, Lord Trenchard, who came with the head of Bomber Command, and later visitors included three American Air Attaches, and numerous other 'top brass'. On the left, top: Air Chief Marshal Sir Edgar Ludlow-Hewitt awards the first DFM of the war at Marham. Middle: Claude with the Secretary of State for Air and Jack Baldwin, AOC for No 3 Group. Bottom: Claude watches Baldwin decorate a wireless operator with the DFM.

At the bottom of every bill for purchases comes that significant little item – the price! As I listen to the heartening news of the spectacular successes of our air forces, I have grown to wait with fear in my heart for the last words. When I hear "All of our aircraft have returned safely", I breathe a sigh of relief, but when the news ends with "One of our aircraft is missing" or "Two of our aircraft failed to return", I know that this is the price. It probably passes unnoticed by many of the thousands who listen to that news, but how bitter it is to those of us who <u>know</u>.

In April 1940, Claude's squadrons were hunting for and then attacking the German cruisers, including the Scharnhorst, in the Norwegian fiords, although some moved to more northerly air bases to do this. Eventually, they had huge success, but the price paid was high. On 11th April Claude reports that two planes were lost, but that others, despite being shot full of holes, had got home safely.

It was young Chester-Master, the rear gunner, who had parachuted from Wickencamp's aircraft. His wife had pathetically wired me, asking if there mightn't be a chance of his being a prisoner. I dared not encourage her to hope, and yet Mills now says that there might be some tiny chance of his having been saved, IF the Germans didn't shoot him on the way down and IF a merchant ship in the vicinity managed to get to him. I wonder! Please God it may be so.

One of the new widows, Jean Wardlaw, who had been married less than a week, came to stay with Claude and Gwen. Only two days later, another raid on the Norwegian fiords led to more losses, including Barber, whose plane had just been patched up from the previous raid, and also Claude's personal favourite, Squadron Leader Nolan, with his second pilot Maybury and his gunner Brundish.

All newly married, and Nolan the soundest of the sound, and as gallant and charming a man as one might wish to meet. His influence was splendid: his example shining. His loss hurts me more than any of the others. Today Jean Wardlaw asked if she might bring Mrs Maybury to stay with us, as she was 'in a bad state', and her parents were not treating her in the wisest of ways. We agreed. At tea-time Bruce, my adjutant, rang up, and said that Mrs Brundish had just motored over to see her husband! He had broken the news to her, and she is also staying with us tonight. A sad house of young widows, with both of us sorely put to it to know how to be as kind as we possibly can. In the afternoon Gwen and I had visited the survivors of Stathan's and Powell's crashes, in Littleport Hospital. All are doing well, except poor Carter, and truly it were better he might die.

So many and such difficult 'human problems' have had to be faced and dealt with as best as we could. We are in a particular position, in that we are working active operations from this station, set in the English country. The COs of Army or RAF detachments operating in France or abroad never come into contact with widows and relatives of those who are killed on service. Here it is unavoidable. Distraught widows bring their troubles to my wife and myself, and I have to help them gather up the threads of their lives, and face a future which appears to them to be utterly blank. In all this my wife is just splendid, and a tower of strength to me.

Next day they lost another aircraft and crew, though this time there was only one widow to inform and console. Mrs Brundish returned to Leicester, Mrs Tucker-Bell was placed with colleagues, and Claude sent for Mrs Maybury's parents. Poor Carter finally died.

A week later, Claude and Gwen were still embroiled with sorting out widows. Mrs Maybury had refused to see her mother, and was proving a very difficult presence round Claude's house; Claude wrote "*I don't like her and nothing would induce me to let her stay here. I consider her a selfish, bad type*". Meanwhile Jean Wardlaw, who had been to school in San Remo with Gwen's niece, proved to be brave and delightful. '*Brave little*' Mrs Nolan had visited them, and there had been the sombre church services, including a funeral for Carter, whose father, who had lost a leg in World War I, attended. Claude arranged for 'poor broken' Mrs Tucker Bell, who was 'in a bad way, and her needs were urgent', to be given a place in the WAAFs, and Claude sent his Medical Officer over to see her.

On 3rd May, Charles Graves of the Daily Mail came over to Marham to do a feature on the air crews there. He interviewed Claude, who told him that the air crews should get duty free tobacco as the forces serving overseas enjoyed, and also gave the journalist a word picture he had written for a painting that was to be done for the Marham mess. Claude was disappointed by the results: Graves said that he was going to use Claude's word painting in his upcoming book, which Claude was unhappy with, stating that he owned the copyright, and as for the Mail article:

Charles Graves only produced one article on this place, and it was utterly feeble. How can he get paid for such stuff? He used most of my description for Turner's picture in his article.

"Marham takes off for Berlin"

In May, with Germany's invasion of Holland, attention switched from Norway to targets in Holland and the Ruhr. There was a brief period before the Germans organized their defences in these areas when the bombing was relatively safe and productive, and then the casualties started to mount again. Claude was also ecstatic that the fighters that he helped to arm were proving very successful:

Marvellous news: six of our 8 gun fighters set on 24 enemy aircraft and routed them, shot down many and all our six got safely back! What are those people feeling now, who opposed us when I was at the Air Ministry and fighting to get 8 gun fighters approved?

The fighting intensified:

23rd May 1940: So much happens in such a short while these days, that I get muddled in my memory of events. Yesterday I snatched a short 24 hours respite, and dashed up to London, stewed off nearly 2 lbs in a Turkish bath and attended my Lodge meeting in the evening. We had an almost a record small meeting – only eight, but it was nice to see familiar faces again. Marham has been on almost 'maximum effort' during the past week – doing no good to the German lines of communication! This moon has been a gift for location of targets at night, and the many burning Belgian and French towns have acted as beacons to direct our fellows. For three nights I averaged two hours sleep, so the days were pretty grim. I fell asleep in my bath on Sunday morning!

In the same entry, Claude detailed three more crews lost that week, and the widows and children left behind. The international news was grim, with France falling to the German advance. However, he maintained that the spirit at Marham was *'splendid'*. During one of the operations, there was the annual Sergeant's Ball, which Claude attended with Gwen and her sister Elfrida, but Claude had to keep leaving to supervise the operation.

Coming out after one such visit, I was hailed by a slightly sozzled 'Tommy'. "Show me the way to Hut 103, chum," he pleaded. "I would if I knew it," I told him. Then he drew back and looked at me carefully in the moonlight. He gasped out, "Lord God Almighty," and fell back. I laughed and told him, "You're quite wrong. It's only the Station Commander." "Aye, but that's a ruddy sight worse, for me."

We had several fat targets in the Ruhr area last week. The night wasn't good, but most of our lads did good work. Strangely, the area wasn't well 'blacked out', and although there were myriad searchlights, the AA was feeble. The humour and the joy of the pilot's verbal reports never get into the cold official reports. The atmosphere of the operations room, as the crews come in, is astounding. The air is heavy with smoke. Mountains of sandwiches pile the table. Everyone is clutching a mug of tea or cocoa or Bovril. Lounging wearily, still in their flying kit, they swap yarns of their efforts. Rank is mutually forgotten. The variety of accents is amazing. Canada argues it out with New Zealand. Australia differs with Scotland. Little Sergeant Gibbs has enjoyed himself thoroughly: "I found two oven doors open, sir," he told me, "so I put a parcel into each, and the whole ruddy works came up and nearly hit us." He had scored three direct hits on a coking oven. Quiet rugged Donaldson, who hails from Vancouver, did a pretty piece of work when he found an MT park in a forest and let them have it with all he carried. "I started no ordinary fireworks amongst them, I surely did," he told us. Gerry, his ever smiling 2nd pilot who hails from Alberta, had taken out a flash camera to record the results, but hadn't had any luck on that trip. Five months ago I asked for those cameras, and they have only just come.

Once again, Claude was ahead of the curve: a few weeks later, word came from the ministry that taking photographs was now 'frightfully important'.

And then, later on, perhaps all are down except one or even two. In the bustle and excitement of interrogating the returning crews, one may forget those who have NOT returned. I go outside and strain my ears for the sound of aero engines. So selective and sensitive my ears have become, that I can now pick out a returning aircraft long before most people. I locate myself where I am sheltered from the rustle of the wind around the walls or among the young poplar trees, which are planted around the heavy blast proof walls of the operations block. I hold my breath until my every heartbeat sounds like a sledge hammer in my ears. Then I catch a faint rhythmic drone and turn to establish from where it is coming – murmuring a prayer the while. But I am sometimes fooled, for we are not the only station involved in these nights, and it may be a stranger who is seeking the shelter or our vast aerodrome, rather than face an extended journey to his own base up in the Yorkshire area. The cold grey dawn will be breaking when I am out, listening for those who have not yet shown up. Strange figures stagger about, clad in their cumbersome flying clothes ...

On 27th May Claude reported a *'grand do'* attacking Brussels and Antwerp, after which Donaldson was feted by the BBC anonymously for his exploits. It was a day of national prayer called for by the King, so Claude got *'a bellyful of church-going'*. In early June Marham cancelled its Sports Day, because they were on flat out operations, but the widows whom Claude had invited came to stay anyway. Claude had to have his creaky hip x-rayed in London – he defiantly writes that he can still play hockey and squash 'with a few twinges'.

On 2nd June, Claude was visited by Harry Balfour, Under-secretary of State, with his parliamentary Private Secretary, Wakefield. Claude knew and liked them both: Balfour went to Claude's old school, St Lawrence, and Wakefield had been at Cranwell with Claude. However, Claude may have blotted his copybook with them by showing them how Marham could not be defended in the event of a German attack without new equipment. He was told that none was available. Lord Trenchard visited Marham four days later with a personal message of support for all there.

On 4th June, Claude wrote about two of his pilots who had been killed on 30th May at the evacuation of the BEF at Dunkirk. The first was the daredevil Glencross, who survived being shot down, and then survived hiding out in a forest which got bombed by the British, only for the British destroyer that rescued him to be sunk by a German submarine. The second pilot killed that day was Vivian Rosewarne, who became very famous:

Young Rosewarne failed to return from co-operation bombing which we were doing to help the BEF get out of Belgium. It wasn't a good night, as there was cloud about. Donaldson and the others said they saw what appeared to be an aircraft, on fire amidships, going down from about 6,000 feet, and Rosewarne was in that locality at that time. Please god I may get news that some have escaped ... Here is an amazing letter left by Rosewarne to be sent to his mother. I had to read it, to check the contents, in case anything forbidden was disclosed. It just made me want to go out and weep when I read it. I am going to ask if I may get it published anonymously. Comment on such a letter would be sacrilege, but it makes me feel I am not fit to have licked his boots. What must that poor mother be feeling to have lost such a son!

The letter was indeed published and went on to become the most famous piece of propaganda in the whole British war effort. The following is taken from the Wikipedia article on the letter:

On 30 May 1940 a force of 17 Wellington Bombers from RAF Marham took off to provide close ground support to the British Expeditionary Force as they withdrew from the beaches of Dunkirk. Aircraft R3162 from No. 38 Squadron RAF was shot down near the town of Veurve in Belgium and the six-man crew were killed. The co-pilot, Flying Officer Vivian Rosewarne, was reported missing, believed killed on 31 May 1940. His station commander, Group Captain Claude Hilton Keith, found a letter among the missing airman's personal possessions. It had been left open, so that it could be passed by the censor. Group Captain Keith was so moved by the letter that, with the mother's permission, it was anonymously published in The Times on 18 June 1940.

On this day Winston Churchill announced, in his *"This Was Their Finest Hour"* speech to the House of Commons that the "battle of France is over. I expect that the Battle of Britain is about to begin". The Times was inundated with over 10,000 requests for copies in the first few days after publication. The letter was subsequently published in a small book by The Times Publishing Company Ltd (as An Airman's Letter to His Mother) and reprinted three times. By the end of the year over 500,000 copies had been sold. King George VI wrote personally to the mother. In the

USA the book was reprinted 12 times by E.P. Dutton & Co. Suggestions that the letter was fictitious and propaganda eventually led to the identification of Flying Officer Rosewarne and his death notice was finally published on 23 December 1940. In 1941 Michael Powell released a short documentary-style British propaganda film, also called An Airman's Letter to His Mother, featuring the voice of John Gielgiud. A portrait of Flying Officer Rosewarne (painted from his mother's photographs) by Frank O. Salisbury was unveiled on 18 September 1941 and although his mother attended she wished to remain anonymous desiring to be known only as "the mother of the young unknown warrior". Rosewarne's letter continues to inspire and his letter features in the RAF's publication *Leadership*. The following pictures of Rosewarne come from his Commanding Officer Group Captain C. H. Keith's personal copy of the published book and are published here for the first time.

On June 8th, Claude wrote about the tensions that were now sweeping Britain about German attacks or invasion. He had to go to the village of Foulden, where the villagers had 'bleated' that the RAF beacon was a bait for German bombers. They claimed that they had been bombed by the Germans the previous night, but it turned out to be falling British AA shells. Claude was also refused entry onto a neighbouring air base at Watton, and the sentries there reported to the police an attempted entry by a 'bogus RAF officer'!

This afternoon I went to tackle Mr. Rayns, the Executive Officer of the Norfolk Branch of the War Agricultural committee, about ploughing ditches across cropped or ploughed fields which might be used by enemy to land troops. The Air Ministry has forbidden this, but Rayns is a grand fellow, and having been wounded in the last war, he was full out to co-operate in doing anything to harm the Hun; such a blessing, as I have already disregarded my orders and have ditched three fields, and plans are in hand for many, many more. As soon as I can must go round and preach war to the farmer owners.

I am troubled by the bad state of defence of my station against an invasion by parachutists or de-planed troops. As things are, if they send a big force, say a thousand, I fear we shall all be wiped out, and these 'Marham Memories' may end abruptly. I shall arrange for Flint to bury them in the garden if trouble comes, and for my Gwen to be told where to dig them up after – if there is to be any afterwards, for her or for any of us, if we lose this war! [by this time, Gwen had been evacuated to stay with her brother Cecil in Paulerspury, near Towcester].

I hear that the Hun has adopted the idea I tried to get accepted in 1932 – of making bombs create a fearful noise as they fall, to stir up panic. Our people turned down my idea, as 'un-English'!

Another problem caused by the German threat was that his own aircraft were now sometimes fired upon by 'friendly' AA batteries mistaking them for Germans. Also, one of Claude's planes got transfixed in British searchlights, and was shot down by Germans. Claude's crews reported that it was safer flying over Germany than it was over 'hysterical' Britain.

The casualties kept piling up. On 24th June they buried 'young' Leach, a rear gunner who had bled to death in his turret during the flight home, and who they had to hack out of his mangled harness. Leach had been a rear gunner for just two days. Flight Commander Marwood-Elton was very down, believing himself to bring bad luck to his charges, as he had already lost seven complete crews, while Hawkins had 'gone bad' and had to be replaced. A lot of the other pilots that had been at Marham had already been transferred and Claude reckoned that there would be a completely new set of personnel by Christmas. The officer's mess was designed for 36, but had 110 living there, with another 20 living out with their families. Claude comments on how this impacted on dinner seating and a lack of sufficient cutlery.

After 24th June, Claude's 'Marham Memories' abruptly ends, with just his word painting and Rosewarne's letter appended. This is presumably because in July and August the Battle of Britain had become so hectic that he had no time for keeping a journal. In September 1940 he himself followed many of his men in being transferred away from Marham. The reason for the transfer is not recorded, but the RAF had a policy of rotating commands, as it was very easy for pressure to get to those in command, as Claude's writings confirm. Also Claude was older than most commanders, and not in good health. However, it may have been his independent mind that had got him into conflict with the higher authorities. He himself wrote:

I ran my Station commands as a dictator – a benevolent one, I hope – and I built the efficiency of my units through the happy, hard work of my airmen. They knew I should bite them when they deserved it, and fight like hell for them when they merited it. I have always refused to be a 'Yes Man' when it affected my doing what I thought to be right for those under me. That is probably why I am in plain clothes as I write this book."

The Battle of Britain was underway, and things were going to get even tougher than they had been in the opening year of the war. Claude had already stated in his 'Marham Memories' that he loved his 'fatherland', Canada, and that he would be happy to answer any call Canada made on him, and that is precisely what happened.

Chapter 20 The Bard of the Blitz

There is no suggestion that Claude's move from Marham in September 1940 was prompted by anything more than the normal schedule of rotating commands – indeed he was mentioned in dispatches for his work there. His new job was to be President of the Air Crew Selection Board; this involved sitting in an office in London each day, interviewing the flood of volunteers who wanted to join the RAF at the height of the Battle of Britain and Blitz.

They came from every walk of life, from every trade and profession, and represented some of the finest manhood in the country – and a few who were 'not so good'... some of them became almost dumb through nervousness – often those who were the most keen. Some were cocksure, with no justification, others, with magnificent qualifications on paper did not possess the quick mental resourcefulness we were looking for. I was astonished to find a science master from a technical school completely unable to work out a simple problem we set him. He evolved a formula for its solution, took seven times as long as normal to get his result – and then it was wrong! On the other hand, I remember a cheery freckle faced red headed young laundry van driver who came before us quietly determined to be accepted. When I heard of his very scanty education, I warned him that there was not much hope ... to his very great credit he got correct answers by sheer perseverance and ingenuity, without having the slightest idea of the orthodox methods. We took him, for I knew that if he could once get through his training, his was the nature which would beat the Hun every time. Gallantry and keenness are not sufficient alone to make a successful air-gunner ... it was heartbreaking to have to explain this to some of those we had to turn down.

Most of them wanted to become pilots, although the educational standard necessary for the training of an observer had to be higher. The type we welcomed was the lad who said "I'd like to be a pilot, but if you can't take me for that, I'll go for observer or air-gunner or anything you like, so long as I can become a member of an air-crew, and have a crack at the Hun." On the other hand, some came up before us when they were just on the point of being called up for national service: they undoubtedly felt that if they were accepted for pilot, they would have a comfortable year in training before they had to face a Hun gun. This sort would not volunteer for air-gunner as an alternative, for they knew that the period of training was only quarter as long, and three months might see them flying over AA in Germany. We generally rejected this type, and put a secret red sign on their papers. This scuppered all hope of their being taken into the RAF for ground duties, as airmen.

Undoubtedly rejections were a great sorrow to many who were unfortunate, but often I felt it was mainly a matter of wounded pride. This type were in the habit of getting questions asked in the House [of Commons], and then an official enquiry might filter down to the Board which made the rejection. There was not always an honest purpose behind volunteering. I was staggered by one young gentleman who admitted to me that he would not risk his life except as a pilot, because there was no future for the other categories after the war! "So you mean to tell me that you are here to get free training through your war service, with the idea of its enabling you to get a civilian job after the war?" I roared at him. He spread his hands, shrugged his shoulders and I quickly made the red mark on his papers. A young cinema actor came up to me in the way I suppose he had found it paid to approach a producer – which merely made me long to get up and kick him out of my office.

Tragedy came into my office the day that one volunteer answered my query by throwing down in front of me a pair of tiny baby's shoes. He swallowed and did not say anything for a moment. Then he pointed to the shoes and exclaimed, "That's why. They got my wife and they got my baby, and now, by God, I'll get them." He passed, and I do not envy the Hun who met him in the air.

One of the other duties Claude had during the Blitz was to be on duty in the War Control Room at the Air Ministry. He was on duty there on 29th December 1940, the night of the most disastrous incendiary attacks on London by the Luftwaffe, known as the Second Fire of London. Over 10,000 incendiary bombs were dropped – 300 per minute of the attack. This is his account:

Deep down in the bomb-proof dungeon which housed the Air Ministry, messages had been pouring in all night, and many senior officers had paid hurried visits and many important people had rung for news. It was known that a big number of enemy planes were started off for England and the direction of the beams [tracking beams for bombers] showed that their target was the heart of London. The weather at home was uniformly bad and low cloud we knew would render difficult any interceptions by fighter aircraft.

More and more signals came in. More and more plots of approaching aircraft, from continental aerodromes all round the coast. The whole of the London area then went 'red' and we knew the foremost aircraft must be getting near. We could but wait. There was nothing more we could do. It was maddening to be shut up, safely beneath ground when we knew that those above ground would be in imminent danger of violent death. We might be a world apart. The continuous buzz of electric fans kept up an irritating monotone background of sound. Everyone was alert and everyone jumped as telephones rang. There was an air of suppressed tension, and the fact that there was nothing to do but wait jarred everyone's nerves.

After waiting patiently for an age, I rang up the Home Security Control Room, and asked for news. The reply was laconic: "The heart of London burns," and yet no sound of bursting bombs had shaken our subterranean depths. I wondered whether all was well at our home, and hurriedly put in a call. My wife answered me, and said that a ghastly pink glow was lighting up the sky so that everybody could read a newspaper by its light. I felt caged, and telling one of our officers that I'd be back in a few minutes, I danced off up the stairs, along deserted corridors, until I reached the roof exit door. I stepped out into the biting chill of a December night, but my heart went colder still when I saw the ghostly pink flickering light which was lighting up the sky and throwing horrible shadows against the roof parapet. In an agony of apprehension, I clambered up until I was high enough to look around. Away to eastward the sky was brilliant with an angry mass of roaring red flames, twisting to and fro, like tentacles of some hellish monster. Fanned by a light breeze, these ghastly red arms curled round the black outlines of familiar buildings, and I gasped as I saw them groping both behind and in front of St Paul's. Fascinated, I stood and gazed in horror and then a strange impulse sent me to my knees to make a hurried yet fervent prayer for the London that I had known so long and loved so well. On the cold cement roof I knelt, forgetful of the possibility of enemy aircraft being exactly overhead. Then I shivered and remembered I was playing truant. One last look at the red inferno, and I dashed off back to the brilliantly lit security of the War Room. They asked me what I'd seen, and I could but answer: "The heart of London burns."

We knew our own fighters were making a wide sweep across the area, and anxiously awaited further news. The enemy were in retreat, it seemed. The weather was deteriorating, and others still incoming had turned back. So we might be spared the agony of a high explosive attack following the incendiary one. With a feeling of guilty impotence, one wondered how it fared amidst the crowded buildings of the city. London went 'white' and I again sneaked up to the roof. The sky was still aglow, but the fury of the flames was spent, and I could still make out the dome of St Paul's. And again I knelt on that chilly roof, but this time to thank God that destruction had been stayed.

At this time, for the first time in his life, Claude took up writing poetry. He wrote poems about his experiences at Marham, and he wrote a poem based on his account of the night of 29th December, which he called 'The Heart of London Burns'. Another poem tells of a journey across London in the early days of the Blitz:

A Cockney Taxi Driver

She'd telephoned and asked me out to dine
There was so much to talk about – could I be there by nine?
In London I had just arrived a few short hours ago
But she was sweet and she was young and very nice to know
The night was dark though clear the sky
My hostess said with scolding eye
"Tonight we'll have a raid for sure
You'd better stay and be secure"

I said I'd come and meet her anywhere
But as I dressed the wailing moan of sirens filled the air
A ghastly sound that heralds ill and shakes one's very heart
But she was now expecting me – I had to make a start
With tin hat on and torch in hand
I started off as I had planned
The night was dark, there was no fuss
But when I looked, I found no bus!

I stepped out not feeling very brave
The streets were dark and empty too – as silent as the grave
And then above, up in the sky, I heard a droning sound
And all the guns gave tongue at once, and shook the very ground
I hurried on, my thoughts on her
I hoped to reach Victoria
For there I thought there might be found
A train on London's Underground

With panting breast and bathed in icy sweat
At length I reached the entrance gate, and lit a cigarette
The gate was shut and barred and locked, no trains were running now
But I had got thus far and vowed I'd carry on somehow
There were still four miles still to go
For I was making for Soho
To go on foot was much too far
Somehow I must locate a car

Then I saw coming down Victoria Street
A taxi-cab with his blue light, which I dashed out to meet
He pulled into the side and I asked him if he would go
Through all the hell that was now on, and drive me to Soho
He laughed and said in Cockney broad
"Refoose yer dibs I can't afford
I'll drive yer there or anywhere
So long as you can pay yer fare"

Although he wore four ribbons on his breast
No tin hat graced his head, and I felt sorely overdressed
He rattled on past traffic lights with no one there to see
"Ole 'Itler's on the job ternight," he shouted back to me
"'E's lit 'isself a a fire, I'm told
Because 'is feet are feelin' cold"

And as I looked a flame shot high
In angry red, which dyed the sky

He turned sharp right, to dodge a barricade
We kept up speed through flash and crash, and never seemed dismayed
And when we reached that distant street, I duly said a prayer
His clock was showing two-and-six, but I asked his fare
"It's on the clock," he snapped at me
"This 'Itler show, I chuck in free"
I handed him a one pound note
He turned and fumbled in his coat

"I'm grateful for this trip you're done tonight,"
Said I to him, "And I should say it's worth a sovereign, quite"
"I ain't one to profit out of 'Itler's 'ymn of 'ate –
'Ere's yer change – maybe you'll need it when you celebrate"
And then I turned and rang her bell
She said just what I hoped she's say;
"Tonight, of course, you'll <u>have</u> to stay!"

It's impossible to know whether the mysterious female is a fiction, or whether Gwen's absence caused Claude to look up old flames. Certainly when he was alone in Canada, later in the year, he wrote a torrent of poetry about his old flames, some of which he sent off to the subjects. He also wrote a poem about his cousin Pauline, which although it is entirely innocent in content, seems rather creepy. There is another to 'Jean', whom he sees in a filmy night-dress, and although there's no incriminating action detailed in the poem, it is hard to escape the uncomfortable conclusion that it's about Jean Wardlaw, the pilot's widow who after the loss of her husband came to stay with Claude and Gwen.

Other poems are about more stirring patriotic themes – the funeral of gunner Leach [see last chapter], the recruit with the baby's shoes [see above], widows in the WAAFs, and this one:

Feed The Brute

The night had been sticky one
With cloud and ice and rain
But still they'd bombed their target well
And crews were back again

I tackled one and asked him how
The trip had gone with him;
I knew he'd had a gruelling time
His faced was tired and grim

He stood to attention and

Looked hard and straight at me
"The sandwiches were stale, sir,
No sugar in the tea"

I laughed out loud to think that on
This very strenuous raid
The only things that worried him
Were just those things he'd said!

I knew his wings had piled on ice
And he had lost control
And plunged headlong a thousand feet
But still he reached his goal

I knew for anti-aircraft fire
He did not care a hoot
But still he proved the saying true:
"You have to feed the brute"

Some poems are more reflective, including one called 'How Can I Face My God?', and this one, about an arms factory:

<u>The Factory of Death</u>

I walked through the shops of this factory of death
My heart seemed to stop and I gasped for breath
For out of the din and into my brain
A voice seemed to cry in a dreadful refrain:
"Never enough – never enough"

The wheels were all turning, and turning so fast
The men who were tending them seemed so outclassed
They seemed to be slaves to this dreadful machine
Themselves to be ruled by its tragic routine
"Never enough – never enough"

I felt as I looked at the shining new shell
The Devil was here and that his must be Hell
For how could one think that these efforts of man
Were other than run for the Devil's own plan?
"Never enough – never enough"

A million or more is the output, they say,
Of cartridges made in the course of one day

And how many lives do you think it will take
Before we find we have made a mistake?
"Never enough – never enough"

I went out the doors, in the joy of the sun
I started to walk, but I wanted to run
The grimness of all I had felt where I'd been
Was still like a pall; I could still hear that scream
"Never enough – never enough"

There is a bitter diatribe against civil servants, of which the following is an extract;

Sniff
If you can't peep ahead or even look about you
Or use your wits as common people do
If you can't trust yourself and most men doubt you
And there's reason for their doubting too
If you were born too tired to earn your living
Or, knowing the whole facts, prefer half lies
Or constitutional taker, shrink from giving
And yet can talk that good or look that wise

If you can't think – and precedent's your master
If you can't dream that life's a soldier's game
If war won't make you move one knot the faster
And overtime's the only treat you claim
If you can't bear strict orders, straightly given
If all you're built for is an office stool
Worn out and stooping, soft skinned for a token
You're one tenth twister and nine tenths a fool

If you daren't mount the clouds or keep sea station
If handling a Bren hurts you over-much
If all you know about administration
Is how to muck up everything you touch
If you can merely fill the unfilled minute
To pass and pass and pass, till Kingdom come
Yours is the Civil Service. Up and in it
And snitch one KBE the more, you bum!

This is an outpouring of bile and frustration that probably many servicemen felt about the civil servants who ruled their lives from the safety of their desks. The last line also suggests that Claude, who had never received any honour or major decoration to that date, resented the honours hoovered up by civil servants. This poem is also a useful illustration of how Claude's attitude to authority might land him in hot water.

Claude's poetic style reminds the reader of Rupert the Bear cartoons. He tried to get his war poems published in both Canada and Britain under the title Per Ardua Ad Astra, but he was turned down by publishers.

Chapter 21 A bittersweet exit

In the spring of 1941, Claude was briefly without a job. He had been due to lead an air crew training establishment when the scheme collapsed. Instead, he was asked to command an Air Gunnery and Bombing School, then being transferred from Pembrey in Wales to Picton in Ontario, Canada. Claude accepted the post, which was for two years, and set sail in a captured German ship across the Atlantic on April 13th. The ship was too slow to sail as part of a convoy, and was carrying amongst other items 3,000 'lease lend' Norwich canaries. The voyage was uneventful. When Gwen followed Claude in a convoy a month later, four ships were sunk in that convoy.

After wartime England, Picton was *'a paradise for fat and comfortable living'*. It is situated on a peninsula on Lake Ontario, with golden beaches, lake fishing, and ski runs in the winter. There was no food rationing, and Claude particularly enjoyed the absence of any night blackout. He and Gwen had a full on social calendar, both within the establishment and out in Canadian society.

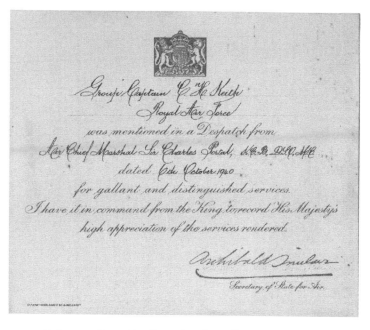

Being mentioned in dispatches for gallant and distinguished services while at Marham would have put an extra spring in his step. The fact that he was personally honoured by the Duke of Kent, who was on a visit to Canada, together with the article in the Canadian paper, which mentions his Canadian origins, would have added the gloss.

Claude set about establishing this new school, and his competitive streak led him to ensure that his RAF establishment would produce aircrew who scored higher marks than the already established Canadian RCAF aircrew schools. He found it very useful that because he had been born in Canada he could technically claim Canadian citizenship when disputes arose. He designed a comfortable English pub style mess [see below – Claude and Gwen are seated in the inglenook] and held social gatherings [below].

Nearly everything was going perfectly, but Claude couldn't resist rocking the boat. The RAF personnel serving in Canada were disadvantaged by a tax system that left them clearly worse off than their Canadian counterparts, so Claude put forward 'twenty points of hardships'. He got no support from the RAF Liaison Officer in Ottawa, but Claude managed to win six of the points for his men. Then abruptly, a year early, and with no reason given, he was recalled to England.

Above: Claude hands out 'Wings' in Picton. Right: clearing snow at Picton.

Claude knew that he had been doing a good job in Canada. The RCAF assured him that they had not requested that he be recalled. The RAF Liaison Officer in Ottawa said that he had nothing to do with it. Claude had met all his targets and had worked very hard. So he was furious when he set sail for England in April 1942, after only a year of his two year posting. He reported to the Air Ministry where Air Marshal Philip Babington was *amazingly vague* about the reasons for his recall, but Claude found out later that Babington had tried to have Claude immediately retired, years before he was eligible for a pension.

Left: Claude in Picton, summer 1941. Right: Claude serving the Picton airmen at their Christmas dinner, 1941

Of course, it is obvious that it was Claude's twenty points of hardship that did for him, and it's possible to see both sides: Claude was only fighting for justice and to get the best for his men, and was doing a good job. On the other hand, from the perspective of the RAF in England, where they were stretched to breaking point in a desperate war for survival against the Nazis, having to deal with someone sitting in comfortable safe Canada whining about tax breaks would be an irritant that they would rather be without.

Briefly, Claude was left without a job, but he was quickly snapped up to command the RAF Central Gunnery School at Sutton Bridge in the Fens. This school dealt with training existing aircrew in advanced skills. He was told that his new command was *'dirty, unhappy and inefficient'*. He quickly learned that this assessment was true!

Claude got down to sorting out the school. He describes his work as being *'expecting to turn out lovely bricks without sufficient straw'*, but he got some experts preaching good practice, and arranged for the trainees to cascade the good practice when they returned to their squadrons. In the absence of anyone who could teach the mathematics of air combat, he got an expert seconded. He used cine film to record training so that *'exhaustive resurrections'* could take place after each mock battle.

But the past was catching up with Claude. His creaky hip had not done well in a Canadian winter, and now, after X-rays in Ely Hospital, he was sent to a Buxton clinic to recuperate. He wrote a poem about gaunt and grim doctors, antique porters, shy giggling nurses and wise matrons in the place, and he alleges that his stay there completely sorted out his problems.

However, the RAF doctors disagreed and said that he would need to have his next posting in the south of England, which scuppered his commanding officer's idea of him taking up a command in Barrow-in-Furness. With no other command on offer, Claude was listed as a 'supernumerary' based at the RAF Uxbridge depot.

Sir Alexander Seton, Claude's commanding officer in Canada, had returned to England, and wanted to know why Claude had been recalled to England. Without reference to Claude, he had two questions about it asked in the House of Commons. This is the Wikipedia account, based on the transcripts in Hansard:

In the House of Parliament on 3 February 1943 Tom Driberg, MP, asked why Keith had been recalled and why it was proposed to retire him, saying, "Is it not a fact that this officer was brought back from Canada after serving eight months, although it had been laid down that he should serve not less than 18 months, and that he was given the highest tributes, officially and unofficially, for his efficiency? ". The Secretary of State for Air replied that a policy had been in place since "the summer of 1941, under which senior officers must give way to younger men when circumstances so require", and deplored that individual officers were named. Tom Driberg responded by saying "Is it not more deplorable that they should be treated unjustly?"

Claude wrote that the first he heard of the exchange in the Commons was when he was sent by Seton a copy of Hansard covering it. Claude commented:

It was perhaps unfortunate for the Secretary of State that he must have been supplied with incorrect information for his answer to the first question, and his answer to the second was not borne out by what was then happening in the RAF.

This is coded language to say that the politician had lied to the House. With such a bitter debate about his career going on in the Air Ministry, Claude realized that it was time to make a dignified retreat.

With the greatest war in history being waged, I spent several idle months at my home, whilst being 'supernumerary' at the Depot. I was by then again medically fit for full flying duties as a pilot. I had no intention of whining, although from a the country's point of view, it seemed a little wasteful that my knowledge and experience of so many years should be of no further use to the RAF. I went off after another job.

Claude's new job was with the BBC:

I wanted a complete change, so I tackled the BBC to see if I could get a job with them as an announcer. I made two short recordings of the reading of news bulletins for their Director of Presentation, and the Controller of Programmes asked me if I could take up the new work at once. I saw John Breen, once my junior but by now become Director-General of Postings with the rank of Air Vice-Marshal, and told him that if I were to be retired, he need not drag out the agony – that I had not anything to ask for. Within a few months I was retired and became a Home Service Announcer with the BBC. So ended nearly twenty-eight years varied service with the RAF – and in the midst of war at a time when I was still under retiring age! I refuse to sour my future with vain regrets, and prefer to count my blessings, which are many. Beyond doubt my insistence in Canada for a removal of hardships affecting those under me rendered me very 'inconvenient' with higher authority. I had been the cause of two special meetings of the Air Council, but they led to the final concession of all the points I had raised and so justified my action. I came out of uniform with clean hands, and that is more than some of the people with whom I had to deal will be able to say!

Despite his protestations that he refused to sour his future with vain regrets, this passage, published in his book, showed that he obviously was very bitter about the way that he left his beloved RAF. Over a year after he had left the RAF, on 1st September 1944, in a letter to an American friend, Suzanne Bavard, he wrote:

This job I now have is the softest I have ever had, and I feel rather badly at doing such with a war on, but my being out of the RAF is not my doing. The row about my retirement is still burning brightly, and a very awkward question to the Secretary of State for Air is due to be asked in Parliament quite soon. I have no personal interest in it, but I do think that the two very senior officers responsible ought to get thoroughly scrubbed for what they did. And I think they will.

It's not recorded as to whether anyone got 'scrubbed', but the chances are that the establishment protected their own.

Chapter 22 Flibs, the BBC, and domestic bliss: 1943-1946

Claude had found the early days of the Blitz an adventure, with his accounts of a taxi ride across the city during a raid being an example. But in the latter years of the war, with responsibilities for a wife, house and dogs, the bombing became a nightly terror, especially when the V2 Rockets, or 'flibs' as Claude called them, began to take a toll:

I'm sitting in our morning room, and Gwen is asleep on a camp bed in the adjoining kitchen, with Bunji on the bed. I can just dimly see them through the open door. I'm keeping a solemn, fateful vigil as I write. We are now in what used to be called the 'silent hours' of the night, and my clock has just chimed half past three. In my day I have kept many night watches and I hope I have always kept them faithfully, but tonight the dire risk of my failure is so great that it sharpens my every nerve, and drives away the inclination to sleep or slacken my second-to-second watchfulness. On my vigilance depends the very life of Gwen. Gratefully fallen into a heavy and much needed sleep, she did so lulled by the feeling of security because she knew I was on watch, ready to call her instantly if I could see that death was threatening. Any moment it may, as I sit in the stillness of this room, straining my ears to catch the first faint vicious murmur which swells into a hollow roar as the flib gets nearer. The only sounds, as I write, are the irritable ticking of the clock, the hiss of steam from the slow-boiler in the kitchen and the deep slow contented snoring of Bunji. The sound I am waiting for is unmistakable: a faint rhythmic vibration at first, but rapidly swelling in volume until it is a threatening roar, as the flib dashes on towards us, hurtling through space at seven miles a minute.

Usually my first warning is a dull cannonade of guns – a muffled rat-a-tat on the windows and a sullen earth tremble. Then I stop writing, as even the scratch of my pencil may obliterate the sound I am waiting for. Once I hear the flib, I rush off upstairs to my study window, which faces the direction of their approach. Standing close to the panes, I gaze out to the south. The leaden pane divisions give me the impression of looking out through prison bars. Above the dark fringes of our chestnut trees, which I have cut so low that they only just eclipse the distant rising ground about a mile away, there stretches the infinite bowl of night, a vast monotonous dome of dull indigo, upon which is suspended the jewelled pattern of the stars. But also it is criss-crossed by the white fingers of many searchlights, stretching skywards and immovable, like silver bars across the heavens.

The flib is more audible now, and I open the windows, letting in a chill blast of night air, which dowses me like a cold spray of icy water. Beyond the hills I see some flashing diamonds appear in the sky, as AA shells burst. Then a string of red balls fly up, as tracer shell is fired. The rumble of many guns comes to me and rattles the window – just the sound children would make, romping on the floor overhead. Then, like some evil will-o'-the-wisp, up pops the flib, with its brilliantly flaming tail light. Anxiously I look to see whether it moves to the left or the right. If it does, then all is well, and it will pass us by. If it doesn't, I have but a few seconds in which to arouse Gwen and get her into our larder, which has been shored up as a makeshift air raid shelter. But tonight a fresh south-westerly wind has sprung up and so far every flib has passed us well to the east. Forging its relentless way to London, the sound of its hollow purposeful roar is terrifying. When it passes out of my sight, I rush to the front of the house and wait for it to reappear. There it comes, like a shooting star behind the dark trees. Its sound grows fainter and I strain my ears to catch the warning splutter which precedes its devilish dive to destruction. Yes, it's petering out now – all is silence. I wait to see the vivid silver flash as it explodes, stop-watch in hand. There it is – like summer lightning, and I start the second hand of my watch going. The sound of the explosion is so long in coming that I think I must have missed it. But no, here it is, shaking every loose thing with a violent angry rap, and quite involuntarily I press the stop catch of my watch. I note that the flash came from the NNE of us and then I see that the sound took 27 seconds to reach me after I'd seen the flash. With sound travelling at 1060 feet per second, that means that the damage has taken place 5 ½ miles away, and on my map I can

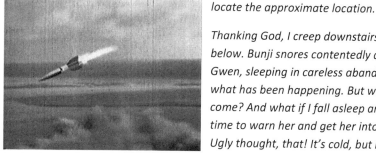

locate the approximate location.

Thanking God, I creep downstairs again. All is peace below. Bunji snores contentedly and I can just see my Gwen, sleeping in careless abandon, unconscious of what has been happening. But where will the next one come? And what if I fall asleep and don't hear it in time to warn her and get her into the larder-shelter? Ugly thought, that! It's cold, but I won't switch on the heater in case it makes me drowsy ...

Another? No, it's a great noisy goods train, winding its ponderous way towards the coast, probably laden with deadly weapons for our invading armies – let's hope it may help them kill more and more of these foul Huns. I don't trust trains on these nights of flib raids, as they mask the sound for which I wait. Once a flib got dangerously close, creeping in, muffled by a train. My busy little cuckoo in the hall has just popped out to tell me it's half past four, but neither Gwen nor Bunji stir. They are used to these nocturnal declamations. Now a steam engine outside is puffing away under a heavy load. What I'd not give for an 'all clear' siren and a cup of cocoa, and then ... bed! But it won't happen like that: this will go on, fraying my nerves until the sun is high in the morning sky, and I, weary and with heavy red rimmed eyes, shall flop into a dull and dreamless sleep. But my Gwen will be safe, please God, and the better for her kitchen sleep. She'll be up and feeding the hens, and then she'll come softly and wake me for a wondrous hot breakfast, which I shall devour unshaven and in my pyjamas, thankful that we are both alive and able to enjoy the sunshine of another day. The canary, now sleeping so trustfully will be flashing from perch to perch in his cage, and twitting to have the radio turned on, so he can sing it down!

I'm so lucky in my home, so truly blessed in my wife. In our present danger perhaps I value both the more. What has the future in store for us? What shall I do – feel like – if Gwen should go, in a pile of dust and rubble and shattered glass, and I escape? That just doesn't bear thinking *about. As I write, just for a short spell, it is peaceful. It is Sunday, the 'day of rest'. God grant that it may be so for us.*

They must have suffered a near miss later, because on 11th April 1945, Claude wrote to Suzanne Bavard in America:

I think the enclosed cutting may interest you. It shows from what we have been saved. It is a blessed long time since we heard the last shattering bang and we only pray that no more may come. It will be grand when we can feel that the possibility of our home being brought down on our heads in dust and rubble is really over. On the whole we must feel very thankful that we suffered no worse damage than we did – and that is all repaired except for painting the newly plastered ceiling.

The canary was not so fortunate: later Claude wrote that it had been eaten by the cat!

They could not escape the bombing by going to live in their house in Helford, Cornwall, because Claude was working for the BBC. He did not write anything formal or published about his time at the BBC, partly because he was busy writing 'I Hold My Aim', and then going through the lengthy process of proof-reading, wrangling with publishers over advances and over illustrations, and finally having it vetted by the censors. In the summer of 1945 Claude complained that 'I Hold My Aim' should have been published in autumn 1945, but the publisher was delaying publication until spring 1946, citing post war paper shortages, and was offering him only $175 as an advance, so he was looking for another publisher. At the same time he had nearly completed another book on the early days of the development of radio *'as I know it'*, which he was planning to call 'Radio Angle'. He was also making money from newspaper articles, which he said were shorter and paid much better: $130 for a 1,500 word article.

When Claude joined the BBC in 1943, he worked as an announcer for the radio Home Service. I possess some very scratchy recordings on acetate discs of Claude reading propaganda broadcast by the BBC. In one he intones in a very plummy voice "Bones, Mrs. Jones, bones! We want your bones." He then explains that this is an appeal for housewives to hand in their meat bones, which will have the phosphorus extracted from them in order to make explosives to drop on the Hun.

However, by September 1944 he had a completely different role. In a letters to Suzanne Bavard, typed on BBC headed notepaper and written while at work, he described his job thus:

I do one day [24 hours] duty and then have 48 hours off duty. I censor the programmes of the American Forces Radio Network, which is a low power service for the US Service Units. The network is housed at 80, Portland Place [which is where I am now] and was equipped by the BBC for US forces as a sort of 'lend lease' in reverse, but it is entirely operated by US personnel, except us three censors. On duty, except when I go to Broadcasting House for meals, I only mingle with Americans. ... My job should last until the Jap war is ended. The network consists of a great number of very short range transmitters all linked up by telephone lines, and placed to give typically American programmes and news to the American forces in this country and in the various continental countries. When this job dies on me I don't want to take on a job which would mean travel to work six days a week, and ordinary office hours. If I can transfer to a 'shift job' as a news writer for the BBC, I think I should like that and be able to cope.

On 21st August he wrote:

VJ Day crashed my job as Censor with the BBC, and, unless they can fit me into another job, I shall join the unemployed on 1st October. We rather think that we should try and buy a former farm-house at Helford in Cornwall, where living will be cheaper and where we can augment our income by taking in a few paying guests during the summer. I am not lit with the idea, as I love my London, but Gwen will adore to be in the depths of the country, and she loves village life, which bores me to sobs. But, unless I can get something to do to earn me a little, we just CANNOT stay on in this house – even without a servant. I've only got my pension and a third of that has to go to a voracious ex-wife, and half of it to the Inland Revenue as Income Tax!

There is no record of Claude being fitted for another BBC job when October 1945 came round and his censor's job ended. However, we do know that he and Gwen remained in Purley until his death thirteen months later, so he must have found some way to finance living there, while keeping his cottages in Helford. Certainly, he enjoyed living in Purley.

While enduring enforced idleness, Claude threw himself into home-making. The last pictures in his last photograph album are all of The Smithy in Purley, South London, where he and Gwen were able to indulge in their tastes and Claude could lay out all the treasures he had acquired over his life. The Smithy, in Old Woodcote Village, was part of a model village built in 1903. It was set round a village green that had a temperance inn, faux whipping post, stocks, and seesaw! The architect and visionary William Webb had insisted on a working smithy with a chestnut tree shading the door of the forge, and had dug up a 25 year old tree to plant next to the smithy. This is the tree that Claude had chopped low. Below is a picture of the Smithy Claude commissioned from the Cornish artist Ernest Oldham, with the Keith and Dunkerley family coats of arms.

Claude appears to have been very happy with his new home:

I LOVE my home, Suzanne, and am as happy as a sand-boy when I can be there with Gwen, doing odd jobs in old clothes, around the garden. I ask nothing better, and having meals out of doors with Gwen is about as close as I shall get to paradise on earth.

In addition to the gardening, he took on the project of building an extension to the Smithy: a garage and a maid's room:

September 1944: There are some 3,000 bricks to lay, and the floor and roof to be done. The garden is doing fine, except that two successive mild and dry winters have given us far too many destructive garden grubs. I've just acquired a hive which is said to contain 50,000 bees – with 50,000 stings! The honey will be useful in the house, and they are easy and interesting things to keep. ...

April 1945: I am inveigled into trying to grow mushrooms. There is a new process of cultivating spores, and they say it gives a guaranteed crop in three months. I am not out for profit, but I shall be glad if I can stock our own larder with them, as they are so useful in the kitchen. My bees fell prey to Acarine Disease [Isle of Wight Disease], and I had to dose them. I think they're all right now although I lost dozens of them. Still, a hive is said to contain 50,000 to 70,000 of them, so I suppose they won't be missed.

July 1945: I still spend busy hours as a builder. I have finished the garage, except for the doors, have got bricks to do the maid's bedroom over it, and am now started on the porch over the back door. I won't start the maid's room until I've had my summer holiday. It is hard work for an old man, as I am now become, but at least it does get done and done the way I want it done, whereas if I waited for builders it might take years – they are busy renovating bombed homes.

It wasn't easy to persuade servants to live in bomb threatened London [especially with the maid's room above the garage not yet built]. Perhaps Claude and Gwen, a former expert for Good Housekeeping, were not the easiest employers:

September 1944: I have persuaded our silly old maid, Martha, to return to us for a week or ten days on the 11th, and am sending Gwen off for a change, which she is due. ... I forget whether I told you we contemplate taking on as our servant a former WAAF Corporal who inconsiderately borrowed someone else's husband to have a baby! It'll mean taking on the baby too, but anything which will alleviate the eternal household grind is worth trying. She'll be ready to come to us in December, as far as we know.

April 1945: Our Bavarian maid is an amazingly hard worker, and seems happy and docile, but is very temperamental. I expect the war news is not very pleasant hearing for her. It is a mercy that she has taken the greatest interest in the hens and ducks, and also the Pekinese and the cat ...

July 1945: Our days are easier in the house now we have the Bavarian maid, Cecile Schuder, but she is a typical Hun in thinking that she always knows best. She is honest, clean and good natured, but likes to do everything in the way she thinks is best, and it is hard for Gwen to get things done when she wants it and in the way she likes. She is good at German cooking, which I have always disliked, but she won't learn anything from Gwen because she is convinced that German cooks are the best in the world! Gwen will be glad when she goes, but I say let's keep her until we get a replacement, which seems quite hopeless the way things are now in England.

August 1945: We still have our 'Hun', but she is often a sore trial to Gwen. She is so convinced that she, being a German, must always be right. She forgets and she is clumsy and the world champion at breaking anything. She does what she likes, when she likes. Yet she is good natured, a religious woman, fantastically clean in herself and the way she keeps everything, a terrifically hard worker, and in many ways, capable. But she does get on Gwen's nerves and they have the most awful wrangles. In desperation Gwen sacked her, but she went into floods of tears – and stayed on. We can't get rid of her, so we are in the position of having a maid we can't get rid of, whereas most people would give their eye-teeth to have any sort of maid!

Below: Claude with Bunji, and Gwen in the drawing room of the Smithy.

VE Day, 8th May, 1945, was of course a day for celebration:

I was on duty for VE Day, but Gwen and neighbours, Squadron Leader and Mrs Tom Mammatt, came to my office during the forenoon with two bottles of Veuve Cliquot, which the Mammats had saved from their wedding, five years ago. So we celebrated in good liquor. I lunched them at the BBC and during the afternoon I managed to get out and we all went to the Thanksgiving Service at St Paul's. Afterwards we loitered along to Green Park, mingling with the gay and happy crowd, who were quite good natured and orderly. At night we all went to see the floodlit Buckingham Palace, where the King and Queen came onto the balcony and waved to the dense and cheering crowds. They are amazingly popular with everyone in the land. Mercifully it was a fine sunny day for hundreds must have slept out in the parks, as no late transport was put on. Gwen had to walk from the Palace to Notting Hill Gate with me, to reach her sister's place for the night, and then I had to foot it back to the BBC at Portland Place at about 1 am. But weren't we all glad that the bombing risk had left us forever!

Despite the euphoria of the victory, peace did not bring unalloyed joy for Claude. VJ day meant the end of Claude's BBC job, and he felt that things were moving in the wrong direction in the country. A few days before the General Election of 5th July 1945, Claude was confident that Winston Churchill and the Conservatives would win, but he reported that the campaigns were being *'fought with lies and bitterness'*.

If Labour got in and did all they threaten to do, I think it would squeeze us out of England for ever and aye, and I should turn my eyes to Jamaica again, as a future home. Our own Conservative candidate is Michael Astor, son of Lady Astor, the first woman MP. I met her in 1919. He has enjoyed all the many advantages of being a millionaire's son, and has had some service in this war. I hope he may get in, for his Labour opponent is a nasty piece of work.

It's interesting that Claude regarded being a millionaire's son as a qualification for Parliament. Astor was duly elected, but Labour won the election, which Claude called an *'ugly surprise'*:

I blame the Conservatives for being too complacent. I think that the Labour Party are in for a terribly difficult five years – any party would be. The trouble with Labour is that their most virile people are not up to the educational standard to fill many of the big ministerial posts, especially when they have to act internationally. To cope with this, they welcome any 'sahib' who will join them, and shove him in a big office for which he may be educated but has not the moral fibre.

Claude did not live to see the Labour Party introduce the National Health Service, but he complained about meat rationing and about not having enough money to be able to afford any liquor apart from beer, so cocktail parties and entertaining Americans properly were quite out of the question.

In most ways, Gwen is the ideal wife and an example and inspiration to me. I only wish I were better off in that it would enable me to give her a better life – but our class is going to the wall in England. It is the 'commercials' who have all the money these days, and the way they chuck it about is often a public offence...

These are bewildering days, and it takes a brave heart to face up to the future. The solidity of human integrity seems to have gone out of the young generation, and I fear it is because they lacked proper religious training as children and were brought up by parents who were too selfish to look after them properly. We are become too materialistic and apt to value everything by the price it would fetch. Well, the years are fast clocking up for me, and as my boy seems to have forsaken me for his mother, I have no direct interest in his rising generation. It is a million pities Gwen never had a babe, as she would have been an ideal mother. As it is she lavishes enough affection on the pekes to have brought up a happy family! But I don't think the world is growing a better place and civilization isn't a great credit to human nature.

This swipe at the younger generation and his own son does Claude little credit. His son Colin [pictured] was out in the

Pacific fighting the Japanese as he wrote these words, and was in Tokyo Bay when the Japanese surrendered on VJ Day. He was away for a full year, so he couldn't be with his father anyway. Colin had a very difficult time with his mother, and may have welcomed a more concerted effort by his father to re-establish relations. Maybe Claude saw himself as one of the 'selfish' parents, but it's unlikely.

We cannot know how much Claude knew about his ill health in the years leading to his death. He mentions several times in his last letters that he has been losing weight and was 133 pounds by August 1945, but he puts this down to *'hard, manual work'*. He had two serious illnesses earlier in his life – typhoid as a child in Wales, and a serious lung disease in Tierra del Fuego in 1914 – and either could have left him permanently weakened and susceptible to another fatal bout. He tended to over-dramatize elements of his life, but he also wanted to play down any ill health when the RAF was trying to retire him. So it is hard to assess the following pieces of writing. Did he have a genuine foreboding of his death, or was it just idle musing? If he had no idea of his mortality, then these jottings are unusual for a man as young as Claude was – only fifty-three years old.

6th August Glasgow 1943

Gwen, my beloved wife, I am going to make a habit of writing to you whilst I am away from you: not to send to you, but to leave for you to read when I am beyond earthly recall, and have already started to become a memory to you.

I don't mean to be morbid in doing this, but I feel that you may like to have these letters to read to yourself when you start to feel the loneliness which must come to you when we are forever parted on this earth. I don't feel I am going to depart tomorrow – I look forward to many, many more happy years together. But each year passed means one year less to go, so I might as well start my letters now.

A day ago I was listening to a very old song on the radio, which I have known all my life: 'When you go down the Vale', and the words set me thinking ... 'the last long vale of tears' – I set to wondering how it will all come about. I hope that you may be with me to the very end, and that I'm sensible and have not been a slowly sinking anxiety to you. I'd hate to die far from you – though perhaps this would be kinder for you. I expect it will be in our own snug little 'Smithy' home. I'd like it to be in one of the chairs in our bright morning room, with your hand in mine.

I have come to think of dying as much as I should resigning myself on an operating table for an anaesthetic. It's got to be faced and one might as well go to it without whimpering. I hope I shall. Already I have run the gamut of life's sensations and experiences, that I feel most new experiences are behind me, and I am happier living in the past than worrying about new sensations and experiences. I am supremely content with just you, in our own home.

Our intellects are so feeble that it is difficult to think of what might lie for us in the great unknown, beyond the grave. With all the possibilities that even our puny knowledge of science shows us can exist, I feel that we shall not be extinguished utterly. My hell may well be our being parted in the world to come, for I cannot claim to have qualified for heaven, but I am sure you have.

Darlingest, we have known the truest happiness in our mutual days and my greatest sorrow is my not having known you years and years before I did, and in your not having had a babe to comfort you when I am no more. You came into my life as the greatest compensation the Almighty could send me for all the beastliness of my days with Angel. Even with the grave facing me, I can find no good thing to say of Angel. She must have been sent on earth as a veritable 'Devil's disciple'.

The second piece is undated:

You must not let sorrow at my going spoil your own sweet life. I should hate to think that this might happen. I am not worthy of your tears, my darling. You have always benefitted those around you, and when you are freed from me you can still go on being a help and comfort to those near you.

I often wonder if your marrying me was for your sweet best, and the doubt at times has worried me. I'm afraid I haven't been a good husband as many men might have been, not have I been able to do for you what many men might have done. I have loved you, true, but so many men might have done that also!

If you quit the Smithy and go to spend your days at Helford, every path and cliff down there ought to be able to talk to you of me from my boyhood days, and many will hold memories for you of happy times we two have spent together there. I hope the villagers will take you to their hearts, and I am sure that they will all come to love you.

I had once meant to do so much in this world, but I have done so little. I have frittered my time and energies, and achieved little of lasting worth. I wonder if, yet, I shall ever get down to writing more books. I'd like to, but shall I?

I know you so well that if thought is still possible for me [after death], I shall so often 'live by your side'. I shall see you on your knees at night, and I shall hope the good god will heed the prayers I know you will make to Him on my behalf. I shall need them!

I wonder if my Michael [his son Colin] will be with you, in your life? If he should develop with his mother's characteristics, have none of him. I still feel that it is probable that I shall outlive him, but of that I cannot be certain. I don't expect myself to die for many years, but who knows the span of his own life with any certainty?

Don't lose grip of your own sweet life, my Gwen, when I am gone. It would worry me to think of that happening. Try still to enjoy the things we enjoyed together, and I am certain that everyone will be kind to you and love you – as they do now.

Bless you, my darling, for all the years of sweetness you have given me, for your example and your tolerance. May god have your days in his keeping and ease your earthly footsteps until His time shall come for you, your own sweet self, to follow me through the grim portals of the grave. And then, please God, it may be His mercy that we may again know each other in the great hereafter.

The paragraph about expecting to outlive Colin is strange. He had only met Colin a couple of times since his son's infancy, when he had taken him out for day outings from his prep school. Colin said many years later that the experiences had been very awkward for both of them: they were total strangers, and neither knew what to say to the other. In the event, after Claude's death Gwen got to know Colin well, and they adored each other; Gwen also enjoyed her step-grandchildren. She sold her cottages in Helford, and moved to live near Colin and his family in the New Forest [ironically only a few miles from where Angel lived in total isolation]. The picture shows Gwen with Claude's grand-daughter, Olivia.

Claude died suddenly at home in The Smithy, as he had wished, on November 18th, 1946, aged fifty-seven. The cause of death was a cerebral haemorrhage.

CERTIFIED COPY OF AN ENTRY OF DEATH

GIVEN AT THE GENERAL REGISTER OFFICE

Application Number COL661745

REGISTRATION DISTRICT	Surrey Mid-Eastern		
1946 DEATH in the Sub-district of Beddington and Coulsdon	in the County of Surrey		

Columns:-	1	2	3	4	5	6	7	8	9
No.	When and where died	Name and surname	Sex	Age	Occupation	Cause of death	Signature, description and residence of informant	When registered	Signature of registrar
120	Eighteenth November 1946 4 upper woodcote Purley Coulsdon & Purley U.D.	Claude Hilton Keith	male	57 years	Group Captain R.A.F (Retired)	1a Cerebral Haemorrhage certified by H.M.W. Shirley M.D.	Mary Mammett Present at the death 5a Smith ambotton Road Purley	Eighteenth November 1946	Surbook Registrar

CERTIFIED to be a true copy of an entry in the certified copy of a Register of Deaths in the District above mentioned.

Given at the GENERAL REGISTER OFFICE, under the Seal of the said Office, the ....24th........ day of ....October........ 2006

DYB 213514

See note overleaf

Chapter 23 Evaluations

I had once meant to do so much in this world, but I have done so little. I have frittered my time and energies, and achieved little of lasting worth.

So Claude wrote in his final piece, but it's hard to know whether he really believed it. Of course, it's easy to see from reading this biography that he did not fritter his life away, and that he did effect some lasting achievements, especially in his arming of the RAF before World War II, though he died before the full importance of resisting the Nazi threat was fully apparent. Claude was acutely aware, even obsessed, with creating his own legacy, and all his writings seem to be focussed on painting a picture of himself for future generations. Perhaps if he hadn't lost touch with his son at such an early stage he wouldn't have had this driving need. Sadly, Colin was never interested in his father's writings.

Claude spent a lot of time living in the past. He spent a huge amount of energy in his later years researching his family tree. He 'discovered' what was almost certainly a bogus connection between the Keith family of Yorkshire yeomen and labourers to the aristocratic Keith family of the Earls Marischals of Scotland. This connection was published in a genealogy book with wide circulation in America. He was desperate to know more about his father whom he never knew. He researched Gwen's family too, and was very welcoming and supportive of all the distant cousins he could find.

Although it's possible that he embroidered certain 'yarns' about his own past and those of his relatives, it can't be denied that he led an extraordinary and full life. It would be simplistic to assert that he was merely caught up in the 'great events' through which he lived – including

two world wars, because Claude was always out to grab opportunities for adventure. He started as a lowly apprentice in a factory in Dalston, and it was through his energy and ambition, not just his education and background, that he hauled himself up to the heights he scaled.

We have no idea whether being an active and enthusiastic Freemason gave Claude significant help in his career, because such things are secret. He was initiated into the Middlesex Lodge in 1916, and was their 'Worshipful Master' in 1921 to 1922. He founded at least two branches of Masons, and his Freemason CV is a lengthy one. He is pictured [left] in London Rank Full Dress Clothing in April 1938.

Claude held many views and did many things that would be roundly condemned today, but we must not fall into the trap of condemning him using standards that weren't commonly accepted in his day. His anti-Semitism cannot be condoned, but although he had an imperial outlook and an innate belief in the superiority of his own race, he got on very well with foreigners of all nationalities, and was very critical of racial discrimination and stereotyping when he encountered it.

His views on relationships with women would outrage feminists [and others] today:

Collectively I consider women an abomination; singly they alone make life worthwhile... Man in the optimistic pursuit of woman is at the zenith of his being. Pursuit and achievement is tonic to all his faculties; possession merely dulls them.... I consider the modern trend of the feminine sex ruinous to all that men should revere in women, and that man should glory in woman's successful competition with himself is but proof of his own decadence.... Often I have seen the pitiable sight of a man made puppet of some worthless woman solely because he has forgotten his manhood... every man should fight with all his strength against being dominated by any woman, and there are times when he should let his pride in his own sex control his own natural desires, rather than give way to female caprice... Be kind to women; be sympathetic; make allowances for the natural caprice of their nature, but never let them run you!

Although this is outrageous to today's sensibilities, several points need to be remembered before we judge Claude on it: firstly, he wrote this as advice to his son when he

was in his desperately unhappy marriage to the combative Angel. His approach with Gwen would suggest that he changed a lot of his views once his experiences with women improved. Secondly, he did read a lot about women and sex, and a lot of what he writes merely reflects the widely held theories of the time. Thirdly, he was a very good looking young man who was undoubtedly chased by women, so some of his comments are definitely coloured by having a more than average number of available women. Fourthly, Claude spent a lot of his life in RAF messes, in all-male social environments where *'men hung together'*, and this was especially true when he wrote the above piece.

Lastly and most importantly, Claude adored women and was adored by them throughout his life. His mother he viewed as a saint, and his beloved aunts, Lotty Rogers and Nell Keith, were very close to him. Although Claude chased many women, he was always respectful and often worshipful of his quarry, and he remained on very good terms with almost all of them long after their relationships ended – he always remembered them with great [maybe excessive] sentimentality.

Some of Claude's political views would have drawn encouraging nods from the Nazis he fought. After World War II, in the final chapter of 'I Hold My Aim', he outlined some ideas for the future:

Talk about 'a war to end all wars' is wishful thinking ... There is not a hope of equal economic prosperity for all nations: some will grow fat as others grow lean. I'm afraid we must accept this unpleasant reality. Are we to starve ourselves so that others may prosper? Would not this be national suicide? There is no hope of being able to argue with a hungry man: when he gets hopelessly hungry he will fight, and nothing will stop him. Our only hope for future peace is to be so strong that no other nation will dare to attack us. ...

If we are to survive as one of the great nations, our position must rest upon the firm foundation of common honesty ... but common honesty is not promoted by laws. It must spring from the childhood training of every individual. Its inculcation is the responsibility of parents, and its development can only thrive against a religious background of sound moral teaching ...

The physique of a nation must be maintained to a certain standard if that nation is to survive. To ensure this the start must be made even before the cradle. Couples of inferior fitness cannot be relied upon to produce children who will be an asset to the nation .... Every mentally deficient child that is born is a liability to the community, so it is merely sound business to do everything possible to avoid such liabilities occurring ...

Systems which provide minimum wage scales and enforce restricted output are broad highways to national decline ... Whilst every Briton prizes liberty, the inclination to give everyone an equal say in the running of everything leads to 'conference control' and hampers efficiency; class hatred is usually the outcome of ignorance of true conditions ... by all means offer better conditions for everybody and assistance for those who suffer some unavoidable misfortune, but better conditions should be the reward of personal effort, and not be regarded as a national gift.

Those of us who have commanded large RAF Stations have had the experience of controlling fairly large communities as autocracies. I consider this a useful training ground for the study of national control and organization.

This was written at a time when Britain was about to vote out Winston Churchill and vote in the first ever Labour majority government under Attlee, which would bring in the NHS. Many ex-servicemen were feeling bruised and confused, but it is extraordinary how Claude was still peddling such Fascist ideas after fighting them in the war.

However, Claude was certainly a visionary. In the same chapter at the end of his book, he outlines how in 1938 he discussed with Professor G.P. Thompson, one of the scientists who had successfully split the atom, whether they could make an atomic bomb for the RAF. Thompson thought that such a bomb would have to be too heavy. Claude went on to ask if they could harness nuclear energy to produce electricity, but he was horrified at the risks involved, and he notes *"can one shut one's eyes to such frightful possibilities?"*.

Claude also understood that war was about more than killing people. He showed that it would be much easier to blind [maybe temporarily] opposing aircrews with rays than to shoot them. He suggested panic inducing bombs, rather than high explosive one, if the purpose of bombing was to sap civilian morale. Claude, when asked about new armour cladding for the Air Ministry in London in 1936, was the person who suggested that all military command centres should be in deep underground bunkers – he suggested under Welsh hillsides. Of course, this idea is now commonplace.

There are three surviving obituaries of Claude, and although they mainly concentrate on the details of his career, and are all written by men who personally supported Claude, they contain some heartfelt praise. The non biographical details are below:

The Times [21st November 1946]: *Claude Hilton Keith, 'Happy' Keith to his RAF comrades, was a personal friend of mine for 30 years, and I have seldom met a man with greater singleness of purpose – namely, the efficiency of the service for which he lived. His unique knowledge of navigation, signals and armament gave him mastery over most fields of RAF activities ... The armament developments which he initiated in 1933-1936, which stood the test of war, proved that he was a man of foresight and vision. In addition to these technical qualifications, he possessed a deep understanding of humanity, with the result that his generosity, sincerity and charm ensured the happiness and efficiency of all units he commanded.*

The Aeroplane [29th November 1946]: *Claude Hilton Keith was one of those quiet, earnest, hardworking officers to whom the RAF owes more than it knows. Public fame never came his way, but to him the success of his work meant more than the publicity. He died suddenly at his home on 18th November ... he never had an active command again, which was, in a way, a pity, because his men in 70 Squadron loved him. His send-off from Ismailia when he left for home, was that odd mixture of enthusiasm and pathos which only a truly popular officer achieves ... Nobody would accuse Claude Keith of being a literary stylist, but he had a naive way of telling a yarn, whether about nomad Arabs or sprees in the mess, or big-time crooks in the armament racket, which make his books easy and educative reading. After his retirement he settled in The Smithy, Woodcote Village, Purley, where he took an active part in local community life. Also he was a keen Freemason who practiced the tenets of the craft. So there seemed to be many years of active life before him. We need many more such useful men as he.*

The Cornishman [December 5th 1946] : *Man With A Fine Vision*

HE INSPIRED OTHERS

Do you remember in 1940 a letter written by a young airman to his mother, left behind for his commander to send on when he was reported missing? In it he wrote: "I have great faith in the philosophic and scientific reasons for a Supreme Being and the after-life." The Times of June 18th published the letter. Group Captain Claude Keith was the Bomber Station Commander who had the insight to realize that the letter was something so outstanding and inspiring that it could not be lost. Through him, the letter was published and translated into nearly every language.

Keith himself had all the gentleness and vitality of a man of faith and a man of action. He had the understanding of young people that is rarely found; he knew their approach to sorrow and he tried, in his duties as station commander, to give sympathy and sanity to the young people who were so bewildered by a war-life in which death might be round any corner of any day. Keith tried to help them keep faith when reason grew terrifying.

In the text of one of his BBC broadcasts he says "We shall never solve the riddle of human existence, but at least we may be able to convince ourselves that there is good reason that a satisfactory answer does exist. Surely it is much easier to convince ourselves that a divine power does exist than to think that our universe runs haphazard?"

In all his actions, in his abilities and in his vital beliefs and religion, Claude Hilton Keith kept faith, and tried desperately to understand the universe and the uncertainty of existence; and towards the end of his life he was able to say "Nothing I have learned has shaken my faith." His death will be felt most deeply in Helford, where he spent his all his school holidays with his Aunt, Miss Charlotte Rogers, at Mimosa Cottage. After his schooldays he worked with Marconi for a time, and he and his aunt travelled abroad a great deal.

Friends of Keith at Helford write "To many of his friends must have occurred the thought that death came to him as he would have wished, as it came to so many of his airmen, with a neat swiftness and a deep peace at last."

His Wikipedia entry, which was compiled and posted by an RAF historian, says this of Claude:

'a man who, perhaps more than any other individual can be said to have 'put the fire in the Spitfire'.

He did not fritter his life away.

The obituaries are fine tributes, and there are adjectives within them that seem to give new perspectives to Claude's character: quiet, happy, gentle, generous, along with other attributes that shine through his own accounts of his life – charm, vitality, popularity, conviction. Claude was a thinker as well as a doer, who wore his heart on his sleeve. I am sad that I never knew him, partly because he would have been thrilled that the Keith line was being continued, and partly because [as long as we avoided talking politics] I am certain that he had many more ripping yarns to tell a grandson. However, I'm very grateful that he left so much behind, so that I could get to know him.

Self

Printed in Great Britain
by Amazon

32897511R00122